Breaking into the Lab

Breaking into the Lab

Engineering Progress for Women in Science

Sue V. Rosser

NEW YORK UNIVERSITY PRESS
New York and London

NEW YORK UNIVERSITY PRESS
New York and London
www.nyupress.org

References to Internet websites (URLs) were accurate at the time of writing.
Neither the author nor New York University Press is responsible for URLs that
may have expired or changed since the manuscript was prepared.

Library of Congress Cataloging-in-Publication Data

Rosser, Sue Vilhauer.
Breaking into the lab : engineering progress for women in science /
Sue V. Rosser.
p. cm.
Includes bibliographical references and index.
ISBN 978–0–8147-7645–2 (cl : alk. paper)
ISBN 978–0–8147–7152–5 (ebook)
ISBN 978–0–8147–7153–2 (ebook)
1. Women scientists—United States.
2. Sex discrimination in science—United States.
I. Title.
Q130.R674   2011
500.82'0973—dc23   2011039757

New York University Press books are printed on acid-free paper,
and their binding materials are chosen for strength and durability.
We strive to use environmentally responsible suppliers and materials
to the greatest extent possible in publishing our books.

Manufactured in the United States of America
10 9 8 7 6 5 4 3 2 1

To academic women, scientists, and engineers

Contents

Acknowledgments

Without the perspectives, ideas, and guidance of so many people, this book would not have been possible. The mentors during my own graduate, postdoctoral, and professional careers who directed me and shared their insights and opinions helped me to understand academia, science, and the profession. I am particularly grateful to the many Professional Opportunities for Women in Research and Education (POWRE) and Clare Booth Luce (CBL) awardees, as well as the Association for Women in Science (AWIS) Fellows, who willingly shared with me their professional and personal experiences as women scientists through interviews and email surveys. Their comments and responses facilitated my understanding of which issues were structural, common, or unique. More importantly, they led me to consider how those obstacles and barriers almost all women in science face might be overcome by institutional changes. I thank my own family, especially Pat, my daughters Meagan and Caitlin and grandsons Charlie, Cole, and Graeme, for reminding me not only that issues of balancing career and family continue for the next generation, but also for allowing me to see that, from the perspective of a senior woman academic and grandma, a wonderful family makes the balancing act completely worthwhile. Finally, I would like to acknowledge the guidance of editors Aiden Amos and Ilene Kalish at NYU Press for bringing this volume to publication.

%% 1 %%

Introduction

Why Women in Science Are Still

Controversial after Thirty Years

In 1968, when I applied to four graduate schools and was accepted to all but Harvard, I wondered why Stanford had failed to provide me with support, since both Berkeley and Madison had. When I called the chair of the department to inquire about this, I was told that they had accepted me only because of my very high grades and GRE scores, since normally they did not offer a place to a married woman who was likely just to have children and "waste" her graduate education.

In 1971, I was directed toward a dissertation topic on fossil rodents based primarily at the Field Museum in Chicago because my major professor assumed that, since I was pregnant with my first child, I would not want to go to Africa for dissertation field research as most of his other students did. In 1975, when I became pregnant with my second child, my postdoctoral advisor suggested that I get an abortion. He said the timing for having another child at that point was not good for the research; he said we needed to collect more data to improve our chances of getting the grant renewed.

Despite these and other obstacles, I did go on to have a successful career in academia, culminating in my serving as a dean of liberal arts at a research I institution for ten years before attaining my current position as provost at a large comprehensive university. The types of barriers, obstacles, and discrimination that women scientists, engineers, and I faced 30 or 40 years ago, and some that slightly younger women faced 10 or 20 years ago, now appear overt and obvious. While today's obstacles seem covert and less clear, my junior colleagues continue to face similar issues, just manifested now in different forms. This volume explores these similarities and differences and their impacts upon the careers of women scientists and engineers.

The Impact of Summers' Remarks

On January 14, 2005, I was an invited speaker at the National Bureau of Economic Research at Harvard University where President Larry Summers delivered his now infamous speech. Summers drew on anecdotes and popular outdated or pseudo-science to make three points explaining the paucity of women scientists and engineers: (1) women are unwilling or unable to work the 80-hour weeks required for success in science at top-flight academic institutions; (2) innate or biological factors, rather than socialization, probably account for sex differences in mathematical aptitude and also for adult preferences for choice of academic study and occupational field; (3) discrimination, which he defined as a "taste" for hiring people like oneself, does not exist in academia because that would be eliminated through market forces by lesser institutions hiring highly qualified women and minorities, thereby gaining a competitive advantage.

The following quotation from the transcript of Summers' remarks captures the essence of his argument: "So my best guess, to provoke you, of what's behind all of this is that the largest phenomenon, by far, is the general clash between people's legitimate family desires and employer's current desire for high power and high intensity, that in the special case of science and engineering, there are issues of intrinsic aptitude, and particularly of the variability of aptitude, and that those considerations are reinforced by what are in fact lesser factors involving socialization and continuing discrimination" (Summers 2005).

Of the some 40 people present at the closed, invitational meeting, most of us, individuals who had worked and conducted substantial research on women in science for more than two decades, were appalled and shocked by his remarks. From the media accounts, some of the Harvard faculty at the meeting, and a few other individuals, mostly economists, agreed with the remarks he made during his prepared presentation that lasted more than one hour.

Despite his resignation from the Harvard presidency and appointment as head of the National Economic Council in the Obama administration, Larry Summers' comments generated a firestorm which continued for several months and still persists. On June 7, 2010, John Tierney began his *New York Times* article, "Daring to Discuss Women in Science," in the following way:

The House of Representatives has passed what I like to think of as Larry's Law. The official title of this legislation is "Fulfilling the potential of women in academic science and engineering," but nothing did more to empower its advocates than the controversy over a speech by Lawrence H. Summers when he was president of Harvard. (Tierney 2010a)

Hundreds of editorials, op-ed pieces, and TV interviews, as well as articles in professional journals, have excoriated Summers for faulty logic, use of dated studies, and political naïveté. Equally large numbers, including John Tierney, also praised him for his courage, for defying political correctness to tell the truth about why relatively few women hold senior positions in science and engineering, especially at elite institutions.

I'm all in favor of women fulfilling their potential in science, but I feel compelled, at the risk of being shipped off to one of these workshops, to ask a couple of questions: (1) Would it be safe during the "interactive discussions" for someone to mention the new evidence supporting Dr. Summers's controversial hypothesis about differences in the sexes' aptitude for math and science? (2) How could these workshops reconcile the "existence of gender bias" with careful studies that show that female scientists fare as well as, if not better than, their male counterparts in receiving academic promotions and research grants? (Tierney 2010a)

The one point on which all agreed is that President Larry Summers focused significant attention on the issue of women and science. His announcement on May 16, 2005, of the decision to designate $50 million over the next decade at Harvard to support initiatives to recruit and support women faculty and minorities in pursuing academic careers provided increased focus and the promise of action on the issues. His comments have extended attention outside of academia to the situation for women scientists in industry as well (Weiss 2008). Many believe that his comments on women and science became the final straw that led to his resignation and the appointment of Drew Gilpin Faust as Harvard's first woman president.

Summers' remarks and the national debate spurred Congress to find a way to determine whether discrimination occurs against women in science and engineering. The legislation "fulfilling the potential of women in academic science and engineering" that passed the House represents one example of such action. Continuing reports from the National Academy of Sciences (2007), the Council on Competitiveness (2005), the National Science Board (2008), and the National Academies (2010) suggest that the United States lags behind other countries in producing scientists and engineers needed for our increasingly technological society. The events of September 11, 2001, as well as the improving educational systems in developing countries such as China and India, mean that the United States can no longer depend on individuals from other countries to staff its academic and industrial workforce in science and technology. The United States cannot afford to lose the talents of women and other under-represented groups in science, technology, engineering, and medicine because of discrimination.

As President Obama has emphasized, the United States needs to increase the percentages of Americans graduating from college overall, and especially needs to increase the numbers of scientists and engineers it graduates to compete economically in the global market. After sitting at the technological frontier for decades, the United States now faces increasing competition in science and technology. At one time the primary source of the world's high technology, the country has become a consistent net importer of high technology, with new competition from high-tech firms in Israel, Taiwan, Finland, Ireland, and even parts of the developing world. Since the dot-com bust, the annual U.S. productivity growth has slowed, and U.S. high-tech small business formation has dropped in every sector (National Science Board 2008). These shifts are especially troubling since economists attribute half of America's economic growth since World War II to new technology.

Although gaps in science funding may be partially responsible for the decline, the main source of the problem appears to be the drastic reductions in graduation of competitive scientists and engineers. Fewer U.S. college students pursued engineering degrees in 2005 than in 1985, despite a rising undergraduate population (National Science Foundation 2010). In 2000, more than 25 countries had higher percentages of 24-year-olds with degrees in science and engineering than did the United States. At the PhD level, U.S. production of scientists and engineers peaked in 1997. As a result, even top U.S. high-tech firms now look abroad for talent and move their research and development to India, Israel, and Ireland. As an Intel spokesperson said, "We go where the smart people are" (National Academy of Sciences 2007). A 2006 Duke University survey of American firms that outsource science and technology jobs found that approximately 40 percent considered the U.S. supply of engineers inadequate, suggesting a strong correlation between the recent relative decline in U.S. technological competitiveness and the drop in the U.S. science and technology workforce (Wadhwa, Rissing and Gereffi 2006). The U.S. scientific workforce needs to change from being predominately white and male to reflect the diversity of the demographics of the population as a whole. Individuals from groups currently underrepresented in the science, engineering, technology, and mathematics (STEM) workforce will not be the only ones to reap the benefits of the relatively good salaries obtained by scientists and engineers. Increasing the diversity in the STEM workforce may also lead to benefits for science and engineering itself, since people from different backgrounds and experience may bring diverse approaches to problem solving and innovation. This represents one of the many reasons that the issues of women in STEM are so important to everyone, not just to women.

Statistics on Women in STEM

During the last three decades, the overall percentage of women receiving degrees in science, technology, engineering, and mathematics (STEM) has increased dramatically. This increase tends to mask at least three other aspects of the demographics of the science and technology workforce. First, when data represent U.S. and immigrant scientists only, and are not disaggregated by gender, they mask the decrease in the number of U.S. white men—the group from which the United States traditionally has drawn its STEM workforce—that has occurred during the last decades. This decrease seems to be the result of white men entering other fields such as law and business, which are perceived to command better salaries, as well as an overall decrease in the percentage of men obtaining degrees from college at all levels. Unless more men of color and women enter the science and engineering workforce, the United States will not produce the number of scientists and engineers it needs to sustain its workforce without importing them from other countries.

In the United States, women currently earn more of the bachelor's and master's degrees than men (see table 1.1). In 2008, women earned 57.4% of the bachelor's degrees in all fields (NSF 2010 table C-4) and 60.6% of all master's degrees (NSF 2010 table E-2). Beginning in 2000, women also earned more of the bachelor's degrees in science and engineering (S&E), although they earned only 45.6% of the master's degrees in science and engineering in 2008. In 2008, women earned 61.8% of the PhD's in non-science and engineering fields, but only 40.7% of the PhD's in science and engineering received by U.S. citizens and permanent residents (NSF 2010, table F-2). The many reasons for these shifts in the demographics of degree earners in the United States include more equal opportunities for women in higher education and the need for dual-career families to make ends meet financially. Predicted to continue, these trends suggest that the issues raised in this book will only become more pressing as the disconnect between those earning degrees in science and engineering and those climbing the ranks in STEM in academia and industry continues to grow.

Second, the aggregated data mask the wide variance of women's participation among fields in STEM. Major gender differences occur in distribution of the genders across the disciplines. Overall, at the bachelor's level, women earn the majority of the degrees in the non-science and engineering fields such as humanities, education, and fine arts, and in the S&E fields of psychology, the social sciences, and biological sciences. Men earn most of the degrees in the physical sciences, earth, atmospheric, and ocean sciences, mathematics and statistics, computer sciences and engineering (NSF 2010).

At the level of the master's degree, women earned the majority of degrees in 2008 not only in non-science and engineering fields, but also in biological sciences, psychology, and the social sciences. Women earned less than half of the master's degrees in earth, atmospheric, and ocean sciences, mathematics and statistics, physical sciences, computer sciences and engineering (NSF 2010).

Women still earned less than half of the science and engineering PhD degrees in 2008 in all fields except psychology, biology, and a few social sciences such as anthropology, linguistics, and sociology (NSF 2010, table F-2). Women earned 50.6% of the PhD's in biological sciences. Unfortunately, the social and life sciences represent areas with constant or decreasing numbers of tenure-track positions and relatively tight federal funding, leading to intense competition. This does not represent the situation in other fields such as computer science and engineering, where women earn about 22 percent of the PhD's (NSF 2010, table F-2). Many PhD's in computer science and engineering obtain positions in industry, making the competition for tenure-track positions less severe in these fields where federal funding is also relatively plentiful. Earning more of the PhD's in these fields would give women greater access to these positions and funding.

TABLE 1.1. Women as a Percentage of Degree Recipients in 2008 by Major Discipline and Group

	All Fields	All Science & Engineering	Psychology	Social Sciences	Biology	Physical Sciences	Geo-sciences	Math/Statistics	Engineering	Computer Science
Percentage of Bachelor's degrees received by women	57.4	50.3	77.1	53.5	59.8	41.3	40.7	43.9	18.5	17.7
Percentage of MS degrees received by women	60.6	45.6	79.2	55.8	58.7	35.8	45.4	42.8	23.0	26.8
Percentage of Ph.D. degrees received by women	50.4	40.7	72.0	48.6	50.6	29.3	35.7	31.1	21.6	22.0

Source: Calculated by author from data in NSF 2010, Women, minorities, and persons with disabilities; Table C-4 for BS, E-2 for Masters, F-2 for doctoral.

In short, in many of the social sciences and the life sciences, women have reached parity in the percentages of degrees received. In other areas such as the geosciences, as well as mathematics and physical sciences, the percentages of women continue to increase, although they have not approached parity. In contrast, in engineering and computer sciences, the percentages of women have reached a plateau or dropped during the last decade, especially at the bachelor's degree level. Unfortunately, these STEM areas, particularly computer science and engineering, represent the fast-growing areas with the greatest workforce demand in our increasingly technological society. Industry and government hire large numbers of computer scientists and engineers with BS and MS degrees. Reaching parity in the percentage of degrees received in these fields would provide more women with opportunities to compete for these positions.

Finally, aggregated data mask the attrition of women at every phase of the educational and career STEM pipeline. Despite grades and other academic attainments equal to or surpassing those of the men who remain in STEM, more women leave science and engineering compared to their male counterparts. While the many reasons that women leave science and engineering will be explored later in the book, some of the difficulties of balancing career and children and the problem of finding satisfactory dual-career positions become particular issues for women scientists and engineers. The dual-career situation especially is an issue for academic women scientists, since a majority of them are married to, or partnered with, another scientist or engineer, often in the same field. In contrast, most men in academic science are not married to, or partnered with, another scientist or engineer. A 2001 survey of American science, technology, engineering, and mathematics (STEM) PhD's found that single men and single women participate about equally in the STEM workforce. In contrast, a married female PhD is 13% less likely to be employed than a married male PhD. If the woman is married with young children, then she is 30% less likely than a single male to be employed (Long 2001).

The following case illustrates why women scientists with young children may leave the field.

Suzanne Lorenz never thought she'd have to choose between work and family. But in April 2001, expecting her third child, she closed up her office and walked away from a 17-year career. Years of dealing with an employer that offered minimal support for family needs, a salary that persistently lagged behind those of her male peers, and

TABLE 1.2.

Percentage of Women Doctoral Scientists and Engineers in
Academic Institutions by Field and Rank in 2006

	All Science & Engineering	Psychology	Social Sciences	Biology/ Life Sciences	Physical Sciences	Engineer- ing	Math & Statistics
Assistant Professor	40.2	62.7	50.5	40.8	28.1	18.9	38.9
Associate Professor	31.2	60.7	37.1	29.0	23.9	13.7	23.1
Full Professor	16.2	29.7	19.4	20.7	9.6	4.1	10.9
Total (includes Instructor/ Lecturer)	32.6	54.8	35.6	35.3	18.8	11.9	15.1

Source: Calculated by author from data in NSF, 2010. Women, minorities, and persons with disabilities, Table H-25.

the pressure of trying to juggle her roles as both a dedicated scientist and a dedicated mother had finally worn her out. She saw little alternative but to quit. Had Lorenz been a lawyer, businesswoman, or government official, the gender bias she faced would be troubling enough. But she was an assistant professor of research medicine in a top-ranked department at a midwestern university. When she quit her job, she left behind a half-million-dollar laboratory, several hundred thousand dollars' worth of training and experience, and a productive research program seeking a cure for blood-pressure disorders. Her story offers vivid evidence that when female scientists and engineers lose the struggle to balance career and family, scientific resources are lost as well. (Rosser and Taylor 2009, M17)

Such losses ultimately result in very few women in senior and leadership positions in the STEM workforce. Within academia in the United States, at four-year institutions in 2006, women made up 40.2% of assistant professors, 31.2% of associate professors, and 16.2% of full professors (see table 1.2) in science and engineering. Doctoral research-extensive institutions (formerly research I institutions) as defined by the Carnegie Classification system have fewer women professors.

Several studies (Nelson 2005; Rosser, Daniels, and Wu 2006) have drawn attention to the failure of the elite research institutions to hire women faculty in general, and women science and engineering faculty in particular, at rates comparable to the PhD production of women from the science and engineering departments of those institutions. Many have sought to explain the small number of women in tenured positions relative to the percentage of qualified women with PhD's and the reasons for their relatively larger percentages in industry (Catalyst 1999; Etzkowitz et al. 1994), small liberal arts colleges (Rosser 2004; Schneider 2000), or in non–tenure track positions such as research scientist or lecturer in research institutions (Arenson 2005). Although some disciplines such as physics and astronomy appear to be hiring women into tenure-track positions at doctoral extensive institutions at approximately the same percentages at which they receive their PhD's (Ivie and Nies Ray 2005), other disciplines such as chemistry (Nelson 2005) hired an exceptionally low percentage of women into tenure-track positions relative to the percentage of women PhD's produced by those same institutions. For example, at the top 50 PhD-granting institutions in chemistry, women accounted for 21% of assistant professors, 22% of associate professors, and only 10% of full professors (Marasco 2006). These sorts of institutions are the ones where most research, innovation, and patenting occur.

Many of these PhD women scientists or engineers who leave academia go on to work in industry, which they see as more family friendly because of the nine-to-five workday, the absence of competition between the biological clock and the tenure clock, and in some cases, better benefits, including on-site day care. Some simply change paths to pursue careers in unrelated fields such as finance, using the math skills from their science background.

Title IX

Title IX, a law passed in 1972 that requires gender equity in every educational program that receives federal funding, provides one means to determine whether discrimination based on gender does occur in academia. As John Tierney noted in his July 15, 2008 *New York Times* article, "A New Frontier for Title IX: Science," most people don't realize that Title IX applies equity to all of education, not just sports: "Until recently, the impact of Title IX, the law forbidding sexual discrimination in education, has been limited mostly to sports. But now, under pressure from Congress, some federal agencies have quietly picked a new target: science" (Tierney 2008).

As Tierney outlines, some federal agencies such as the National Science Foundation (NSF), NASA, and the Department of Energy (DoE) are investigating potential discrimination against women scientists by looking at federal grants—the place where research universities would definitely be hurt in terms of both dollars and prestige:

> The National Science Foundation, NASA and the Department of Energy have set up programs to look for sexual discrimination at universities receiving federal grants. Investigators have been taking inventories of lab space and interviewing faculty members and students in physics and engineering departments at schools like Columbia, the University of Wisconsin, MIT, and the University of Maryland. (2008)

Tierney made the point that these compliance reviews are controversial and that some fear they will lead to a quota system:

> Applying Title IX to science was proposed eight years ago by Debra Rolison, a chemist at the Naval Research Laboratory. She argued that withholding federal money from "poorly diversified departments" was essential to "transform the academic culture." The proposal was initially greeted, in her words, with "near-universal horror."
>
> Some female scientists protested that they themselves would be marginalized if a quota system revived the old stereotype that women couldn't compete on even terms in science. But the idea had strong advocates, too, and Congress quietly ordered agencies to begin the Title IX compliance reviews in 2006. (2008)

Instead of a quota, the reviews seem to have led the 2010 Congress to propose workshops, as part of the reauthorization of the America Competes Act. When Congress passed the revised, stripped down bill on December 20, 2010, the workshops were removed.

In emphasizing the conservative view, that women's lower participation rates in science emanate from lack of interest, Tierney raises the question of the quality of evidence for discrimination:

The members of Congress and women's groups who have pushed for science to be "Title Nined" say there is evidence that women face discrimination in certain sciences, but the quality of that evidence is disputed. Critics say there is far better research showing that on average, women's interest in some fields isn't the same as men's. (2008)

He ultimately suggests that the gender gap is due to choice:

The gap in science seems due mainly to another difference between the sexes: men are more interested in working with things, while women are more interested in working with people. There's ample evidence—most recently in an analysis of surveys of more than 500,000 people—that boys and men, on average, are more interested in inanimate objects and "inorganic" subjects like math and physics and engineering, while girls and women are more drawn to life sciences, social science and other "organic" careers that involve people and seem to have direct social usefulness. (Tierney 2010a)

Framing the issue of women's not entering science compared to other fields as one of "choice" makes the case of discrimination difficult to prove. In my day, most girls who "chose" not to play sports really believed that they preferred other activities. Until Title IX made women's teams, scholarships, and facilities more equitable in high school and college, most girls did not choose to undertake the activities in elementary and middle school to make them competitive in college sports. Individuals who favor application of Title IX to insure that space, equipment, and graduate students of women scientists equal those of their male peers believe this removal of discriminatory barriers will lead more women to choose science as a career. Summers' cavalier ignorance of the actual research and his blunt articulation of discriminatory attitudes, coupled with the current resistance of Tierney and others in the media and scientific establishment even to collect data on whether discrimination occurs at elite institutions via Title IX compliance reviews, underline the idea that women in science remains a controversial topic.

Differing opinions also greeted the 2009 publication by the National Academy of Sciences of *Gender Differences at Critical Transitions in the Careers of Science, Engineering and Mathematics Faculty* (NAS 2009), which showed that women who remain at elite research institutions have similar resources to those of their male colleagues. The co-chairs of the report, Claude Canizares of MIT and Sally Shaywitz of Yale, viewed this report as confirming that the disparities revealed by the MIT Report (Hopkins 1999) between women scientists and their male peers at research institutions have been largely rectified.

As Tierney states, "last year a task force of the National Academy of Sciences concluded from its investigation of 500 science departments that by and large, men and women 'enjoyed comparable opportunities within the university'" (2010b).

The MIT Report

In March 1999, the Massachusetts Institute of Technology released "A Study on the Status of Women Faculty in Science at MIT" that caused a stir well beyond the boundaries of that institution. Five years earlier, senior biology professor Nancy Hopkins (1999) initiated the collection of evidence documenting that the 15 tenured women faculty in science had received lower salaries and fewer resources for research than their male colleagues. Dean Robert Birgeneau recognized that, in addition to salary disparities, the data in the report revealed systemic, subtle biases in space, start-up packages, access to graduate students, and other resources that inhibited the careers of women scientists relative to their male counterparts. Release of the report struck a nerve with administrators and women faculty on campuses across the nation. Headlines such as "Women at MIT Create a Movement for Female Academics" that appeared in *The Chronicle of Higher Education* (December 3, 1999), also echoed in *Science*, the *New York Times*, and countless other publications, fueled questions about the status of women scientists at other academic institutions and in the broader profession.

More than one year later, MIT President Charles Vest hosted a meeting of the presidents, chancellors, provosts, and 25 women scientists from the most prestigious research universities (California Institute of Technology, MIT, University of Michigan, Princeton, Stanford, Yale, University of California at Berkeley, Harvard, and University of Pennsylvania) at MIT. At the close of the meeting on January 29, 2001, they issued the following statement: "Institutions of higher education have an obligation, both for themselves and for the nation, to fully develop and utilize all the creative talent available," the leaders said in a unanimous statement. "We recognize that barriers still exist" for women faculty. They agreed:

To analyze the salaries and proportion of other university resources
provided to women faculty,

To work toward a faculty that reflects the diversity of the student
body,

To reconvene in about a year "to share the specific initiatives we have
undertaken to achieve these objectives."

To "recognize that this challenge will require significant review of,
and potentially significant change in, the procedures within each
university, and within the scientific and engineering establishments as a whole." (Campbell 2001, 1)

For the first time, in public and in print, the leaders of the nation's most
prestigious universities suggested that institutional barriers have prevented women scientists and engineers from having a level playing field
and that science and engineering might need to change to accommodate
women. This watershed moment came about because of both the data
collected by the tenured women full professors at MIT and the willingness of MIT President Vest and Dean Robert Birgeneau to convince their
counterparts at other prestigious institutions to take the data and their
implications seriously. The data and leadership from MIT, set against
the backdrop of affirmative action debates, set the stage for such a public proclamation. The statement had a large impact on the public debate,
finally opening up the conversation to create possibilities for real change.

Almost simultaneously, the NSF initiated ADVANCE, a new awards
program, which provided funding of $17 million for 2001. The goal of the
program is to "catalyze change that will transform academic environments in ways that enhance participation and advancement of women in
science and engineering" (NSF 2001). It was also established to "develop
systemic approaches to increase the representation and advancement
of women in academic science, technology, engineering and mathematics (STEM) careers, thereby contributing to the development of a more
diverse science and engineering workforce. ADVANCE focuses on ensur-
ing that women faculty with earned STEM degrees consider academia as
a viable and attractive career option" (NSF ADVANCE 2011). While not
intended to directly impact the STEM pipeline before the level of entry
to the professoriate, ADVANCE supports projects that focus on institutional transformation, as well as partnerships and collaborations.

By 2009, the fourth cohort of institutions had received awards: "the NSF
has invested more than $135M to support ADVANCE projects at more

than one hundred different institutions" (NSF 2009). The program offers an award for institutional, rather than individual, solutions to empower women to participate fully in science and technology. The NSF encouraged institutional, rather than individual, solutions because of "increasing recognition that the lack of women's full participation at the senior level of academe is often a systemic consequence of academic culture" (NSF 2001, 2).

Tierney quotes Christina Hoff Sommers, a resident scholar at the American Enterprise Institute, as criticizing NSF for ADVANCE: "She criticizes the National Science Foundation for sustaining this industry over the past decade with more than $135 million from its Advance program promoting gender equity" (Tierney 2010b). Sommers' critique reflects her conservative stance that no changes in the status quo of institutions such as flexibility in the tenure clock, mentoring, or data collection should be made to understand disparities based on gender and to level the playing field for women.

In contrast to Claude Canizares and Sally Shaywitz, who authored the 2009 National Academies Report, others, such as Phoebe Leboy, president of the Association for Women in Science (AWIS) and professor emerita from the University of Pennsylvania, did not view the disparities revealed by the MIT Report as having been rectified. She pointed out the basis of the 2009 National Academies report in statistics of women scientists successful at research institutions. "The report 'focuses on only that sub-population of women who have the nerve to apply for these positions,' and largely ignores the implications of the data showing that so many do not apply to those institutions or for any number of reasons work off the tenure track. 'It's really distressing that they have ignored so many issues about women in STEM fields'" (Jaschik 2009, 1).

Leboy raised questions about the women not hired by research institutions. For example, why do a relatively higher percentage of men who receive their degrees from the most prestigious educational institutions obtain tenure-track positions in comparable institutions, while relatively more women who receive degrees from those same prestigious institutions obtain positions in less prestigious institutions or in government or industry? What happens to those women who are hired, but are unsuccessful in promotion and tenure in research institutions? What about the women who leave such institutions "voluntarily," before the tenure and promotion decision, for opportunities at other types of institutions or "choose" to switch from the tenure track to the research track, while remaining in the same institution? None of these categories was included in the report. The controversy generated by this and other reports documents that discrimination against women in science remains a hot topic.

Why hasn't the women in science question been resolved after millions of federal and foundation dollars spent to encourage women in science and engineering and years of debate? What is the evidence for discrimination in academia, since many more women now earn degrees in science and engineering compared to thirty years ago? Is it simply a matter of time until these increased numbers of women earning degrees in science and engineering eventually translate into more women professors at elite universities? Will the percentage of women full professors in science and engineering at research I institutions remain constant at 10%, as it has for the last five decades? What difference does it make if women continue to be less attracted to some areas of science and technology initially, drop out of the science workforce, or never attain senior and leadership positions at elite academic institutions?

Importance of Male Mentors

The demographics of academia, where the overwhelming numbers of full professors in science and engineering are men (90% in doctoral extensive research institutions), mean that women pursuing a career in science will encounter mostly male mentors. Although men scientists face some obstacles in their careers similar to those women face, such as the pressure to constantly write grants, the threat of publish or perish, and the need to balance competing demands of teaching, research, and service, on the whole, women experience more and different barriers than their male peers. Helping male mentors to understand the experiences women scientists encounter so that they can more effectively guide these women in their careers serves as a primary impetus for this book.

In her interview immediately after receiving the Nobel Prize in Physiology and Medicine on October 5, 2009, Carol Greider emphasized the significant impact that a supportive male mentor can have on an entire field, as well as on an individual woman's career:

ADAM SMITH: I wanted to ask about women in telomere research because it's been commented before that it's a field where, happily, a large number of women have contributed. Is there something particular about the subject, do you think, that has made that happen?

CAROL GREIDER: I don't think it's necessarily about the subject. I think it's one of those examples of a jackpot effect, where you have somebody that trains a lot of women, and then there's a slight gravitation of women to work in the labs of other women. I don't think it's a large effect but a small effect. And so, because the founding group was women, it tends to then, you know, sort of grow out as a jackpot effect. So then, Joe Gall, with whom Liz Blackburn worked, was extremely supportive of the women that worked in his lab and he trained a number of telomere biologists—Liz and Ginger Zaklan and others. And so, I really think that the fact that he sort of founded a group of strong women that then went on and had other women in their labs was most likely the reason that there were so many in the telomere field.

AS: Right, right, so . . .

CG: It's a founder effect, sort of.

AS: Exactly, from small seeds, yes. And is it something that you continue to propagate? You said that there is a sort of slight gravitation. Is it something that one has to actively promote, do you think?

CG: I think actively promoting women in science is very important because the data has certainly shown that there has been an under-representation and I think that the things that contribute to that are very many social . . . subtle, social kinds of things. So, yes, I think that one should definitely be cognizant of that and be aware of it. (Nobelprize.org 2009)

Although the numbers and percentages of women scientists, often referred to as the pipeline, have increased in all fields of science, technology, engineering, and mathematics (STEM) since the 1960s, the overwhelming majority of women scientists will have a male mentor, given the relative numbers of senior men and women in academia. Guiding male mentors to understand both larger obstacles and everyday micro-inequities their women mentees face remains critical to enabling mentors to avoid unintentional discouraging remarks and behaviors and to help their mentees overcome obstacles in order to continue in science. Although most male mentors try to remain sensitive to the ways to encourage their female mentees, sometimes these same individuals will also engage in negatively discouraging behaviors. This may leave women feeling ambivalent about their decision to become a scientist.

A senior male scientist who heads a foundation program that provides funds to advance women in science and engineering sees barriers and changes over the last three decades. Of course, his personal career path differs substantially from that of the senior woman scientist, partially because of his decision to enter the foundation world rather than academia, but perhaps also because of his gender. He reflects on gender issues in ways that may be helpful to male mentors.

Foundation Program Office Ned Bluesky*

Ned Bluesky started his career with an interest in theoretical physics. As a Canadian, the undergraduate education he received focused strictly on science and mathematics for four years. Despite the reservations of his family, who would have preferred he pursue a career in business, he attended graduate school in physics at a private Northeastern research I institution in the United States. Basically he did not like the situation there in the physics department. Although he liked the students, there was little interaction between the faculty and the students. He decided that he wanted to be neither in theoretical high-energy physics nor academia. His time there coincided with the Vietnam War era, and he wanted a more practical, social component for his work. A faculty member suggested he talk to a chemist in political science. That individual became his mentor when he switched from physics, after receiving his MS, to political science, where he received his PhD.

The head of the center for international studies helped him obtain a postdoc at another major private research institution in the same city. After completing the postdoc, he returned to his PhD-degree granting institution as a faculty member in science, public policy, and arms control. He took a leave to go to Washington to work with the science advisor to President Carter; by this time he had also married an American. He returned to his home institution and wrote the book required for tenure. Unfortunately, his colleagues decided it was too policy-oriented, so he did not receive tenure. His colleagues helped him obtain a non–tenure track position in another major Northeastern city at a private research I institution, running the program on international security policy. Because of his non–tenure track status, he remained in that position for eight years before having to leave. Because his wife was now well-positioned in her career, his mentors

---

* Names and indicators have been changed for this individual and all interviewees in the book to protect identity and privacy.

from his PhD granting institution helped him obtain a position at a major private foundation so that they would not need to relocate. The portfolio he manages for the foundation has little to do with his prior experience in international science policy and security; instead he oversees the programs on women and minorities in science and engineering and work-life balance.

Certainly balancing work with family ranks as a major issue for junior women in science and engineering. In light of some changes made, partly due to guidance from the foundation, I now see other issues of major importance such as climate in the departments, isolation and loneliness, absence of professional soul mates, as well as pressures to decide not to marry or not to have kids. Because of the life choices women felt forced to make, the foundation supported a pre-tenure leave fellowship program, so that women could imagine the possibility of combining career and family; many institutions and individuals still seem reluctant to use the program.

I see many senior women who have postponed having kids until they received tenure. They then learn it's not possible to get pregnant, that they can only have one child, or face other consequences. Many women in their forties then deal with elementary-aged school kids. The issues differ from those of the junior women, because the senior women are now established, but they still have issues.

I believe that although tenure provides a particular obstacle for academia, actually it's not so different from other professions. For example, in both law and accounting, the partner-track has a similar time-limited up or out type of period for junior people.

I believe that personal interactions differ between men and women. Obviously, this constitutes a gross generalization with many exceptions. However, I find men, on the average, more willing to put themselves forward. Since women tend to interact more with other women, they tend to be disadvantaged in the professional world because they are uncomfortable promoting themselves. Thus, they end up with the conditions enumerated in the MIT Report of smaller offices, less money, and fewer graduate students. Because many little decisions in academia remain secret, multiple opportunities exist to accumulate disadvantage.

A related phenomenon results when women do not move up to senior administrative positions. Such positions do require going out into the political fray and subjecting oneself to other things. I have observed that many women are not willing to do that.

Some of the same issues of not holding senior administrative positions, unwillingness to cope with the political fray of the corporate/industrial world outside the academy, and hesitancy about promoting themselves may provide partial explanations not only for difficulties faced by senior women in science and their reluctance to enter senior leadership positions in administration, but also for women scientists' lower rates of patenting and commercialization of science relative to their male peers. Reasons traditionally used to explain the dearth of women in science, such as balancing work with family, lack of mentoring, and active exclusion from male networks, appear to be equally, if not more important, for the gender gap in patenting and commercialization.

As documented in chapter 6 of this volume, in all countries, across all sectors and in all fields, the percentage of women obtaining patents is not only less than that of their male counterparts, but it is less than the percentage of women in science, technology, engineering, and mathematics (STEM) in the field in the country. Since science, both in the United States and globally, has moved more toward commercialization and technology transfer, the dearth of women obtaining patents appears to signal women's absence from leading-edge and lucrative areas in science and technology. Just as women were not as likely to be mentored in graduate school 30 years ago to write grants in the same way that the male students were, today the women are less likely to receive mentoring to commercialize their work. This appears to be a new face of an old issue that results in the potential creative contributions of women to science and innovation not materializing.

During the past three decades, many of the same issues have persisted for women in science and engineering, although perhaps presented differently. In 1988, I expressed the loneliness I felt at being one of so few people focused on women and science: "For years I have always felt an outsider at national professional meetings in either science or women's studies" (Rosser 1988, 105). Now, most campuses boast women in science and engineering (WISE) programs for students. Each year numerous conferences, journals, and anthologies focus on women and science, and the National Science Foundation (NSF) and other federal agencies award multimillion-dollar grants to facilitate institutional transformation to advance and retain women in science and engineering. These programs, the increasing numbers of women in science and engineering, and the insights gleaned from individual women scientists willing to share their experiences document considerable success for women scientists and engineers.

Each individual mentor and woman scientist needs to do all she or he can to remove obstacles and open pathways to provide opportunities to enhance success. However, as long as efforts remain at the level of individuals, the institutional barriers and structures remain untouched. The dearth of women scientists and engineers, despite 20 years of NSF programs (Rosser and Lane 2002b) such as the Professional Opportunities for Women in Research and Education (POWRE) to support careers of individual women scientists, which many of these interviewees do credit with advancing their careers, documents the need for institutional, in addition to individual, approaches. Some of these institutional changes include family-friendly policies, more flexibility in the tenure clock, and support for dual-career hires. These are important interventions aimed at shifting the structures that impede the prospects of all, rather than forcing individual women to negotiate with their department chair for an extra year of time toward tenure after the birth of a child or for a position for her spouse/partner who is also a scientist. Women scientists and supportive mentors must work to transform institutional barriers, while supporting the careers of individual women scientists and engineers.

I offer this volume of my experiences as a woman scientist and dean at a doctoral research extensive institution, who has worked in women's studies for 30 years. My experiences are complemented with data from interviews of current scientists, both junior and senior, in response to the questions about why there are so few women scientists at elite research institutions, what happens to successful women as they become senior and consider going into administration, and whether women are excluded from leading-edge work in commercialization of science and technology transfer.

In the next chapter, seven vignettes from my experiences establishing my career some 40 years ago are paired with interviews from young women academic scientists currently working to achieve tenure. These vignettes illustrate that similar issues and themes persist, presented in different language, actions, and structures. Some decisions or behaviors hold enough impact to set a career trajectory in a negative direction that becomes almost impossible to reverse. Experiences drawn from interviews of current women scientists and engineers underline pitfalls to be avoided.

Chapter 3 continues the theme of juxtaposing experiences from 30–40 years ago with their current manifestations. The vignettes in this chapter focus on positive comments or behaviors from male mentors that hold the potential to further the careers of women scientists and engineers. This chapter serves as the counterpoint to the previous chapter by using experiences from interviews of women scientists currently establishing their careers to illustrate decisions and situations that place and keep their careers on a positive trajectory.

Chapter 4 describes the new set of filters that senior women scientists and engineers often encounter as they establish their careers, achieve tenure, and garner reputation in their profession. Interviews with Association for Women in Science (AWIS) Fellows reveal the parameters of the barriers they face and how they differ from those encountered by their junior women colleagues and their male peers.

Chapter 5 focuses on the question of why women scientists have particular skill sets and experiences that prepare them for top positions in academic administration. Interviews with women presidents, provosts, deans, and department chairs reveal why women seek these top positions and some of the risks they encounter in such leadership positions.

Chapter 6 explores the data that reveal that in all countries, across all sectors and in all fields, the percentage of women obtaining patents is less than their male counterparts and also less than the percentage of women in the discipline. This chapter questions why women do not obtain patents at the same rate as their male counterparts and what policies and practices might be changed to close the gender gap in this area.

Chapter 7 uses the lens of feminist theories to examine the impact women have had on basic science and technology. Do women ask different questions, use different approaches, and propose different theories because they have different experiences and backgrounds than the men who have traditionally done science?

In the concluding chapter, I suggest that women not only have had an impact, but will be critical for the future of science. The national focus on attracting and retaining women in science and the particular shortages in the science and technology workforce in the wake of September 11 have spurred many institutions of higher education to review and reform their policies and practices. The experiences of women scientists chronicled in this volume suggest that the institutional reforms that may help junior women establish their careers, while balancing their family priorities, differ from the institutional changes needed for the careers of senior women scientists and engineers to flourish.

Attracting and retaining women in science and high-tech entrepreneurship will require changing the culture of science to make it more family-friendly and less belligerent. Both men and women must recognize that women who want families don't have the luxury of waiting to have children until they've established their careers. Scientists of both genders must realize that networking and commercialization represent aspects of a productive career in science and technology, rather than manifestations of "selling out." Scientific graduate training should include understanding risks and processes of commercialization, lab management, and marketing of ideas to venture capitalists. Institutions must redouble their efforts to insure that mentoring makes technology transfer appealing and transparent so that women scientists are not excluded from the leading edge in commercialization of science.

〃 2 〃

Starting Careers

Plus Ça Change,

Plus C'est la Même Chose

B iologist Martine Ryeson completed her PhD at age 24 in Britain; unfortunately, this coincided with Thatcher's reforms of the British educational system. She became part of the brain drain and took a post-doc at a Canadian university. After 3 1/2 years as a postdoc, she decided to stay in North America, obtaining a tenure-track position at a large, public university in the Southeast.

> Although I did not marry until after I achieved tenure, one of my col-leagues asked me if one child wasn't enough when I became pregnant again, this time with twins. Unlike the young male colleague whose record of achievement was less than mine, the department did not put me up for early promotion, although I still did make professor within 10 years of being hired. I felt that the chair and dean did not support women. I left the institution to become a dean at a public institution in the Midwest. Now I'm the provost at a research institu-tion in the mid-Atlantic region.

Her colleagues' negative reaction to her pregnancy impacted Mar-tine's decision to leave the institution. The security of tenure permitted her the luxury to choose the timing so that she could move up in the profession. Women who lack the seniority and job stability to have such options when biological issues of pregnancy, childbirth, and nursing arise, often are forced into less career-enhancing moves and choices.

The differences in the experiences of women and men scientists and engineers are undoubtedly extensive and well documented, but it can often be difficult to sort out origin and impact. How much is due to the individual's scientific discipline? How much results from the era in which the woman received her education and training? How much do mentors impact women's experience? What effect does family, including family of origin, have? In short, what contextual surroundings help us understand these experiences? Fortunately, scholarship in women's studies helps provide some of the context to understand the experiences of women in science.

Context to Understand Experiences of Women in Science

During the past 30 years, the women's movement and its academic arm of women's studies have had an impact on higher education research and teaching, as well as institutional policies and practices. Women's studies and feminist perspectives have transformed theoretical approaches to knowledge and mandated inclusion of women and a focus on research subjects of interest to women, also leading to more inclusive pedagogy in the classroom and curricular content and increases in hiring, promotion, and tenure of women faculty in humanities and social sciences. Although to date women's studies has made less powerful inroads in the sciences, it provides the perspectives to understand that the comments made by Larry Summers, and echoed by the support of others, simply represent old arguments rehashed and presented in new language. As one of the individuals (Rosser 2000, 2004) who contributed to the new body of research on women and science that evolved as part of the burgeoning new scholarship on women during the last quarter-century, I'll briefly summarize my perspective on the development of women and science and feminist science studies to place these experiences and interviews in that broader context of evolution from individual to institutional solutions.

Although women's health concerns became one of the forces motivating the women's movement in the 1960s, women scientists and engineers tended not to be very heavily represented in the leadership for women's issues on campus. Directors of women's studies and much of the scholarship on women emerged initially from the humanities (Boxer 2000), followed by the social sciences, and only more recently from the sciences (Fausto-Sterling 1992b; Rosser 1988, 2000). This dearth of scientists resulted partially from the very small numbers of tenure-track faculty women in senior and leadership positions in science, technology, engineering, and mathematics. Strong cultural traditions of masculinity and objectivity in science threatened to keep women's studies separate from the theories of cultural and social construction of knowledge production acceptable in the humanities and social sciences. In many ways, the scholarship on women and science mirrors the categories of scholarship in women's studies as a whole and the emerging development of the field.

History of Women in Science

Lost texts and figures that have been recovered characterize some of the earliest scholarship in the late 1960s and early 1970s, when women's studies emerged as the academic arm of the women's movement with the establishment of the first programs in 1969–70 (Hedges 1997). The search for where and why women were missing from all fields was a necessary first step in beginning to understand how their absence led to flaws, distortions, and biases in each discipline. History of women in science and their impact upon the different disciplines and subfields continues to be an active research area today.

Current Status of Women within the Professions

Recognition of basic data on the numbers of women relative to men receiving degrees in science, mathematics, and engineering, and their employment status, rank, salary, and professional progress and attainments, was crucial to women and science and came early. After a successful lobby of Congress, the Science and Engineering Equal Opportunities Act of 1980 was passed. The National Science Foundation was required to collect data each year on the status of women and other underrepresented groups; in the 1990s the data collection expanded to include persons with disabilities in science.

Building on these foundational data, current scholars provide statistical documentation and analyses of more subtle factors and obstacles that now deter women. The dearth of women faculty can be traced only in part to relatively small numbers of women graduating with undergraduate and graduate degrees in many areas of the sciences, engineering, and mathematics. (See chapter 1 for the current numbers and percentages of women at different ranks and in different disciplines.)

The stories of senior women, particularly in chapter 4 of this book, reveal some of the obstacles in everyday life that may result in decreased numbers of women at the senior levels. Indicator data on salaries, space, start-up packages, time to tenure, time to promotion, and numbers of endowed chairs for women scientists and engineers compared to their male counterparts form a crucial portion of all projects to provide quantitative data critical for judging progress for women in academia.

Inclusions and Exclusions:
Gender Differences and Diversity among Women

The revelations from the data on numbers of women coupled with documentation of differential socialization, environmental, and educational environments for women and men scientists lead to questions about the impacts that these differences might make. Do women's differing interests, life experiences, and perspectives lead them to ask new questions, take different approaches, and find alternative interpretations leading to new theories and conclusions?

Just as women's studies scholars revealed that the assumption that male experience coincided with human experience constituted a form of androcentric bias that rendered women invisible and distorted many research results, these same scholars mistakenly assumed that the experience of all women was the same (Harding 1998). Women of color, working-class women, and lesbians pointed out that their experiences as women and as scientists did not fit the depictions that emanated from a white, middle-class, heterosexual perspective. This revelation led to the recognition that gender did not represent a homogeneous category of analysis and that gender needed to be studied in relationship to other oppressions of race, class, nationalism, and sexual orientation.

Age or developmental stage becomes another aspect of diversity that can modify the experience of even the same woman throughout her life course. The comments of senior women scientists and engineers in chapter four reveal the new, subtle forms of gender discrimination and discounting they encounter, after successfully overcoming barriers to establishing their career and balancing with family responsibilities.

During the past 15 years, we have begun to recognize the influence of globalization and the significance of understanding international perspectives and movements. In much the same way that early on, in its eagerness to discover the influence of gender, women's studies suffered from the failure to recognize diversity among women, scholars now acknowledge the constraints of not understanding the experiences of women in different countries as well as the cultural contexts and contribution of scientists in Southern continents (Harding 1998).

Although enrollment of foreign graduate students in science and engineering increased by 35% from 1994 to 2001, it peaked in 2001 (NSB 2004). In 2001, 41% of doctorates awarded in the United States went to non-U.S. citizens. The number of doctorate recipients continues to decrease and dropped 3.5% from 2008 to 2009 (NSF 2009). Although nearly 30% of the actively employed science and engineering doctorate holders in the United States are foreign born, as are many postdocs (NSB 2004), very little research has focused on immigrant women scientists. One study (Xie and Shauman 2003) found that immigrant women are only 32% as likely as immigrant men scientists and engineers to be promoted, partly because the women tend to immigrate for their husband's career.

Some of the junior women scientist and engineer interviewees who were recipients of NSF Professional Opportunities for Women in Research and Education (POWRE) awards and/or Clare Boothe Luce (CBL) Professorships comment explicitly on their experience of becoming established in the United States after immigration and compare the relatively favorable status of scientists in their country of origin with that of U.S. scientists. Only a few of these women provide insights that shed light on how the experiences of immigrant women scientists differ from those of their U.S.-born colleagues.

Revealing Male Subtexts and Building Alternative Models

As women's studies entered a stage that focused on the analysis of gender as a social category, critics began to question the ways in which gender determines the structure of social organizations, systems of cultural production, and the roles and definitions of masculinity and femininity. Scholars explored how the scientific hierarchy, including the language and metaphors of scientific theories and descriptions used, both reflected and reinforced gender roles. They uncovered the historical roots of modern science in a mechanistic model in which objectivity became synonymous with masculinity (Keller 1983, 1985) and that encouraged the domination of male scientists over women, nature, and organic models of the world (Merchant 1979).

Theory into Practice

Many scientists (Koertge 1994) rejected the postmodernism espoused by their colleagues in the humanities and social sciences. Many women scientists and engineers, while appreciating the issues raised about objectivity, questioned the translation of "high theory" into practice of science and the relevance for such theories in their own lives as scientists (Koertge 1994), where they still encounter substantial discrimination. The science wars that developed from postmodern theories and increasing globalization drew attention to the necessity for the re-fusion of theory and practice. For many women teaching and practicing science, this dichotomy between theory and practice appeared to be a false separation. Grounded in laboratory practice, the fusion of theory and practice in science classrooms and laboratories has a long tradition.

Feminist Science Studies in the Daily Lives of Women Scientists

Further evidence of the fusion of theory with practice comes from a current focus of feminist science studies on the personal experiences and daily lives of women scientists (Daniell 2006; Evans and Grant 2008; Gornick 2009; Mason and Ekman 2007; and Monosson 2008). These studies also reflect interdisciplinary approaches in their use of postcolonial theories, oral histories, and ethnographies as theoretical and methodological approaches to science studies. This volume falls within this category.

Messages to Women Scientists

Women interested in the natural, physical world who find themselves attracted to a career in science and engineering typically receive mixed messages. Encouraged to become one of the few today who dare to follow in the footsteps of the pioneering greats such as Marie Curie, Dorothy Crowfoot Hodgkin, Jane Goodall, Rosalind Franklin, or Maria Mitchell, women also receive realistic cautions about difficulties in combining family with a scientific career and less than subtle hints about how to be perceived as feminine in the masculine domain of science and engineering. These messages emanate from a variety of sources, including family, the media, and peers, as well as teachers and professional scientists and engineers. A lifetime of such messages discourages most girls from becoming scientists and engineers. For those women able to ignore or overcome these background negative messages to pursue scientific careers, the messages of their teachers, mentors, and colleagues in the profession become particularly significant. The important role such individuals play, and the impact that their words and actions have on aspiring scientists, make comments such as those made by Harvard's President Larry Summers especially damaging for young women.

Several studies (Mason and Goulden 2004; Mason, Goulden and Frasch 2009; Rowe 1974; Sandler 1986; Valian 1998; Xie and Shauman 2003; Zuckerman, Cole and Bruer 1991) have documented the detrimental impact of the cumulative effect of micro-inequities on the careers of women in general and women scientists in particular. The original articles written on this subject by Mary Rowe in the 1970s defined micro-inequities as "Apparently small events which are often ephemeral and hard-to-prove, events which are covert, often unintentional, frequently unrecognized by the perpetrator, which occur wherever people are perceived to be 'different'" (Rowe 1974, 3). Bernice Sandler enumerated the ways in which individuals are "either singled out, or overlooked, ignored, or otherwise discounted" in the classroom and academia because of their gender (Sandler 1986). These behaviors are particularly applied to women scientists who are "different" because of their relatively small numbers compared to men, who have dominated science for centuries. Over time, the cumulative effect of micro-inequities can damage self-esteem, impair a person's performance in the classroom or workplace, and may lead to eventual withdrawal from the situation or profession.

In this chapter I provide examples of comments made to me at critical junctures in my education and early career formation by key male mentors. Some of these comments were very negative and would be clearly illegal or defined as harassment and grounds for dismissal by today's standards. More commonly, the mentor actually thought he had my best interests at heart and/or believed that he was complimenting me. Sometimes the very same mentor who had encouraged me to pursue science, at a later date engaged in discouraging behavior, which he may or may not have realized left me with ambiguous feelings about becoming a scientist. In all cases, the statement revealed considerable evidence of the mentor's inability to see beyond traditional views of women and of science to grasp issues significant for women and women's studies in general and women scientists in particular.

Within the last two years, although dated by the language and circumstances of the day, I have heard or observed the current version of each of these comments made by male faculty and colleagues to women students, postdocs, or junior faculty. I provide current interview comments from a woman scientist or engineer to demonstrate a recent version of situations similar to what other women and I faced three decades ago.

To learn more about the intertwining of professional and personal career paths, I interviewed a sample of 40 of the almost 400 women who had received NSF POWRE awards. POWRE awardees are women who received peer-reviewed funding from a focused NSF program in fiscal years 1997–2000. They are primarily untenured assistant professors in tenure-track positions at research institutions. The POWRE awards were capped at $75,000, with a typical duration of 12–18 months. I wrote a series of papers (Rosser 2001; Rosser and Lane 2002a, 2002b; Rosser and Zieseniss 2000) documenting the research on 389 of the 598 POWRE awardees during the four-year POWRE program.

I also interviewed a sample of 11 of the almost 50 Clare Boothe Luce (CBL) Professors who had responded to an email questionnaire that I had sent. The CBL Professorships were created by Clare Boothe Luce's bequest to the Henry Luce Foundation on her death in 1987. At the time of the interviews, 133 CBL Professorships had been awarded; most CBL Professors are assistant professors in their first tenure-track positions at liberal arts colleges. At that time, each CBL Professorship provided for the salary, benefits, and a highly flexible career development account administered by the recipient for a period of five years (Rosser and Daniels 2004).

From these 50 interviews, I selected those that seemed similar or parallel to the situations I had experienced. Some of these women pursued other careers before becoming academic scientists; these women are younger than I, but older than some of the young women interviewees, just beginning their academic careers immediately after completing postdocs. The names of the interviewees have been fictionalized and their institutions described generically. (For details of the methodologies used for the email questionnaire and interviews, please see Rosser 2004; Rosser and Lane 2002a.)

Mentors Who Seek to Attract Students to More than the Field

In the late summer of 1965, I returned from my high school graduation present of nine weeks in Europe to register for courses at our large, Midwestern state university. Since the trip had prevented my attending the more leisurely orientation/registration sessions held throughout the summer, many of the courses traditionally taken by freshmen, including all science courses, were closed. Because I thought of myself as a French and English major, the rather bizarre assortment of classes, including Latin, Ancient Religion and the Early Church, Philosophy, French Civilization, along with Honors English, that eventually constituted my first semester schedule, didn't bother me. During the second semester, I signed up for Genetics for Poets, a course for non-science majors officially titled Genetics and Human Affairs. Although I had taken the full complement of college preparatory science courses in high school, including mathematics through calculus, this course for non-majors seemed appropriate to me because I wasn't considering majoring in science. I did very well in the course, receiving the highest grade in the class of over 400 students. My outstanding grade led the professor to ask me to come to work for him in his laboratory. Desperately in need of a summer job that would be more exciting than the babysitting and library assistant jobs that I had landed so far, I agreed enthusiastically.

I enjoyed the relatively menial laboratory work, ranging from washing test tubes through pipetting reagents to accompanying the lab tech to local farms to bleed the cows for the immunology research. Noticing my hard work and dependability, the professor asked me to stay on to work during the semester, explaining how I could fit the laboratory work around my class schedule. Sometime during the fall semester, he began to ask me if I had thought about majoring in science, specifically biology. Although I hadn't considered it, in response to his frequent requests, I decided to sign up for introductory biology in the spring, both to fulfill my laboratory science requirement and to get him off my back. One reason that I was eager to have him stop asking was that he often accompanied the question with a kiss.

In the spring I took introductory biology and became fascinated by the information and new worlds it opened to me. Anticipating the professor's persistent question about the major, I was pleased to learn that I could finish within four years, adding a second major in biology, along with my Honors French major. Because I had taken so much French in high school, I only needed to take one course each semester to complete the French major, leaving ample time to squeeze in the chemistry, physics, statistics, and extra biology courses I needed for the additional major.

I worked in the lab throughout my undergraduate years, enduring the kisses and hugs of the professor, along with the guidance he gave me about my biology major. Although I trusted the information he provided about biology, I never knew how to interpret the kisses and hugs. Had I done something to make him think I wanted him to kiss me? Was it my fault? What did he really want from me? When it came time for graduate school, I stayed at the same institution, but I realized that I was relieved to have a university fellowship, which meant I would no longer have to work in his laboratory.

By today's standards, the professor who kissed and hugged me while I worked for him in his lab was sexually harassing me. Since this occurred in the late 1960s, that terminology did not yet exist. I only knew that I felt uncomfortable when he did this and tried to avoid or resist as much as I felt I could without losing my job. Only in the 1970s in graduate school did I join a consciousness-raising (CR) group of other women graduate students and postdocs. As we discussed our personal and daily lives in the laboratory, we were all amazed to learn that each of us had experienced some form of this behavior (in a few cases from this very same professor).

Historically, much of the power obtained by women and the naming of issues from the women's movement arose from our meeting together in small CR groups without men to explore and understand our personal experiences. Recognizing that each of us was not unique in experiencing unwanted advances from the lab director or professor permitted us to stop questioning ourselves and start interrogating the culture and institutional structures that allowed this. The sharing in CR groups made us realize that often we had no language or terms for what turned out to be common phenomena. Terms such as sexual harassment and date rape emerged and helped us and future generations to define and understand these experiences. The 2006 book, *Every Other Thursday*, chronicles how one such group in the Bay Area, in existence for more than 25 years, has provided a supportive environment for the seven women scientists who often feel isolated in the competitive world of science (Daniell 2006).

The conspiracy of silence around this behavior that was broken in the consciousness-raising group made me realize for the first time that it really wasn't somehow my fault—that my skirt was too short, my breasts too big, or that I had encouraged him in some subtle fashion—that he behaved in this way toward me. Soon we learned that not only had every woman in our group experienced this, but that women in CR groups around the country were discovering this and other common information about their bodies, private, and professional lives by talking with each other about formerly taboo subjects in these safe women-only spaces. Meeting with other women in similar circumstances in CR groups to talk about the intertwining of the professional and personal led to understanding the phrase coined by Carol Hanisch (1970) that the "personal is political." One of these groups coined the term "sexual harassment," giving us a language to label and begin to de-mystify the behavior.

Having the terminology for the behavior made me feel somewhat better. He was the sexual harasser or perpetrator; I was the victim. Virtually all women had experienced this at some time and in some fashion. Actions emerged to stop such behaviors as departments and institutions eventually began to formulate sexual harassment policies and develop sensitivity training sessions. Individuals with well-known reputations as harassers received warning from their superiors and were advised that subsequent incidents might have consequences.

I don't know whether my professor ever understood my perception of his behavior and why it was about power differentials and control. Since he often accused people of being uptight about sex, I suspect that he thought everyone was simply more prudish than ever.

An enduring result of this behavior was that it left me with ambiguous feelings toward both him and science. Many studies (Clewell and Ginorio 1996; National Academies 2006; Seymour and Hewitt 1994) reveal that for many scientists, especially women and men who are racial or ethnic minorities, recognition and encouragement by a teacher or mentor serves as the primary drive for their decision to pursue science. The same individual who recognized my talent and strongly encouraged (even pushed) me into science, also harassed me. This taught me that science, or at least working in the laboratory, can be uncomfortable, possibly something to avoid because of potential dangers of harassment. It is not surprising that I have mixed feelings about science and it partially explains why relatively early in my career I left bench science, at which I excelled and found pleasure, to pursue social studies of science.

Does this harassing behavior still occur? Today, some 35–40 years later, most institutions in academia, government, and industry have sexual harassment policies firmly in place. Although enforcement of these policies and meaningful sanctions against harassers leave substantial room for improvement, such blatant harassment appears to be less common or receives immediate attention and sanctions, as in the case involving the Physics Department at Duke University (Wilson 2004). More commonly now, the harassment is more subtle, may include intercultural elements, and/or occurs where the power differential seems less striking (i.e., between peers who are both graduate students or between a postdoc and a graduate student rather than my situation of an undergraduate and a tenured, full professor who headed a large laboratory).

Although reliable data on frequency and type of sexual harassment remain notoriously difficult to obtain, several studies in different professions and disciplines in science document that many more women than men are harassed and that substantial percentages of women scientists, physicians, and engineers have been harassed during their educational and professional training. Because women scientists are much more likely than men scientists to experience sexual harassment and to have been harassed by a scientist mentor, I believe these experiences leave women scientists with mixed, ambivalent feelings about their careers that may result in their taking different directions from the typical career trajectory of a male scientist.

Recent interviews with women scientists demonstrate how their experience of harassment led them to make a particular decision regarding the type of institution at which they would pursue their careers.

Molecular Biologist Opal Wurtz

When I finally went on the job market after a lengthy postdoc, I inspected my options carefully to be certain that I did not land in another impossible situation. I believe that I avoided a disastrous position at private Midwestern research I, where the dean was insisting that the department hire a woman. The woman who took the position I rejected, eventually sued the department.

This interview and autobiographical accounts (Evans and Grant 2008) suggest that women scientists turn away from elite research institutions because of sexism and harassment experienced there (Schneider 2000). Especially when coupled with the perceived high-pressure research environment, lack of community, and non–family friendly climate, harassment provides a further reason for women to avoid institutions they believe will replicate their graduate experience. They seek the more nurturing environment of small liberal arts colleges; some decide to avoid academia entirely.

A 2009 study of 8,373 doctoral students in the University of California system revealed that both male and female graduate students in science showed decreased interest in pursuing an academic career at top research universities compared to when they entered graduate school. However, significantly more women (84%) than men (74%) expressed concern about the family friendliness of their career choice, and more men still planned to pursue a career at a research institution (Mason, Goulden and Frasch 2009).

Bias/Discrimination against Married Women Scientists

In 1968, the summer between my junior and senior years in college, I got married. I was actually naive enough to believe that being married would facilitate my acceptance to graduate school and that my male lab partners would stop seeing me as a sex object and start treating me as a serious scientist. I thought that my desire to pursue a PhD after marriage would signal my serious intentions about my career as a scientist, since at that time a notion permeating the culture was that many women attended college to get a "Mrs. degree."

My husband and I applied to Harvard, Stanford, Berkeley, and the University of Wisconsin. Accepted at all but Harvard, I was surprised at the differences in funding offered to each of us. Although the University of Wisconsin gave us both fellowships, at UC-Berkeley, he was offered a fellowship, while I was offered a teaching assistantship. At Stanford, he received a fellowship while I received no funding. Because I had better Graduate Record Exam (GRE) scores, grades, and recommendations, I wondered if Stanford had made a mistake. When I called to inquire, the professor informed me that only my exceedingly strong record had persuaded them to admit me at all, since they assumed that as a married woman I was likely to have babies and "waste" my education.

Stunned by this revelation that marriage would detract from, rather than enhance, the perception of me as a serious scientist, we chose to stay at the University of Wisconsin because they had treated us fairly. Fortunately the department's ranking of number one in my field mitigated somewhat the problem of remaining at the same institution for graduate school from which we had received our undergraduate degrees. Of course it's impossible to evaluate the career impact of the options not taken.

In 1969, people commonly made comments like the one the professor at Stanford made to me, since overt gender discrimination in admissions, hiring, and salaries did not become illegal until the lawsuits and court decisions of the early 1970s. Today, candidates never hear such statements, or if they do, they can pursue legal sanctions.

Does this mean that the thoughts behind such statements and antifemale bias in student recruitment and barriers toward married women have been eradicated from academia? Unfortunately, the statements may now be more subtle. Although many academic couples exist in academia, considerable research suggests that dual-career couples face issues.

Several studies (Fleig-Palmer et al. 2003; Schiebinger, Henderson and Gilmartin 2008; Sonnert and Holton 1995) have explored the problems faced by dual-career couples in academia. The dual-career issue becomes especially salient for women in science and engineering because 62% of women scientists and engineers are married to men scientists and engineers (Sonnert and Holton 1995). In the fall of 2009, the Clayman Institute at Stanford released a study focused on dual-career couples in academia, which included data disaggregated for scientists. The study of 9,000 full-time faculty members at 13 leading U.S. universities found that although 36% of full-time faculty had academic partners, women (40%) are more likely than men (34%) faculty to have academic partners. In the natural sciences, they found that 83% of women scientists in academic couples are partnered with another scientist, compared to 54% of men scientists (Schiebinger, Henderson and Gilmartin 2008). Women scientists remain statistically much more likely than their male peers to face the dual-science career situation, as well as questions or hidden biases about the impact that childbearing will have on their scientific research. Perhaps the comments from faculty complaining/fearing that their research will be slowed when their graduate students or postdoc gets pregnant reveal the current, more subtle equivalent of the more overt statements I heard in the late 1960s.

Biologist Sherry Colby

Sherry Colby has an incredibly supportive spouse to whom she has been married for a long time. After receiving her degree in biology, she worked for the government as a physical science technician. She then pursued a MS degree and then a PhD. Although she loved doing research, she had an extremely negative postdoctoral experience with a very sexist advisor. Because of this, she sought a position at a small, teaching-oriented institution.

> After my sixth year at the small college, a woman came through and asked me to write a POWRE proposal to come to work in her lab. I uprooted my family and went to the lab. My husband stayed home with our three-year-old, whom I had delivered at age 39. I learned a great deal from this female mentor, who helped me to get my research back on track and taught me to write successful grants to obtain money. I continue to work in the mentor's lab every summer. Reinvigorating my own research this way also opened the door for me to mentor other women, whom I ask to work in my lab.

Although small teaching-oriented institutions do seem more family friendly, they have different expectations for faculty in terms of how time is spent. Because they typically have heavier teaching loads, expectations that faculty will advise students and student organizations, attend parent weekends, and perhaps even "prep" as well as teach the laboratory sections of all courses, faculty in these positions may find that they spend equivalent time on the job as do their colleagues in elite research institutions. Faculty at small teaching-oriented colleges often end up in a struggle to retain their research, as Sherry did.

Choices Foreclosed: Making the Decision for Me—PhD Dissertation

Just prior to the holidays, in December 1970, I defended my master's thesis and passed my qualifying examination for the PhD. Thrilled and more relaxed than I had been since graduation from college in 1969, my husband and I decided to try to start a family. We visited friends in Boston for New Year's and after attending a live performance of *Hair*, we conceived our first child.

Morning sickness dominated the first six months of the pregnancy. I finally had to explain to the professor who taught my 7:45 a.m. biostatistics class that the baby inside me, not his lectures, regularly caused me to rush out of the class early to throw up. Despite the nausea, I received A's in my courses that semester and began to think seriously about the proposal for my PhD dissertation.

Contrary to my fears, my major professor appeared to respond well when I told him about the pregnancy. Unlike some of the faculty in this all-male department, who refused to accept women graduate students, my advisor welcomed both women and international students, so I had some reason to hope for a positive response.

Typically students studying with him spent the semester after qualifying exams applying for Wenner-Gren or National Science Foundation funding to go to Africa to study *Australopithecine* remains. Concerned that he and I hadn't even begun the conversation about, let alone the preparation of, the grant application by mid-semester, I broached the subject with him the Monday after spring break. He told me that we must be thinking along the same lines because over spring break, he had spoken with folks at the Field Museum in Chicago and arranged for me to do a study of fossil rodent teeth, partly under the direction of the curator of Vertebrate Paleontology there.

Surprised and somewhat taken aback, I inquired why I wouldn't be going to Africa like everyone else to study the fossils there. He informed me that he was just being practical and thinking of me, since Kenya, Tanzania, or even South Africa were no place for a pregnant woman or a new baby. On some level, I felt a sense of relief, partly because I now had a focus for my dissertation, but also because I had worried about going to Africa, given the impending birth. On another level, I felt oddly deprived and controlled. Robbed of the option of choosing the subject and species for my dissertation, I felt that I had no input into a major decision determining my future career, since one's dissertation topic typically defines the research trajectory for at least several years beyond the PhD.

I have no doubt that my major professor intended to help me and that he thought he acted in my best interests by finding a project that would not derail or delay the completion of my PhD. As a professor I have seen circumstances less life changing than the arrival of a baby cause students to fail to take that final step and write up the data, remaining in that All But Dissertation (ABD) phase. I now understand his perspective and admit that he might have been correct. After all, when my daughter was 20 months old, I did receive my PhD, completing it in four years, only two and one half years after earning my master's degree.

Of course, the facts that my daughter arrived as a full-term healthy baby and that I was a healthy 24-year-old who experienced no post-partum complications, greatly facilitated my completing the PhD. As the stories of the various women scientists in *Motherhood, the Elephant in the Laboratory* (Monosson 2008) and in *Mama, Ph.D* (Evans and Grant 2008) document, a baby born prematurely, and/or with disabilities, as well as problems during pregnancy, delivery, and post-partum, can delay research and career substantially.

The part I struggled with then, and wonder about to this day, is his making the decision for me; I have always felt deprived of having the opportunity to choose the topic for my own dissertation. In retrospect, I've pondered whether that contributed at least partially to my decision to choose to pursue a different area early in my career as an assistant professor. Ultimately, I stopped work as an evolutionary biologist and used my biology background to inform my research on women's studies and social studies of science.

Does this happen today? Although some faculty might react to this situation in the same overtly controlling way my major professor did, I believe that more gender distinctions continue to enter dissertation work in covert ways. Reports of women steered toward less challenging or interesting topics than their male colleagues and anecdotes about major professors reluctant to critique women's research because they want to avoid "dreaded tears" in their office may represent the "modern" version of this differential "kindness" to women students.

Geologist Sue Perimeter

Sue believes that the confidence that her professor demonstrated in her as an undergraduate allowed her to persist in science after a very negative experience at the big state research university where she attended graduate school. Because she was married and had a baby, people perceived her as a "joke" who wasn't serious about science. Conversations with her undergraduate mentor provided her with the courage to seek a new advisor, when her initial advisor let her go. The new advisor enabled her to complete her MS. Because of this, she always tries to convey positive impressions to her students about the possibilities of combining motherhood and science.

> Despite this negative experience, I applied for the PhD program at a major university in another state. Told by the faculty and students at my MS-granting institution that I would fail at my new institution, I did not. I believe that the absence of preconceived notions about the inability of women and mothers to become scientists at my PhD institution allowed me to succeed and earn my PhD.

Pregnancy: About More than My Family

Late in 1974, in my second year of postdoctoral research, I realized I was pregnant with our second child. Using the word "realized" makes it sound as if I lacked awareness of the possibility or that contraception had failed. Although a rocky marriage, coupled with the absence of a tenure-track position for both my husband and me, made the timing less than ideal, our older daughter had just turned three. One thing that my husband and I agreed on was the desirability of having two children, so one night we mutually "allowed" an evening of unprotected sex.

Already having had a child enabled me to recognize the signs of pregnancy right away, even before I missed my period. Since I had taken a postdoc at the same institution where I had obtained both my undergraduate and graduate degrees because my husband still had not completed his PhD, we had some marital and financial worries. Still, I felt excited about the pregnancy.

About a month after the holidays, I decided to share the news with people in the lab before I began showing. Of course I first approached the professor who headed the laboratory. Although I didn't imagine that he would be thrilled with the news, I completely failed to anticipate his reaction, no doubt influenced by the Supreme Court decision, the previous year, legalizing abortion even in the very conservative state of Wisconsin. He told me to get an abortion because the pregnancy came at the wrong time in the research, since we needed to gather data intensively over the next several months in preparation for renewal of the grant.

His comments stunned me and shook me to the core, especially since it made me realize that my professional situation was equally, if not more, precarious than my personal situation. When the flu, followed by a sinus infection that wouldn't clear, landed me in the hospital, I asked the doctor whether the baby was likely to be harmed by my illness, wondering if perhaps the professor's suggestion of an abortion might be heeded. When the physician reassured me that he thought the baby would be fine, perhaps a bit small but OK, I proceeded with the pregnancy.

Soon I learned that the professor's new, third wife was pregnant. Since he already had two grown children from his first marriage, at age 50 he was not eager to become a father again. In contrast, his Latina wife, never previously married, did not view the marriage as consummated unless they had children. His secretary, my age and also pregnant with her first child, and I eventually pieced together that anger toward his wife about her pregnancy provided the source of the inappropriate, negative comments he had directed at each of us throughout our pregnancies. This became particularly evident as the birth times (all within two months) approached, and he began to talk about feeling abandoned by everyone. Since he had a lab full of technicians, grad students, and another postdoc, the secretary and I couldn't imagine what he meant until we realized that all of them were male. What he was really saying was that he felt abandoned by all the women who worked for him. The secretary and I kept his professional life running smoothly, while his wife managed the home front.

Although in retrospect I realize that the professor's comments reflected his own problems, at the time his comments made me feel that becoming pregnant had jeopardized my career. Since the baby he suggested that I abort graduated with a degree in chemistry from Harvard and is now a physician, I believe that my decision to ignore him resulted in a positive decision for both society and my family.

The political controversy that has surrounded abortion in the United States and current discussions and focus on family-friendly policies in the workplace mean that women scientists don't hear suggestions as blatant as "get an abortion because it's the wrong time in the research" any more. However, several indicators suggest that repercussions or fear of repercussions from childbearing remain rampant. Women report being asked certain leading questions during interviews for graduate school, postdoctoral, or faculty positions. They recognize that questions such as "what are your future plans?" code for "do you plan to have a family?"

In the United States, scientists have very few federal or institutional supports that their colleagues in other countries have to support childbearing and rearing, such as paid leave for both mothers and fathers, on-site nurseries, and making it mandatory to hold the position while on leave. Instead, children become an individual responsibility. Using 17 nationally representative data sets drawn from different stages of the life course, Xie and Shauman (2003) found that balancing career with family slows career advancement of academic women scientists, but not men scientists, with preschool children. In their study using data from the 1979–95 National Science Foundation's Surveys on Doctoral Recipients, Mason and Goulden (2004) found that male faculty members who start families within five years of receiving their PhD's are 38% more likely to earn tenure than are women who do the same. Only one in three women who takes a fast-track (elite or research) university job before having a child ever becomes a mother. In contrast, the group that they defined as "second tier women PhD's—those who are not working or who are adjunct, part-time, or 'gypsy' scholars and teachers" have children and experience marital stability much like men who become professors (Mason and Goulden 2004).

Every time I'm on a formal panel to talk about my career, I'm asked my opinion about the ideal time in the career of a scientist to have children, as many professional women still feel unsure of how to plan their futures. Anecdotes also underline the trepidation women feel when trying to decide whether to take advantage of policies such as stop the tenure clock and active service modified duty that evolved to help maintain career momentum during childbearing. The United States lags behind many European countries and Canada in having paid family leave. Many institutions have now instituted family-friendly policies such as "stop the tenure clock" and having a semester off at the time of childbirth or adoption. "Stop the tenure clock" policies typically permit faculty on the tenure track who must come up for tenure by their sixth year or face being out of the tenure-track position (commonly known as "up or out"), to have an extra year because of the birth of a child, adoption, or other major change in family circumstances, that does not "count" toward the time allotment. As Mason and Ekman (2007) suggest, women may actually face or fear a stigma if they take advantage of these policies. "Our study of University of California faculty revealed that the majority of mothers who were eligible for a reduced load—effectively no teaching for a semester following childbirth—did not take advantage of the benefit. They said they chose not to do so for fear of their colleagues' disapproval" (Mason and Ekman 2007, 87–88). Controversy remains over whether automatic stoppage of the tenure clock for both men and women, such as instituted by Princeton University (Fogg 2005), reduces the stigma for women, or simply leads to the men who have stay-at-home wives gaining an extra semester to write up their research, or the decision of both male and female faculty to avoid the stigma by not having children. At MIT, female tenure-track professors automatically receive one-year extensions, while men faculty must request extensions (Fogg 2005).

Will colleagues and the department chair take this out on the women in covert ways because they resent the impact on the students and the department of having to find the adjunct to teach classes during a leave for active service/modified duty? The women also fear repercussions from their male colleagues. For example, if they stop the tenure clock for childbirth, will colleagues expect another year's worth of publications for tenure and promotion? A growing body of research, including that by Mary Ann Mason (Mason and Goulden 2004, Mason and Ekman 2007) at Berkeley and my own work on POWRE and CBL awardees (Rosser 2004), documents that balancing career with family, particularly at the time of childbirth, is perceived to jeopardize the careers of women scientists and engineers more than any other single factor.

Nursing the Baby: Not an Acceptable Way to Spend the Lunch Hour

My training as a biologist made me keenly aware of the positive benefits of breast-feeding for the baby's immune system and overall health. Having breast-fed my first child, I never seriously considered not breast-feeding the second, although I should have recognized that the professor in whose laboratory I had the postdoc might have a problem with it.

One day at a lab lunch, he shocked the secretary and me, who were both nearing the end of our pregnancies, by announcing that he wasn't going to allow his wife to breast-feed, since "her breasts were for him, not the baby." Everyone seemed embarrassed by this remark, and several of the men graduate students and technicians went out of their way to tell me how inappropriate they thought he had been.

Already on guard because of his admonition that I get an abortion to avoid interrupting the research, I returned to the lab with some trepidation, five weeks to the day after the birth of the baby. I carefully selected a babysitter that lived in graduate student housing who would permit me to nurse the baby at her home during my lunch hour, as well as immediately before and after I went to the lab.

Everything seemed to go pretty well for the first six weeks or so until one day at noon. The professor/laboratory head received a call from a colleague in another state who had a question that pertained to my part of the work. Because the call came at lunch time, only one or two people were in the lab. One of the people who was there told me that the professor rushed around the lab, asking where I was. When someone told him that I probably had gone to feed the baby, he became very upset and asked why I would be doing something like that in the middle of the day. I had erroneously assumed that since most of the guys played squash everyday at noon, my leaving to feed the baby would be no big deal.

Venting his anger at me the minute I walked back into the lab, he demanded that I stand by him as he returned the call to the colleague and answered the questions. That incident made me realize that having the baby had made this postdoc untenable. I had to find something else as quickly as possible.

Fortunately, about two weeks earlier, someone from the newly formed women's studies program had approached me and asked me to teach the new Biology of Women course. She had explained that Ruth Bleier, now recognized as a pioneer in feminism and science, had developed the course and taught it once, but that her 100 percent research assignment precluded her teaching it again. Faculty in the women's studies program had heard that in addition to my PhD in zoology, I had participated in a consciousness-raising (CR) group with other women scientists; they wondered if I would be interested in teaching the course.

After the professor's reaction to the nursing, I jumped at the chance. It took about three weeks to work out the details with women's studies. I expected the professor to be relieved when I told him of my decision to leave the lab and go to women's studies. Instead, he hit the ceiling. He told me that I was trained as a research scientist and that I would be making a big mistake to go into something as faddish as women's studies. When I told him that I was finding my role as a laboratory scientist increasingly incompatible with my role as a mother, citing the incident of the phone call when I was out nursing the baby, he told me that I had over-reacted to his remarks. The irrationality of his response and failure to discuss the problem and possible solutions convinced me even more that I needed to get out.

When I stood firm in my decision to go to women's studies, he eventually relented a bit and also made arrangements for me to teach in the genetics department, so that my total salary from women's studies and genetics teaching approximated what I had earned as a postdoc. Teaching in women's studies and my involvement in the first year of what is now recognized as one of the oldest, best-established women's studies programs in the country opened up a wonderful new world to me which set the direction for the rest of my career. I realized that despite my having earned my PhD in zoology and having given birth to two children, I knew very little about my own body. Digging for that information and the feminist critiques of science we evolved proved pioneering work for which others and I have received pleasure and recognition. Despite my successful ascension through the ranks of academia as a tenured professor in a science department, for many years I wondered whether I was a failure because I no longer pursued bench research in science.

For engineer Karen Frost, breast-feeding affected her job search. She believes that the travel and other career demands make it difficult for many women to remain in science and engineering.

Environmental Engineer Karen Frost

Karen began college as a physics major but switched to the College of Environmental Science and Forestry, majoring in Forest Biology. She went to Africa with the Peace Corps after undergraduate school. Back in the United States, she and her husband decided to attend graduate school in engineering at a Midwestern land grant institution.

Since the time to interview for jobs occurred just after my baby was born, I had to ask to go to the bathroom to pump my breasts during the interview. This constraint made me carefully select the number and places to interview. Even though the department consisted of older, entrenched males, I received and accepted an offer from the New England public university where the faculty exhibited no problems with my need to pump during the interview.

Some institutions have begun to establish stations for "nursing moms" at different locations on campus to facilitate breast-feeding or pumping. Georgia Tech used some of the funds from the NSF ADVANCE grant to establish such stations (Rosser and Chameau 2006). Although helpful, the definition by many individuals of such stations as avant-garde or forward looking suggests the difficulties for women attempting to combine an academic career with childbearing.

Collegial Collaboration or Just Helping: A Gendered View?

In August 1969, I began my first of what would ultimately turn out to be three postdocs, in three different laboratories, headed by three different professors in three different departments at the same institution where I had received my PhD in June of that same year. Excited to begin a new project that built upon my PhD research but explored a new problem in a different species, I arrived early at the lab, eager to start each day. When, about a month into the position, the professor/head approached me and asked whether I would be willing to help him with the analysis of some data he had collected, I was thrilled.

He explained that he had collected quite a bit of data for a particular project on the species that he studied. He indicated that he had been told that multivariate analysis might reveal some of the trends he anticipated, based upon his years of study of the organism. Having served on my dissertation committee, he knew that I had used the computer to invert very large identity matrices, applying these "new" multivariate statistical methods to a large amount of data in a different organism. Admitting his ignorance of the methods and lack of theoretical understanding of their bases or implications, he asked me if I would run the analyses and write up the methods and results sections of the paper.

During the next six weeks, I lugged boxes of computer cards back and forth to the Computer Center, enduring the "downs" of receiving a one- or two-page print-out when the program didn't run and the "ups" of thick print-outs that revealed significant variables in the data. Hours of poring over the data, consulting with the professor, and running secondary and tertiary analyses followed these first weeks. Because I had relatively little experience in writing for publication, it took me almost two weeks to write the methods and results sections, as well as to prepare the tables and charts to go to Graphics. A few more days of the professor's reading and editing my sections of the paper and my making suggestions for the sections he had written meant that I had spent much of almost three months of this one year postdoc on these analyses, which had interfered substantially with the initiation of my own project. I consoled myself about the time investment by remembering that this would result in an immediate publication with a well-known person in the field, who was also department chair.

Imagine my shock and dismay when the professor asked me to do a read-through of the final draft before "we" submitted it to the journal and I found his name as sole author and my name in the acknowledgments, along with that of the secretary who typed the manuscript. Very upset, I consulted several friends, mostly non-scientists, as well as my husband, to see whether I was unreasonable to expect to be listed as a co-author on the paper. Fortunately, the next evening there was a meeting of my consciousness-raising (CR) group, composed entirely of women scientists and postdocs. Everyone to whom I had spoken, with the exception of one neighbor who had given up her career to be a stay-at-home mom, shared my outrage and believed that I needed to confront the professor and ask why he hadn't listed me as co-author on the paper.

The next day I went to our regularly scheduled weekly appointment. I asked him whether he had been pleased with my analyses and write-up of the data. He reiterated his gratitude for my help and underlined that he could not have done it without me. Trembling, I then suggested that I was disappointed not to have been listed as a co-author. He seemed amazed, saying that he had just thought of me as "helping" him. When I asked whether the analyses I had provided hadn't been crucial, he indicated that of course they were, just as was the typing done by his secretary. Noting my look of dismay and displeasure, he added that he would be pleased to add my name as co-author if that would make me happy.

He did add my name, but my pleasure at this needed addition to my nascent curriculum vitae was undercut. The incident had introduced doubts in my mind: Why had this happened? Was my contribution really significant? Did I deserve co-authorship? Or had this occurred because I was the first and only woman graduate student and postdoc in this man's 30-year distinguished career? Was this incident another indicator that I would be treated differently as a scientist and have to fight constantly not to be seen as a technician or a secretary? Just as the women scientists in *Every Other Thursday* (Daniell 2006) received support and reality checks from the group that helped them to bolster confidence in themselves as scientists when negative setbacks occurred in the lab or department, the CR group helped me to maintain equilibrium.

Although incidents as blatant as this seem to arise less frequently today, partly because more women graduate students, postdocs, and faculty are in the system, I hear anecdotes and see subtle remnants of similar behaviors: For example, perhaps the reports that abound of women graduate students who are steered toward different, "less challenging" problems to work on for their dissertation reflect a current, more covert version of a continued belief in a different role for women in science. Male professors' statements that they are reluctant to work too closely with women for fear of being accused of sexual harassment may lead women students and postdocs to have fewer co-authored papers with well-known men in the field compared to their male peers. The higher percentage of men graduate students compared to women graduate students receiving patents, even though they have the same advisor, may signify differential mentoring based on gender. These may represent the twenty-first century version of the behaviors I and other women scientists experienced in the 1960s and 1970s.

Interview: Computer Scientist Olga Smolensky

When she moved to the United States from Europe, Olga was already married and had a baby. She received her MS in computer science and began work on the PhD at the same public institution where her husband obtained a faculty position.

> I fought with my advisor who came from Iran; I was his first PhD student. He attempted to control me, and we disagreed over many issues, including publication of papers. Two years of work at the prestigious private university in a neighboring state, working with a famous researcher on robotics, and accompanying my husband on his sabbatical in California, at the same time that I gave birth to our second child, allowed me to complete my PhD, despite my advisor. Ultimately I switched to a different field entirely, which I believe improved my chances of obtaining tenure. I remain happy there.

When the Minimum Is Maximum

My first faculty position at a small liberal arts college for women provided many opportunities, including the possibility of returning to my alma mater to teach summer school. Retaining this connection to the major research institution proved significant for me on a number of professional and personal levels: My children could spend some extended time with my parents and my now ex-husband's parents, since both sets of grandparents lived in the same town. I had access to state-of-the-art computer facilities and other tools crucial for my research and unavailable at the small liberal arts college. I could refresh and maintain significant professional contacts with former professors, scientific colleagues, and my interdisciplinary colleagues in women's studies.

One Monday morning when my students and I flooded out of the classroom for our much-needed 15-minute break in the three-hour class, I ran into a former French professor from my undergraduate years. Although I had pursued my PhD in zoology, after double majoring in French and zoology as an undergraduate, he and I had remained in contact during my years as a graduate student and postdoc because we lived in the same apartment complex. I had not seen him for three or four years, and was delighted to run into him earlier that summer and learn we were teaching at the same time in the same building.

At this latest encounter, he said that his wife had directed him to invite us to their home for dinner the following weekend. I regretted, telling him that we would really like to do that, but explaining that I had to go to UC-Berkeley to give an invited talk that weekend.

"Really," he mused, going on to say that he had heard I was beginning to make quite a name for myself. He continued by saying, "Let me see if I've got it straight about your research area. If I understand it correctly, you've narrowed down your focus to women's studies and constricted it further to where that intersects with biology and health? So you work with this small area of biology with this fraction of the human population. Is that accurate? Is that what all the fuss is about?"

At that point the break ended, for which I was grateful, because I felt upset and needed some time to understand why. On the way home after class, my mind returned to our conversation. I wondered why what appeared to be a compliment from a former well-meaning professor from outside the field, recognizing that my work was getting notice, had left me feeling put down.

As I analyzed what had happened in the interaction, I realized that my former professor had described my area of research as small and narrow. How could he minimize work on women, who constitute half of the world's population, and something as significant as biology and health, which often have life or death consequences? After all, he had spent his entire career studying the eighteenth-century French philosopher and writer Diderot.

Some of my former professor's comments likely emerged from his surprise that a former student, who had chosen her first position at a non-research institution, in the South, no less, was beginning to make a name for herself. However, I believe that most of his reaction genuinely sprang from limitations imposed by his gender coupled with traditional disciplinary training. Having received the classical education for a French literary scholar, this professor had concerned himself not only with reinforcing the boundaries of the discipline, but also with disputes over whether the works of certain authors whose lives spanned more than one century should be studied along with the canon and in the courses devoted to the eighteenth or the nineteenth century of French literature. The disciplinary focus of eighteenth-century French literature on maintaining very strict boundaries provided limited encouragement for the professor to understand the new insights likely to emerge from interdisciplinary boundary crossings, particularly between disciplines as disparate as the humanities and sciences. As a scholar who studied the eighteenth century and the Enlightenment, he had become particularly steeped in notions of universalism. Unaware of the feminist critiques of universalism and its extrapolations inappropriately from men of a particular race and class to women and all races, nationalities, and classes, he probably did actually see "women" as a constricted, non-universal group.

Today most women would be less likely to encounter this sort of reaction. Women's studies has now existed for almost 40 years in the academy, so that most faculty know something about it, even though many fail to understand the significance of studying gender. Now interdisciplinarity forms the cornerstone of research, especially in the sciences. Nonetheless, women scientists in particular are discouraged from affiliating with women's studies, partly because women's studies is now perceived as affiliated almost exclusively with the humanities. Even a move to a different area of science can be perceived as risky, especially for women.

Computer Scientist Irina Schlamansky

Irina grew up in Russia, where science and scientists were held in higher esteem than they appear to be in the United States. She attended a special math- and science-oriented high school in St. Petersburg that was known as the best high school; the ratio of males to females was 2:1. Because her father was an engineer, she was surrounded by machinery; since she liked mathematics, she came to the field of computer science from an engineering standpoint.

Irina then attended an engineering school that had an equal ratio of men to women. In Russia, everyone majored either in engineering or human resources, just as in the United States a majority of students seem to be studying sales and business. While in college, she worked part-time as a computer programmer, which was where she initially became involved in research. Although computer science was not her undergraduate major, she decided to enroll in graduate school for computer science in Leningrad. She received her MS and was accepted for the PhD program, but she then immigrated to the United States with her parents.

For my first ten years in the United States, I worked as a programmer in a brokerage company. My husband, whom I met and married in the United States, worked full time, while pursuing his master's degree in chemistry. After our second child was born, I stepped down from the brokerage company to return to graduate school. Although I had two children at home and was working full-time at Blue Cross, I finished my PhD in six years. Massive layoffs at Bell Labs, where I hoped to work, gave me the idea to combine my computer science skills with the training in medical networks I had developed at Blue Cross. I was hired at a prestigious New York medical school to work in medical networks, one year before I completed my PhD.

Working as a computer scientist in a medical school seemed a mixed blessing. Not holding an M.D. proved to be a disadvantage; being a scientist became an advantage. In the discipline of computer science, I find age as a more significant issue than gender because the field changes so rapidly.

My 30 years of experience as a woman scientist in women's studies whose research has centered on women in science and engineering made me aware that the comments I had received from male mentors were not unique or even unusual. President Summers' remarks and the dialogue they generated made this very clear to the general public and even to women scientists who may have doubted how frequently women experience these situations.

The responses to the email questionnaire I conducted (Rosser 2004) of 450 POWRE and Clare Boothe Luce awardees, followed by in-depth telephone interviews of 50 of these women scientists and engineers, documented that most women scientists and engineers have experienced and endured similar situations during their educational and professional life.

So far in this chapter I have focused on words, behaviors, and timing that male mentors may use that prove harmful to women scientists and engineers. Although some women seem especially sensitive, while others remain relatively impermeable to the actions and reactions of others, none of these actions alone makes or breaks a career.

Numerous researchers (Zuckerman, Cole and Bruer 1991; Hall and Sandler 1982; Xie and Shauman 2003), however, have underlined that cumulative effects of these micro-inequities over a lifetime and career do make a very big difference. In their 1991 study, Cole, Zuckerman, and Bruer found that the gap between men and women in publications increased throughout their careers, because women received more negative micro-inequities and men received more positive micro-inequities or kicks. Over time, this accounted for a significant portion of the publication rate difference between men and women scientists.

Positive kicks or additions such as getting a paper accepted, being invited to deliver a prestigious talk, receiving a generous start-up package, and obtaining a grant on the first try, accumulate to move a career along a positive trajectory. Negative kicks and setbacks, such as failure of a major piece of equipment required for research to arrive for a year, having to move labs after the second year in the position, discovering that your department chair thought Larry Summers' remarks were on target, or a senior colleague who wanted his protégé to receive the position instead of you, make the path less smooth. When these professional kicks combine with positive or negative differences in personal life such as a supportive or non-supportive spouse/partner, an easy or difficult pregnancy and childbirth, presence or absence of a support network of relatives for child care and other emergencies, the effects may converge and multiply well beyond the micro-inequities to derail an initially promising scientific career. The stories of women scientists in *Mother-*

hood, the Elephant in the Laboratory (Monosson 2008) underline the particular way that the personal and professional intertwine to facilitate or hinder, or actually in some instances to make or break a scientific career.

Some of these decisions and circumstances such as childbirth difficulties or equipment failures remain out of the control of women scientists and their mentors. Some, such as choice of spouse/partner, definitely belong solely to the woman. While most of the others rest primarily with the woman, if both understand the significance of micro-inequities and their impact, the mentor and woman scientist can work to facilitate positive kicks for the career and mitigate negative kicks experienced by everyone at some point. As the Group in *Every Other Thursday* revealed to a member struggling with kicking a student out of graduate school, honesty becomes very important: "We've reminded one another that we do a disservice to both the students and ourselves if we fail to be honest about their abilities" (Daniell 2006, 142).

Only a few decisions fall into the realm of pitfalls so serious that they become a major deterrent to a successful tenure-track career in academia. The following interviews illustrate such pitfalls.

Always Putting Your Spouse/Partner's Career First

Geologist Jean Jones

Jean Jones began her interview by stating that her career differed from that of most women scientists. Instead of placing her career first, she put her husband and family first. Because she taught to help her husband finish his degree, she took five years to complete her PhD, while she followed her husband to his postdoc in Germany. She finished her PhD there and obtained a postdoc in Berlin. Her experience in Berlin plus her postdoc in Spain actually determined her specialty (non-marine carbonates) and gave her a niche, because that specialty is relatively rare in the United States.

After five years in Europe, her husband took a position at a comprehensive Midwestern university. Jean followed her husband and worked at the same institution as an adjunct for about a decade. She observed that although many successful women geologists did not have children, she placed her daughter and husband as her number one priority.

Although I eventually obtained a half-time faculty position that allowed me to continue to spend time with my daughter, garnering respect proved difficult. I managed to hang on, publishing a book, getting money here and there, and using my husband's library card. Many individuals, especially in the college dean's office, helped me, but I didn't really fit.

When I finally obtained a real position, my career blossomed. Although I had applied to NSF for years, my adjunct status made obtaining funding difficult. Right after getting my faculty position, I received the POWRE award which allowed me not only to continue my research, but also to move to the next level. The award also raised my esteem in the eyes of my colleagues and the institution; the president of the university singled me out in his address on the State of the University.

Unfortunately, right in the middle of my POWRE grant, I was diagnosed with cancer. NSF extended my award, and my health is looking much better now.

I believe that since women are the "family instigators," institutions should give women of childbearing age part-time positions. I wish that people would be more open to unusual job opportunities and that institutions would permit stopping the tenure clock and movement from part-time to full-time work more easily. I also believe that funding agencies should be open to funding individuals in non-traditional positions, since money is the key to success.

In addition to the obvious problem of having difficulty in obtaining a desirable tenure-track position because of family constraints, Jean's biographical sketch reveals other difficulties common for the trailing spouse: Circumstance, rather than interest, determined the area of her research focus. Fortunately, her rare specialty gave her a niche, but this might not have been the case, depending upon where her husband's career had taken her. She also experienced difficulties in obtaining funding, because most institutions do not allow adjunct faculty to serve as a principal investigator (PI), even on her own grants. Initially, without a permanent appointment she had difficulty garnering respect for her work and herself as a scientist. Although couples in all fields and particularly those in academia face struggles over career priorities, for women scientists, the issue is especially acute since, as the Clayman Institute report documented, 83% of women scientists are partnered with other scientists compared to 54% of men scientists (Schiebinger, Henderson and Gilmartin 2008).

Taking a Non-Tenure Track Position:
"Just Until My Husband Becomes Established"

Although Jean clearly decided that her husband's career and family would always come first, many women scientists think that they will defer their career only temporarily. They often believe that they and their husband/ partner can alternate who accepts the superior career opportunity. Sometimes the strategy of alternating career opportunities proves successful, as in Vinda's case.

Engineer Vinda Patel

Vinda feels that the most significant influence on her decision to become an engineer came from her family. Because her parents both worked as researchers in national labs, it seemed that everyone she knew was a scientist with a PhD. When she started undergraduate school, she naturally gravitated toward physics and materials science.

She attended graduate school at a major research institution in the Northwest, pursuing her degree in materials science and engineering. She got married right away to another engineering student after she received her MS degree. Her husband was very supportive of her work on a daily basis. Her excellent advisor, coupled with the predominance of outstanding role model faculty who were very active in research, and the surrounding environment of a research I institution, combined to lead her to consider a career in academia. Until she began working on her PhD, she had thought she would go into industry or follow her parents' path to one of the national labs.

> The receipt of the NSF POWRE award proved pivotal for my career. Not only did it permit a move in research focus from ceramics to biomaterials, but it also helped me to obtain a tenure-track position at the same Midwestern institution where my husband held a faculty position. Since we have a child, employment at the same institution is a high priority. I believe that the preliminary research and graduate students I hired with the POWRE grant enabled me to produce papers that were instrumental in my receiving a very prestigious CAREER award from NSF.

Not only does the institution where I work have only two women faculty in engineering, the particular field that I am in also has a dearth of women. Although the absence of women in both my college and field gives me high visibility, I recognize that I must be certain to be perceived as an independent researcher, since my husband's research area is close to mine and we collaborate on several projects.

Although sometimes the non–tenure track position can eventually be converted to the tenure track, not beginning in the tenure track can slow down a career. Unfortunately, many women do not experience the successful conversion Vinda did. Often, the first position sets the trajectory for future career opportunities. A good first job, when one performs well, often opens doors to new, better options; in contrast, a less favorable first position may limit and constrain options. As Mason and Ekman (2007) underline, these second-tier scholars rarely obtain tenure-track positions. More often, the spouse/partner who took the less attractive position gets "tracked" into a series of problematic positions while the other spouse's initial career success translates into a positive upward career trajectory. Unfortunately, the difficulties Sharon Smoakes encountered when trying to stay near her husband are common for many women, although some have less happy outcomes.

Engineer Sharon Smoakes

Sharon Smoakes recognizes that many of her professional and career decisions emerged because of efforts to solve the dual-career situation. After receiving her BS in chemical engineering from a technological institution and her PhD in chemical engineering from a prestigious public university on the West Coast, she took a postdoc there because she was waiting for her husband to finish. Because her husband wanted to go to another institution on the West Coast, she took a second postdoc there, in cell and molecular biology in the medical school. She learned a tremendous amount from this postdoc, and she had four different advisors, all male, who were excellent and provided her with important perspectives.

I found my first faculty position at the state university because my husband was at the flagship institution in the neighboring state. I became pregnant almost immediately. Then my husband received a job offer in the Northeast. The administrative structure began to change at my institution, resulting in my having a bad departmental chair. I began thinking about trying to move to the technological institution near my husband.

After having the baby and experiencing some health problems, I thought more about leaving. I wrote a POWRE grant, which the chair at my institution refused to let me submit. The NSF program officer permitted me to submit it through another organization. I also received a CAREER award from NSF, but the dean and provost refused to let me take a leave and gave me a termination letter. Fortunately, the POWRE award allowed me to begin a collaboration with the State Department of Health that led to the offer of a faculty position near my husband.

Despite the best initial intentions of both partners to alternate positive career opportunities, the initial decision often determines, or at least circumscribes, the trajectory and its direction. The first position determines the options available for the second and subsequent opportunities. Ultimately, economic gaps between tracks may emerge; as Mason and Ekman (2007) document, lecturer and research scientists lack job security and represent the first to go in times of financial crisis. These differences in salaries and job security put pressure on couples to engage in family decision making to benefit all; this often results in the person who took that initial, secondary position never catching up with the opportunities available to the spouse/partner. Desires to remain in close geographic proximity, especially when the couple has children, further complicate the situation. Many of the academic women who switched to second-tier positions did so to accommodate childbearing and rearing (Evans and Grant 2008; Mason and Goulden 2004).

Becoming Romantically Involved with Your Mentor

The dual-career situation for scientists and engineers proves difficult for most academic couples, as suggested by previous scenarios and as documented in the 2008 study from the Clayman Institute. In some fields such as physics, 58.3% of women physicists had a partner in the same department compared to 30.4% of men physicists (Schiebinger et al. 2008). When couples meet in graduate school and are in the same field, this can be especially problematic and often leads to the woman taking the secondary position initially. Being in the same field means that she obtains access to networks developed by a male partner or spouse. Because men have access to wider, more influential networks (Zuckerman, Cole, and Bruer 1991; Stephan and El-Ganainy 2007; Xie and Schaumann 2003), access through a male partner can enhance a woman's career in some ways. However, in addition to the usual dual-career problems, one type of situation can become a particular pitfall, as Kim's case illustrates.

Engineer Kim Rogers

Kim Rogers studied marine biology at a Northeastern public institution. Because she examined the benthic ecology of invertebrates, she became involved with hydrodynamics and coastal engineers. She spent the summer between her junior and senior years at Woods Hole and realized that she needed to attend graduate school in engineering. She became involved with a professor while she was a graduate student. Although they became engaged while she was still a student, they did not marry until she received her PhD. This relationship has determined her decision to stay at the technological institution where she received her degree.

> I believe that receiving the POWRE award from NSF saved me, because it helped me to obtain other funding. Without the POWRE award and the credibility it conferred, I would have had to leave the institution to go elsewhere. Although I have been quite successful in receiving grants from Office of Naval Research (ONR), National Oceanographic Administration (NOA), and the Army, I have been unable to obtain a tenure-track position and promotion at the institution. I have received numerous awards from the institution. The institution also has me teach there as an adjunct, probably because I am fully funded for five years from my grants, but I wonder if I can ever get on the tenure track.

Although Kim perceives the obstacle as obtaining a tenure-track position at the same institution as her husband, one wonders whether having become romantically involved with him while a graduate student would continue to dog her career there even if she were to negotiate a successful move to the tenure track. Would the issue re-surface at the time of tenure and promotion, for example?

Most women scientists report difficulties with time management. In the survey of 450 NSF Professional Opportunity for Women in Research and Education (POWRE) and Clare Boothe Luce (CBL) awardees, time management and balancing teaching, research, and service ranked second only to balancing career and family as an obstacle (Rosser 2004).

Coming Up Too Early for Tenure

After their mentees accept a tenure-track position, senior mentors can provide invaluable career guidance, especially in the pre-tenure period, by protecting junior faculty from excessive service and advising about when to go up for tenure. Male mentors need to recognize that their colleagues may hold different views about when it is appropriate for a female, relative to her male colleagues, to come up early for tenure.

Physicist Susan Emerson

Although support of male mentors helped her in undergraduate and graduate school, some advice from her mentor almost ended Susan's promising career. An unfortunate incident occurred when she was asked to go up early for tenure.

> Angry at the chair, the faculty voted against me, while unanimously supporting a male who came up simultaneously. I believe that institutions must pay more attention to mentoring women, providing money for networking groups, and access to conferences to overcome the isolation that women experience from being so much in the minority. This would also provide some protection or an opportunity for a reality check for poor advice given by mentors.

Jealousy and Competition

Obtaining grants and awards earns respect from colleagues. Although grants have value in the humanities and social sciences, most scientists and engineers have difficulty undertaking large projects without federal, corporate, or foundation funding. At research institutions, funding levels correlate closely with research productivity and publications required for promotion and tenure in most fields in science and engineering. (See table 1.2 for distribution of men and women at research institutions.) As with many career fields, the view that male colleagues have of some of these awards may differ, depending on the gender of the recipient targeted by the award. As Cybele experienced, male colleagues may especially resent grants and awards restricted solely to women, from which they feel unfairly excluded in a competitive environment with tight budget constraints.

Geologist Cybele Blakley

Two interviews at small liberal arts colleges resulted from Cybele's eight or nine job applications, as she finished her PhD. The position offered by the Northeastern women's college suited her well. Hired to replace a retiring senior woman, Cybele joined a department of mostly men. Her colleagues appear to have supported her transition to work in a different area. When she received an American Association for University Women (AAUW) Fellowship, she could take a full sabbatical year that helped her to finish the manuscripts and write the grant proposals that she needed to position her well for tenure.

> Although some of the older geologists accord me some degree of respect because of my Clare Booth Luce (CBL) Professorship, I find that some of the younger men appear jealous of the CBL, as well as the other opportunities such as the American Association of University Women Fellowship for which being a woman makes me eligible.

It's often difficult to assess appropriately the reasons for competition and jealousy of colleagues. If the colleagues are peers, it may be safe to assume that they hope to stay ahead of other competitors in order to obtain tenure, promotion, and salary increases.

Overt competition with a mentor can prove fatal, since he or she may fail to direct opportunities toward a mentee who is perceived to be a threat. Samantha may never know the genuine reasons why the department failed to ask her to lead the project when the principal investigator on the grant left the institution.

Environmental Engineer Samantha Short

Samantha Short attributes her becoming an environmental engineer to growing up in California, where environmental issues and air pollution received attention, as well as to the influence of her physicist father and chemist mother, who encouraged her interest in science generally and directed her toward AP classes in particular. Her sister is also an engineer.

She attended undergraduate school at a public New England university, where she might have fallen through the cracks had a genetics professor not taken an interest in her during her sophomore year and asked her to do research in his lab. He praised her problem-solving skills and encouraged her to go to graduate school, including helping her to decide to apply to a university in the South. The presence of environmental issues in Public Health created a more gender-balanced climate at that institution.

In the final year of my PhD program, my former institution had an opening. When I applied, my professors from my department in undergraduate school facilitated my being hired in engineering. Because my undergraduate degree was in science, I was not perceived as an engineer. The POWRE award helped me overcome this stigma. First, it provided a psychological boost for my confidence to realize that the NSF panel perceived my work as good. Second, it permitted me to work with an internationally renowned scientist who also had a foot in engineering.

In addition to serving as a turning point in my own career that enhanced my ability to sell myself better to others, leading to invitations to consult and deliver papers, POWRE encouraged me to reach out to other women. Although the climate in civil engineering remains tough, I have seen it change during the course of my career. Because I have had two children while in the tenure track, I appreciate the importance of stop the tenure clock and family-friendly policies to remove obstacles for women. The pressures of competition in the private sector have forced them to become more female-friendly because they cannot afford to waste the talent of women; academia lags behind the private sector in this regard. Because of POWRE I mentored five junior women faculty, helping them to win more than $1 million in grants.

I believe that the men in power view themselves as open-minded and not sexist. Because of this, the barriers they create are covert rather than overt. For example, despite my status as co-PI on a grant, when the PI left, the department asked another white male who was less involved in the project to lead it.

It is difficult to assess whether jealousy over Samantha's success generated by her POWRE award caused the department to pass over her and choose a male when the principal investigator on the grant where she served as co-principal investigator left. Sexism or other factors may have triggered the decision. The current environment of tight resources makes it more difficult to walk the tightrope between success and jealousy throughout a scientific career.

These vignettes illustrate some of the pitfalls that women scientists need to avoid to have a successful career. Individual mentors can provide important guidance at crucial steps to aid their mentees in maneuvering around these obstacles. Because of the powerful impact each mentor has on individual scientists' lives, he or she must be certain to understand this literature on pitfalls. Since microenvironments provide the difference in daily lives in the laboratory or department, lab heads and department chairs must insure a positive environment for all, with particular sensitivity to the needs of all women and of men of color. University leaders, in their roles of deans, provosts, vice presidents, and presidents, set the overall tone and climate for the institution. If that climate remains chilly for women, then institutional transformation must be sought.

Since I believe that many times male mentors remain unaware of the negative impacts of their remarks, some male mentors may also be oblivious to positive actions and words they can deliver. In the next chapter, I'll provide examples of such positive support for women scientists and their careers.

Some Behaviors and Messages for Mentors to Avoid

1. Don't de-emphasize or fail to take seriously all complaints. Even those that seem minor may have a cumulative negative effect when coupled with other micro-inequities.

2. Don't kiss, hug, or make comments about the bodies of students or employees or allow employees you supervise to sexually harass others. If a supervisor has been made aware that someone he or she supervises has been accused of harassing and does nothing about it, the supervisor may also be liable for harassment.

3. Don't permit a hostile environment that could constitute gender discrimination by permitting others to have pictures, send emails, or make remarks or jokes that might be offensive.

4. Do not ask only women students, postdocs, or potential employees if they would like information about parental leave and other family-friendly policies. Instead, tell everyone, both men and women, about these policies during their interviews and post the policies in the laboratory and on your website.

5. Don't avoid taking couples in the laboratory and don't vote against hiring an individual because he or she is part of a "two-body problem."

6. Don't "help" your women graduate students or postdocs by steering them toward less challenging research topics and problems when they become pregnant or are contending with family issues.

7. Don't tell students, postdocs, or junior faculty that they should or should not have a child or more children at a particular time or stage of the research.

8. Don't expect an additional year's worth of publications and funding at tenure, if the colleague has had the tenure clock stopped.

9. Don't insist that women faculty use the restroom or their shared office for breast-feeding.

10. Don't expect students, postdocs, and junior faculty to contribute substantial time, techniques, or analyses to a research project without becoming a co-author on the publication.

11. Don't assume that a former mentee's research is not significant because it is in a different area than yours, is interdisciplinary, or uses techniques with which you are not familiar.

Some Behaviors for Women Scientists and Engineers to Avoid

1. Don't always put your spouse's or partner's career first, if you expect to be taken seriously as a professional and scientist.

2. Don't assume that you will find an equally good position to the one you currently have or to the one offered your spouse/partner, if you move because your spouse/partner has received an excellent offer.

3. Don't assume that beginning as a lecturer or research scientist will mean that position can easily be converted to a tenure-track position.

4. Do not date, sleep with, or marry your mentor.

5. Do not assume that additional criteria will not apply if you come up early for tenure.

6. Do not assume that male colleagues will appreciate and understand why some awards and opportunities are restricted only to women scientists.

Positive Interventions from
Mentors and Mentoring Networks

Physicist Mary Vasser credits a male mentor at each level of high school, college, and graduate school for helping her to get through the difficulties in her educational path toward a career in particle physics. When others put her down and harassed her, a powerful senior scientist at the AT&T Bell Labs where she worked in high school, a highly respected male faculty member when she was both an undergraduate and graduate student at a prestigious Ivy League institution, and another well-known physicist at Oxbridge in England where she received her master's degree, supported her and helped her to believe that she could do it.

> After a postdoc in Boston, I took a faculty position at a neighboring institution. The ratio of 4/36 women stacked up favorably for a physics department. The senior faculty gave me opportunities but didn't overload me with committees, which allowed me to establish a solid research career to obtain tenure.

As Mary Vasser indicates, senior faculty can play a critical role in providing opportunities, while not overloading junior women with too many committee assignments. Some male faculty use their positions of power to appoint women to crucial committees. Protecting junior women faculty from serving on too many committees is more helpful than nominating them to large numbers of committees. Because of the dearth of women faculty and the desire to diversify representation on committees, men of color and women tend to serve on far more committees at all levels, compared

---

Parts of this chapter and chapter 4 were taken from a published journal article written by the author: Sue V. Rosser, 2006, "Senior Women Scientists: Overlooked and Understudied?" *Journal of Women and Minorities in Science and Engineering* 12(4): 275–293.

to their white male counterparts (Fogg 2003). This service often provides visibility for the woman, increases her collegial networks, and facilitates her understanding of institutional structures, policies, and practices. Unfortunately, in most institutions such service rarely receives appropriate rewards at the time of promotion and tenure, unless the research record and teaching performance have not suffered because of the excess service. Service overload presents a major threat to junior women faculty.

In contrast, refusing to accept any committee assignments and constantly declining opportunities becomes equally fraught with dangers. Junior faculty must engage in adequate service to be perceived as a good citizen whom their colleagues wish to retain, without losing so much time that research and scholarly productivity are jeopardized. Because knowing when and how to say no can be puzzling and problematic for most junior faculty, and particularly for women, a good mentor can protect from excessive service and advise when a positive response to a service request is critical or at least wise.

Teachers, professors, and mentors hold strong potential to provide positive encouragement and recognition for all of their students. Research (Astin and Sax 1996; Seymour and Hewitt 1994) documents that most women and under-represented minorities in science, technology, engineering, and mathematics (STEM) point to an encouraging teacher or role model who proved crucial in their decision to enter and remain in STEM. Women scientists seek mentoring not only in the early stages of deciding whether to major in science and what scientific field to choose, but also in later decisions about how to obtain promotion and advancement in the particular work sector and setting. In the study of the 450 academic women scientists who had received POWRE or CBL awards at research universities and small liberal arts colleges, "lack of camaraderie and mentoring due to small numbers of women" emerged as the issue cited second most frequently by women in all scientific disciplines as they plan their careers. The only issue mentioned more often and underlined as more significant was "balancing work with family responsibilities" (Rosser 2004).

One woman scientist in that study articulated why mentoring by other women scientists is particularly critical: "Although possibly less now than before, women scientists still comprise a small proportion of professors in tenure-track positions. Thus, there are few 'models' to emulate and few to get advice/mentoring from. Although men could also mentor, there are unique experiences for women that perhaps can only be felt and shared by other women faculty, particularly in other PhD granting institutions. Some examples of this include different, more challenging treatment by undergraduate and graduate students of women faculty than the treatment male faculty encounter, difficulties in dealing with agencies outside of the university who are used to dealing with male professors, and difficulties related to managing demands of scholarship and grantsmanship with maternity demands. More women in a department would possibly allow a better environment for new women faculty members to thrive in such a department through advice/mentoring and more awareness of issues facing women faculty members" (respondent 26 in Rosser 2004, 40).

"Mentoring for junior faculty" emerged as the response most frequently given (41.3%) by Association for Women in Science Fellows, a group of distinguished senior scientists (see chapter 4 for further information about this group) in response to an open-ended question regarding the institutional policy/practice most useful for facilitating the careers of junior academic women scientists or engineers: "Intense, active, continuing mentoring and establishment of support groups (breakfast, lunch, or dinner on a regular basis—i.e., weekly or biweekly gatherings) where women feel comfortable airing their concerns, gripes, fears, questions, to get reassurance, information, advice . . . from their peers" (Rosser 2006, 286).

Considerable research (Valian 1998) has documented that significant differences centered on issues of confidence and validity emerge between men and women in their decision to pursue a career as a scientist or engineer. A regular aspect of group meetings documented in *Every Other Thursday* featured members giving "strokes" or positive statements to other members to recognize their competence and build their confidence (Daniell 2006). As early work demonstrated (Bar-Tal and Frieze 1977; Deaux and Emswiller 1974), most women tend to attribute their success to external factors such as luck or help from others and their failures to internal shortcomings within themselves, particularly lack of ability, while most men do the opposite, attributing their success to their own strengths and their failures to shortcomings in the system or others (Swim and Sanna 1996).

For women considering a career in science, questioning their ability to succeed and fear of failure become especially salient because the choice to become a scientist represents a non-traditional career that goes against gender role expectations. The lack of female role models underlines and exacerbates questions women students have about whether becoming a scientist constitutes the right/good choice and whether they will be able to succeed in the male-dominated profession.

Male mentors and professors can play a key role in building confidence in women and signaling their acceptance of them as valid members of the profession. Although women mentors can provide particular insights on childbirth and career, given the relatively small numbers of women scientists, not only will women students have male mentors, but even those with women advisors should include some male mentors in their network. Research (Stephan and El-Ganainy 2007) documents that male mentors have access to more influential professional networks than their women peers. In the last chapter, I explored several experiences where male mentors and professors unconsciously or intentionally dashed my confidence and made me and other women feel they were less than valid members of the profession. In this chapter, I will explore ways in which male mentors provided opportunities that built confidence and helped others and me to believe we could be professional scientists.

The First Publication

When I finished my PhD in the spring of 1973, I had not yet published. This stemmed primarily from my major professor's declaration the previous year that he planned to move to Australia in the fall of 1973. He encouraged all of his students who had just begun their graduate work either to find a new major professor or apply for admission to the university in Australia. Those of us in the dissertation stage were told to finish everything by the spring of 1973 or to seek a dissertation fellowship that would permit us to spend some time in Australia, writing the dissertation under his supervision, while still graduating from our current institution where we had completed all the course work, MS degree, qualifying exams, and dissertation proposal.

With a baby in tow and a husband finishing his dissertation in another department, my choice seemed clear. Having completed the field work that summer of 1972, I rushed to complete the measurements on the specimens, to run the multivariate analyses of the data, and to write the dissertation during 1972–73. Finishing a year earlier than I originally had planned and three years earlier than the average time for students receiving the PhD in the department, I was thrilled to have received the PhD by the deadline proposed by my major professor.

Today, almost no one finishes a PhD in science without publishing. In 1973, people commonly had not published when they received their degree and even when they obtained their first job. Keenly aware, though, that some of my fellow students had already published, I was eager to publish and a bit apprehensive about how I would find the time to publish the papers from the dissertation, since the postdoc I had accepted was in a new lab and in a different field.

Fortunately, my postdoctoral advisor gave me an opportunity. In retrospect, I realize that he probably recognized that I needed both some time to write and a demonstration from him of his confidence in me.

About two weeks after I had begun the postdoc, he called me to his office. He told me that he had been asked to write a chapter in a book for Cambridge University Press edited by a well-known scientist. He suggested that since phylogenetic evolution of the immune system constituted the topic for the chapter, my background in paleontology and evolutionary biology gave me superior qualifications to him for this task. He asked if he might recommend me instead of him to the editor to write the chapter.

Even then, despite my newly minted PhD in evolutionary biology, I understood that he had the stronger qualifications, particularly in immunology, to write the chapter and that he was generously providing me a publishing opportunity. Buoyed by his confidence in me, I worked night and day on the chapter, finishing it in about six weeks. Both he and the editor were pleased with the results.

After the confidence and success instilled by publishing this chapter, I had no difficulty preparing the papers from my dissertation work in the "down-time" intervals between experiments during the new postdoc. To this day, I'm convinced that this mentor facilitated my career in both the short and long run by giving me the opportunity, at precisely the time I needed the encouragement and space, to publish. By creating a writing task that was part of my new postdoc, he gave me the time and space I needed in the short run to get something in print and the confidence to proceed immediately from that success to publishing papers from my dissertation without delay, while the work remained fresh in my mind. In the long run, the confidence he demonstrated helped me to feel like a professional, since he validated my PhD as a "superior qualification." He also reinforced publishing as a way to open the doors of recognition, prestige, and mobility in the broader profession.

For Rachelle, who had received a couple of rejections when she attempted to publish results from her dissertation, her advisor's suggestion that she try something else for a bit also gave her the space she needed. The time in a different country and successful publication of the results of that project helped to build her confidence.

Geologist Rachelle Spotson

Although Rachelle had a male advisor for her PhD, the presence of a well-known historian of science who was a senior woman made her feel that the women in the graduate program were looked after and that women's concerns received attention. At the end of four years she had collected all of her data. Because a couple of the articles she had attempted to publish were rejected, she began to wonder whether she was ready to function as an independent scientist. Her advisor was supportive and suggested that she obtain a Fulbright and go to New Zealand for a year, although it negatively impacted his own research.

> Upon my return, I had the confidence to enter the job market because I had published the small project that I completed in New Zealand. I received the position I wanted, partly because they perceived me as confident and able to complete my dissertation.

Again, the willingness of her major professor to look beyond his professional needs to suggest an avenue in the best interests of his student allowed Rachelle to publish in the short run. In the longer term, it had the impact of building her confidence to find a job in her field. One function of the group in *Every Other Thursday* focuses on enabling the scientists who are mentoring graduate students, postdocs, and technicians to separate and define their needs and interests from those of their mentees (Daniell 2006).

Responding to Insecurity with Confidence of Expression

In contrast to my slightly later start in publishing, I began teaching undergraduates somewhat earlier than the average. During the second semester of my junior year, the professor in whose lab I had worked at least 20 hours per week since my freshman year, asked me if I would like to serve as a teaching assistant (T.A.) for a discussion section the following semester when he taught his large lecture in Genetics and Human Affairs. Knowing no other undergraduates who had ever served as a T.A., I was honored that he asked me.

Because T.A.'s were always graduate students or postdocs, he had to circumvent quite a bit of bureaucracy at this state institution to make this happen. Ultimately, I received three credits for an "independent study/ research" course under his supervision for attending the lecture, leading the one-hour discussion section each week, and helping to formulate questions and grade the examinations for the lecture part of the course, along with the other T.A.'s, all of whom were graduate students.

Wanting to do an exceptional job as a T.A., both to demonstrate to myself that I could do this and to insure that other undergraduates might be given a similar opportunity, I prepared diligently over the summer. I began the semester with the problems worked for the first half of the course and lesson plans for what I might do during the first month of discussion sections, depending upon the direction he took in lecture. The students in my section responded well; they didn't seem to change their reaction or class attendance even after the fifth week, when one day during lecture the professor casually revealed my status as an undergraduate student.

Even though the students received less than stellar grades on their first exam, all continued to go relatively well. Actually my section exam average was higher than the mean. One day shortly after mid-semester, just as we had begun to work through some relatively difficult problems on population genetics, the professor walked into the discussion section and took a seat at the back of the room.

Although he had warned all of the T.A.'s that he would make an unannounced visit to our section to observe and evaluate our performance, for some reason I was completely surprised when he entered the room. I became very nervous and somewhat flustered, as my quaking voice and shaking hands made very evident. By the time the class ended, I felt like a wreck and couldn't honestly remember the explanations I had given or whether I had worked the problems correctly.

Since the professor had left about five minutes before the end of class to attend a faculty meeting, I didn't have the opportunity to talk with him. All night I tossed and turned, imagining the blistering critique he would render of my teaching and worrying that he would ask one of the graduate student T.A.'s to take over my section for the rest of the semester.

The next day in the lab he didn't even mention the section and appeared to treat me the same way he always did. I wondered what he thought. Finally when he was back in his office at the end of the day, I knocked on the door and asked timidly for his feedback on my teaching. He said that obviously I was very nervous, for reasons he didn't quite understand, but that the students seemed engaged and my explanations were right on target. We talked a bit more about the class, and as I left he asked whether I wanted to teach another section the following semester.

That served as the right question at the right time. By asking me to teach next semester, he demonstrated the confidence in my teaching I needed to face the students in this section and redouble my efforts to insure that they continued to perform at their maximum this semester. More importantly, he restored my belief that maybe some day, after many years in graduate school and as a postdoc, I too could be a professor.

Although many mentors provide a "mixed bag" for their students, women often receive the extremes of the positives and negatives. This mentor, also the one who sexually harassed me, clearly had major insensitivities. Yet, he somehow knew what to say at that time of vulnerability in evaluating my teaching to restore my confidence and keep my dream alive.

For Ulla, professors who also treated her a bit like a graduate student by allowing her to take graduate courses and pursue a research project, while still an undergraduate, encouraged her to pursue electrical engineering.

Engineer Ulla Mysom

Since Ulla Mysom knew that she didn't wish to become a teacher like her mother or a carpenter like her father, she followed the path of her computer scientist cousin. She received her undergraduate degrees in both computer science and technical writing. The major influence on her decision to pursue electrical engineering was the research project she undertook in electrical engineering as an undergraduate.

> Particularly since the overall climate for women in electrical engineering is a bit chilly in terms of the isolation and getting male colleagues to converse at conferences, women must draw their inspiration from the excitement of research. Although the undergraduate research project failed, I learned to love image processing. In retrospect, I recognize that many of the good professors, who encouraged me by allowing me to take graduate courses while still an undergraduate, probably influenced me.
>
> Because I knew that I loved both teaching and research, I went directly into academia immediately after receiving my PhD. As the only woman in the department in the northeastern public institution where I teach, I believe that it is critical to hire undergraduate women to work in my laboratory so that research can inspire them to enter the field.

Although the role of a major professor or postdoctoral advisor remains critical, sometimes a faculty member who is a former teacher, member on the student's dissertation committee, or even just in the nearby lab can fulfill a critical career-guiding role. These individuals may intentionally or unintentionally counterbalance some of the negative insensitivities of the major advisor.

A Tenure-Track Position

By my third year as a postdoc, I knew most of the faculty in the Genetics Department at least somewhat. Since our lab had the best coffee, and very frequently one of us brought in some donuts or cookies, all three of the other faculty on our floor stopped in at least once each day to fill their cups and chat.

The faculty in the all-male department treated me politely, but I could tell that some felt more comfortable than others interacting with me as a colleague, especially in comparison with the way they felt with the male postdocs. The professor in the lab next to ours treated me as a colleague, so I especially enjoyed talking with him. I also knew and held immense respect for his wife, who served as a justice on the State Supreme Court. During this time period of the early 1970s, because of their extreme scarcity, I eagerly sought out and studied any women in high-level professional positions.

One day while chatting over coffee with the professor from the neighboring lab, I made a remark which clearly implied that I planned to stay in this lab for several years, to run the projects of the professor who headed the lab. The professor from the neighboring lab looked puzzled, and asked why I would do that. He inquired whether I didn't want to become a professor myself.

At that moment, I realized that he had succinctly stated an issue that had bothered me for some time and that had floated in my head in a fuzzy, inarticulated form. On some level I knew that I did want to become a professor. However, I had had no role models of women faculty in the departments from which I had received my undergraduate or graduate degrees or where I currently served as a postdoc. Although as an undergraduate, I had taken one English course and three French courses from women faculty, including two full professors, I knew that all of them were not married. Not only did all of the science departments in the College of

Letters and Sciences have no women in tenure-track positions, but also the university actually had a rule prohibiting women from being on the tenure track if their husbands were on the faculty.

In contrast, I knew many women PhD's, including relatively large numbers of women who were scientists. They actually conducted much of the research, writing the grants, planning the experiments, and managing the lab, while the professor and laboratory head taught, attended meetings, and served on dissertation committees. These women held non-tenure line positions with titles such as postdoctoral fellow or associate research scientist. Often married to the professor, the woman kept all running smoothly, in partnership with her husband, both in the home and the lab. Male professors who were not married to a woman scientist in their area of expertise often sought out a bright woman scientist to serve in the role of "lab wife" and to complement the duties of their legal wife who stayed at home or was not a scientist.

The professor with whom I had this current postdoc had a new, third wife who was decidedly not a scientist and definitely wanted to stay home and have a baby. He had talked with me about running the lab in the future because we had just received word that our large National Institutes of Health (NIH) grant had been funded for the next five years. With a child, a husband, parents, and in-laws in town, remaining at the university in such a position provided a future that had definite advantages, one of which was that I could envision it as a possibility, since I knew other women PhD's in similar positions. Although it didn't feel very satisfactory for the long term, I had difficulty imagining other alternatives, since I literally had no role models of married women scientists (with or without children) who were professors.

During the next year, I thought of the neighboring professor's question from time to time. Once I even discussed it briefly with him. Although I suspect that his fear of angering my professor/lab head prevented him from encouraging me too strongly, he did again ask whether I too didn't want to be a professor.

The next year when my second pregnancy and childbirth had caused friction with my postdoc supervisor, and simultaneously my marriage was in trouble, I remembered his query. One night I tossed and turned, worrying about how I could extricate myself from both the professional and marital messes I had created, especially now that I had two babies for whom I was responsible. This question triggered the thought, "I could become a professor."

Although it was May and well beyond the academic job season, the next day I scoured the ads in *Science* and on the bulletin boards. Later that week, I saw an ad for an assistant professor of biology at a women's college in Virginia. I applied, was invited for the interview, and obtained the job. I told my husband that I was taking the position and that he could come or not. By August 1, my two children, husband, and I had bought a home and moved to Virginia.

I doubt very much that the professor from the neighboring lab ever knew the significant impact that his asking that simple question had on me. The respect and confidence that he had shown by asking me whether I didn't want to be a professor had remained with me and bolstered me when I really needed to make a transition to escape a professional quagmire. In retrospect, I also view my obtaining a tenure-track position as one of the first steps that empowered me to leave my problematic marriage, although that took a couple of more years.

Women faculty often serve as mentors to many students and post-docs for whom they are not the assigned advisor or official major professor. Although many of these unofficial mentees are women seeking role models, studies (Burroughs Wellcome Fund and Howard Hughes Medical Institute 2004) document that women faculty are sought out preferentially by both men and women students. Although this unofficial mentoring contributes to retention of students and postdocs, its unofficial status means that this work often fails to be acknowledged by the institution in evaluations and raises. A position at a women's college also permitted Angelina to extricate herself from a postdoc of five years and to attain the personal goal of remaining in geographic proximity with her husband.

Chemist Angelina Longini

Angelina Longini obtained her MS and worked as a master's level chemist for four years while her husband was working on his PhD. This early exposure to the work world convinced her that she must obtain her PhD. Her male boss held very traditional ideas about women, perhaps because he was from India; he looked down on someone who only held the MS degree. After enduring his threats and admonitions to know her place, she decided she must get her PhD.

With a nine-month-old baby, I decided to pursue my PhD in the Midwestern city where my husband worked so that we could cooperate on childcare. During the last two years of graduate school, we had a commuter marriage because my husband took a position on the East Coast. The first of those years, living as a single parent made me feel especially constrained in my work. My husband took our son with him the second year, permitting me to work the long hours in the lab needed to complete my PhD.

Because I was geographically constricted, I sought and remained in a postdoc on the East Coast for five years. My boss used me to run the lab. A position at a women's college in the same geographic area emerged at just the time I was considering leaving the field.

As Mason and Ekman (2007) point out, the numbers and percentages of PhD individuals in non–tenure track positions serving as lecturers and research scientists has increased dramatically in universities since the 1970s. Women constitute the majority in these second-tier positions. Although institution-wide nepotism rules no longer formally exist, some departments have them. This constitutes a further barrier to non–tenure track faculty hoping to receive a tenure-track position. Mason and Ekman cite Leslie, who had two children and began to lecture part-time: "Ultimately she ran into the 'nepotism wall', which is sometimes a formal and more often informal rule that universities should not hire the spouse of a faculty in the same department" (Mason and Ekman 2007, 87).

Even after obtaining the PhD, women may continue to question whether they should remain in science. Because the postdoctoral period represents a time of intense professionalization for scientists, women who remain isolated as the only woman or only woman postdoc in a particular lab may find that issues may resurface about whether it's possible to be a scientist and a woman or mother.

Not Equating Science and Engineering with Masculinity

As I began my first postdoc in 1973, I found myself entering into one of those transition points where I again questioned whether I really belonged in science. In some ways, this seemed ironic, since I had just completed my PhD—the union card to the scientific research profession, as one of my committee members phrased it. In other ways, looking back and questioning seemed only natural and logical, since I now know that many people experience a let-down following the completion of a major project and goal such as the PhD. Furthermore, because I had a young baby and a husband who had not yet completed his PhD, I was beginning a postdoc at the same institution where I had obtained both my undergraduate and graduate degrees. Although I was grateful to have found a postdoc and desperately needed the money, even my general naïveté about the profession did not prevent me from realizing that continuing at the same institution did not constitute a great career move.

Another aspect of the questioning focused on the old problem that had haunted me since my undergraduate days about my choice for a major: Did I really belong in science? The absence of women faculty from tenure-track positions, coupled with the types of negative comments described in the previous chapter coming from male mentors and peers, made me wonder where and if I would fit in. From conversations I had held with the very few other women graduate students, I learned that this question bothered most of us a good bit.

As a biology major, I had always held a keen interest in health and medicine and wondered whether I should consider medical school. One day early in the postdoc, when I felt particularly doubtful about my future as a researcher, I spoke with admissions folks in the medical school. At first the admissions officer welcomed me and responded positively when he saw my transcripts and PhD. Then he learned that I was married with a child. Suddenly his tone changed dramatically. He told me that I would no longer be considered a good prospect. He continued by stating that if I were accepted, I should expect a failed marriage to pay for medical school and asked whether I was prepared to do that.

Leaving the interview, I ran into the father of an old friend of mine from high school. A member of the medical school faculty and head of Internal Medicine, he asked what I was doing over in the medical school. He asked jokingly if I had finally come to my senses and decided to go to medical school, as he had always thought I should do instead of pursuing a PhD.

I told him that I had been thinking of it until the interview, but that now it didn't seem likely. When I told him what the admissions officer had said, he replied, "You're not going to pay any attention to something like that, are you? You know much more about both science and people than that. You know that being a good doctor or scientist has everything to do with brains and commitment and nothing to do with old-fashioned ideas about masculinity, femininity, marriage and careers, don't you?"

His words conveyed precisely what I needed to hear at that moment. As a respected and distinguished Professor of Medicine who was also a trusted family friend, his comments overshadowed those negative comments of the admissions officer and of other scientists who had made disparaging comments to dissuade other women and me from the profession. I decided not to pursue medical school but to continue on my path as a research scientist. His sensible statements and the confidence he exhibited in me allowed me to persist in that time of transition and doubt.

Although women now constitute half of medical students, women scientists today continue to hear remarks that make them question whether engineering or their particular discipline of science is defined as masculine and therefore inappropriate for them. No one likes to feel as if they must give up their femininity, motherhood, or another characteristic they view as core to their identity in order to fit into their profession.

In her interview, Michelle Antonia expressed her own questions about fitting in to mechanical engineering.

Engineer Michelle Antonia

Michelle's father, who was an engineer, guided her toward the profession when he observed that she particularly enjoyed the practical applications of math and science in high school. She found that she enjoyed and fit in at the private northeastern technical institution where she went to undergraduate school. The faculty encouraged her to go to graduate school, and she learned that she loved research while pursuing her MS at the public Midwestern university.

> After receiving my PhD, I decided to pursue an academic position, mostly to prove that I could do it. Eventually I thought I would leave academia to go into industry.
>
> In contrast to my own success, I find the overall climate for women in mechanical engineering difficult. Sometimes I wonder whether I belong in this field with all of these guys. When parents and/or peers suggest that mechanical engineering is dirty and therefore inappropriate for women, I question how the perception of the field deters both me and my students.

Research by Cynthia Cockburn (1983, 1985) reveals how the historical conjoining of the military and engineering, combined with the continued high percentage of men in engineering and computer science, leads women and the public to question women's fit into these male-dominated fields. Research documents that the more an individual deviates from the expectation of what a "professional in the fields looks like" with regard to gender, race, class, age, and other factors, the more others inside and outside the profession will question that individual's professional competence. Since 90% of U.S. engineers are white males over age 50 (National Academies 2007), a young African American female engineer faces many challenges to her competence because she differs in so many ways from the stereotype of an engineer. A savvy mentor who has power and credibility can help establish the competence of such an individual by demonstrating his belief in her competence to other men.

Providing Informal Opportunities to Talk to the Guys

During my first month on the job as the first woman dean at a technological institution, I received a call from the president. He asked whether I would be willing to serve as one of the faculty representatives on the Athletic Association Board. He indicated that although the Board was a separate corporation from the institution, with alumni, community, and student members, as well as faculty, that academics represented the majority of voting members. The president then reiterated the importance of both academics and athletics, an identifying motto for this research-focused institution that also boasts athletic teams in the NCAA Division I football and other teams.

Although I had no personal interest in sports, I knew better than to refuse this invitational request from the president, especially during my first month on the job. Aware of some of the Title IX rules, I imagined that being a woman and a dean played a role in my appointment.

When I casually mentioned this to some of my peers, faculty, and staff, all the men seemed envious and wondered how I had managed to "swing that." My development officer made the prestige of the appointment clear, relishing the impression that the appointment would make on alums and fundraising. He explained that many of my peer deans would give their eye teeth for such an appointment.

When later that same week, the appointment of the second woman dean at the institution was announced, I wondered why she had not received the Athletic Board appointment. Since the overwhelming majority of athletes were alums of her college and since she had risen to her position as dean from the faculty, rather than coming from outside the institution, such an appointment would have made sense.

Quite immediately, I could see that my appointment to the Board provided a certain cachet, particularly with male colleagues and alums. Passing on some of the perks of the position, such as two extra free tickets to football and basketball games, seemed to please chairs or donors to whom I gave these small rewards.

Because of this position, I actually did learn some of the inner workings of the athletics association as well as the Atlantic Coast Conference (ACC). I found myself able to enter into conversations about likely bowl opponents and about why having the most ACC teams going to bowls, including the less prestigious ones, benefited the conference as a whole financially because of the basis of the split. My appointment to the finance subcommittee of the Board proved invaluable for my understanding the layers of complicated finances of the Board, as well as the financial relationships among the athletic association, the institution, and the NCAA Conference.

Eventually, my male colleagues, and even my superiors, respected my knowledge and opinion in this area. They occasionally asked my opinion about how a particular Board decision they had read about in the newspaper would impact the finances or academic program of the institution.

After I completed both of my three-year terms of service on the Board, I reflected back on my initial wonder at why the president had appointed me—a new woman, dean, non-sports fan, and institutional outsider—to this Board. Realizing how many contacts I had made, how much I had learned about sports, and very importantly about the financial interrelationships among the conference, institution, donors, and athletes, I understood how wise the president had been.

As a man, a superb fundraiser, who himself was a big sports fan and alum of the institution, he recognized the importance of this appointment for orienting and educating me in my role as dean. He facilitated my meeting certain powerful donors and alums of the institution who were not alums of my college. He provided me with the opportunity to become knowledgeable about sports in general and their financing in particular. The understanding and mutual respect that this generated helped level the playing field for me as the first woman dean at this institution where 70% of the current students and 80% of the faculty are men.

In contrast, women who do not have some guidance from senior men may miss out on crucial information passed through informal networks. Over the years, Betsy learned about how difficult it is for women to get in the "loop."

Botanist Betsy Courtling

Betsy attributes her career in botany to her fascination with nature as a child and to spending her junior year abroad. In Germany, where botany was highly respected, Betsy first used electron microscopy to study plants. The second woman in the department in a tenure-track position, she became the first woman to have a child.

> Now the department seems to be experiencing an explosion of children, but it was a lonely and somewhat isolating experience ten years ago. I still find some bias against women as power holders. Being out of the loop of informal conversations causes difficulties for women who miss out on crucial tidbits of information. I believe that mentoring from senior colleagues would help junior women learn the ropes about how to approach the dean for cost-sharing, how to negotiate counter-offers, and use end-of-year money to obtain equipment.

In addition to facilitating entry or at least providing contacts and information from the old boys' network, male mentors can encourage women to support activities for women in science. Many women scientists fear they will be stigmatized for attending or leading efforts to support women in science. In shunning women in science and seeking only to be accepted as a scientist, not as a woman scientist, they wish to identify with the powerful who are men. These "queen bees" sometimes go so far in their attempts to identify with the powerful men that they oppose programs to help women scientists, indicating that they made it on their own and so should others. In contrast, powerful male mentors can signal to all women, including senior women, the importance of women in science programs.

Encouraging Continued Focus on Women

When I became the first woman academic dean at the public technological institution where I was hired in 1999, I wondered whether they really knew what they had gotten. Although my curriculum vitae, which at that time included seven books and 80 articles on women and science, not to mention my 20 years as director of women's studies, provided clear clues, I wondered if they understood the implications of that.

During the interview process, I tried to determine this by asking questions of different individuals and groups, in ways that I hoped were discreet: Do you think the institution is ready for a woman dean, I inquired of the other deans? What strategies has the institution developed to attract and retain women faculty, I asked the provost?

Keenly aware that being the first woman dean obviously focused their attention on gender, I didn't want to overemphasize my own research interests on science technology, women, and gender. But I did want to ascertain their readiness to engage in institutional transformation to create a comfortable climate for women, including me. With my questions, I attempted to walk the fine line between appearing obsessed and focused only on women's issues and finding out what I needed to know. I did not want to take a job at an institution where they would be upset when they learned about my work on feminism and science or on development and implementation of policies and practices for women, since one of the many aspects that attracted me to the position of dean was the possibility of continuing this work at a different level in the administrative hierarchy.

The reassuring answers to my questions convinced me to take the position. When I arrived on campus, several of the women faculty, including some in other colleges, made it very clear that not only did they know what they were getting, but that they also had pushed hard for me. They were thrilled I was here because of my background and anticipated great advances for the campus as a whole to come from my leadership on women's issues.

As part of my start-up package, I negotiated three years of funding to support a center for women, science, and technology; during the first year, I convinced Housing to provide a dorm for sophomore women in science, as a variation on a learning community. Pleased with our initial progress, the other women faculty and I began to strategize about ways to insure the permanent future of these efforts, as well as a much larger project to advance women faculty to senior and leadership positions.

Since this larger effort would focus on promotion, tenure, and hiring for the entire institution, success would not be possible without support of key male top administrators, especially the deans, provost, and president. Very aware that this would serve as the real test of how committed the institution was to advancing women, I approached the most powerful male dean of the largest college.

His response stood as some of the strongest institutional and personal support I have ever felt. He not only agreed enthusiastically to support the proposal, but he also offered to approach the provost to see if he would serve as the PI on the grant. Known for his conservative views, the provost would be more likely to endorse the project if approached by the powerful male dean than by me. Although my fellow dean didn't say so, he recognized this immediately and offered to obtain the provost's endorsement to serve as PI. Centered on issues nearest and dearest to faculty purviews and power such as promotion, tenure, hiring, and collecting data on sensitive issues beyond salaries, including start-up packages, space, and salary supplements, the provost had to serve in the critical role of PI to obtain these data and to insure genuine transformation of the entire institution.

By the time the ADVANCE grant funding from NSF arrived, the powerful dean had become provost and served as the PI himself. Working with him in that position allowed us to push institutional advancement of women beyond my hopes and expectations. His confidence and support of me also enabled the college to accomplish outstanding achievements, unrelated to gender, while I was dean.

Like their male counterparts, successful women scientists can also provide powerful encouragement on women's issues. Kara Kockelman perceived that receiving the Clare Boothe Luce Professorship provided her with the entitlement and momentum to encourage other younger women to go into science and engineering.

Engineer Kara Kockelman

Kara Kockelman credits her father, mother, and siblings with encouraging her to be competitive and pursue technical interests. The faculty at the public research I institution in the state encouraged her to think about an academic career even as an undergraduate. Although she had no female mentors until she began teaching, Kara found that the male faculty both in undergraduate and graduate school did mentor her.

Not a member of Society of Women Engineers (SWE) either as an undergraduate or when I began teaching, I fought to become the advisor of SWE. Since the organization already had two other advisors, I knew I had to be a role model and seek out the position. I undertake considerable outreach, using the Expanding Your Horizons Program, the Girl Scouts, and Engineering Week to encourage middle school girls to consider careers in engineering. Because I received the nomination for the CBL Professorship before I started teaching, I have tried to give back by using some of the Luce money to sponsor a forum for future women faculty. I want to attempt to improve the situation for younger women in science and technology.

Reading interviews of many women engineers and scientists from different disciplines also reveals some more subtle circumstances and decisions that appear to be career-enhancing. Many of these fall under the control and responsibility of the woman scientist. Although none of these alone can make a career, when coupled with other favorable circumstances and the intelligence and hard work of most women scientists, a positive trajectory can be enhanced. Awareness of these factors allows both the women and their mentors to appreciate the role they play in career development.

A Supportive Spouse/Partner

Several surveys, coupled with numerous anecdotes, suggest that a supportive spouse/partner may be the most significant help or impediment to a successful career (Mason and Goulden 2004; Rosser 2004; Schiebinger et al. 2008; Sonnert and Holton 1995). Among personal decisions that have primary career impacts, this decision certainly ranks as very important. Mason and Ekman sum up the situation concisely: "almost without exception, married mothers credited their partners as key to their success. 'If you want a career, don't marry a jerk,' a prominent engineer told me" (Mason and Ekman 2007, 55). Among all decisions affecting one's professional life, choice of spouse/partner may be more important than the choice of major professor, postdoctoral advisor, institution, or even type of position.

As the following interviews indicate, Alice and Joan had husbands willing to make major career accommodations, including becoming primary caregivers for their children.

Engineer Alice Hopkins

After majoring in Forest Biology in undergraduate school, Alice and her husband went to Kenya with the Peace Corps. Shortly after she received her MS at a Midwestern state institution in engineering, they had their first child. Her male advisor encouraged and supported her during the PhD and allowed her to do much of her work on nights and weekends to accommodate her and her child.

Although I decided against the international project I wanted to pursue because of the child, I became pregnant with our second child near the end of my PhD research. My advisor remained supportive, despite my relatively slow progress, as did my husband and my fellow students, all of whom were male.

I believe that the expectation that scientists and engineers will work all hours and travel extensively becomes the biggest barrier for women, since most women do not have a stay at home spouse the way many men do and I do. Since most women don't want to give up having a family, they drop out of science and do not pursue administrative positions that demand long hours and considerable travel.

The Stanford Clayman Institute study of dual-career academic couples documents that a major factor that causes individuals to leave an institution or the field altogether results from failure to find an academic position in the same location as their partner or spouse: "A full 88% of faculty who successfully negotiated a dual hire at their current institution indicated that the first hire would have refused the position had her or his partner not found appropriate employment" (Schiebinger et al. 2008). Frequently the woman leaves; in the case of mathematician Joan Berry, her husband left the field.

Mathematician Joan Berry

Joan Berry married another mathematics PhD just before she finished her PhD. They decided to coordinate their careers and move together. Although both put their family first, their first move favored her career, since she received an excellent postdoc.

She studied with another woman with a husband, child, and similar interest who was the perfect mentor for her. Unable to find a suitable position, Joan's husband left mathematics and changed to computer science.

After the postdoc, I took a tenure-track position at a small coeducational college, where I had two children within three years. Although my husband worked full time initially, now he stays at home with the children. I still find balancing career and family as the biggest challenge for women scientists. Despite policies to stop the tenure clock, too many semesters with reduced loads before tenure make it difficult for women who have children to accumulate a strong record during their pre-tenure phase. Child care near or on campus also presents a challenge.

Institutions with policies that permit or encourage dual-career hires facilitate balancing career and family for individuals. The institutions themselves may also reap benefits not only by attracting two well-qualified professionals but especially in retaining them. If one member of a couple has a less than satisfactory position, this may lead that individual or both to look for a better situation at other institutions. When both have satisfying tenure-track positions, the couple becomes much more likely to commit to the institution and stay, since quality of life issues appear to be increasingly important for junior faculty (Schiebinger et al. 2008, 3).

Encouraging, Supportive Parents

Although people cannot choose their parents, those lucky enough to have encouraging, supportive parents hold a definite advantage both in career choice and success. This becomes especially important for women in science and engineering, where the data document that many scientists and almost all engineers have a parent, aunt, or uncle in the profession who served as a role model.

Geologist Lola Cosmos

Lola Cosmos owes her success in science to her parents. Both educators in New York City, they frequently took her to the Museum of Natural History, where she developed her initial interest in geology. While in high school, two teachers, one male and one female, encouraged her interest in science.

The geology department at the Ivy League institution she chose for college proved exceptional for undergraduates, including for the half of the majors who were women, despite its all-male faculty. Lola's enthusiasm for geology increased during her undergraduate years, although she never took a course with a female professor.

Even though the private university where she received her MS degree had a woman in the geology department, Lola's field of geochemistry meant that she did not have courses with this paleontologist. Finally at a prestigious public Midwestern university, she had the opportunity to work with the one tenured woman in the department. Having a woman who promoted her students and supported them exceeded Lola's expectations for a major professor and allowed her to overlook some of the sexist attitudes and relationships that other women students in the department encountered. Being strong-willed, older, and in a committed relationship also helped Lola to thrive.

> I now have an excellent situation at a small liberal arts college as one of two women faculty in a department of five. The CBL Professorship positively impacted my start-up package by paying for laboratory renovations that enabled me to conduct my geochemistry research without going to another building. I appreciate the supportive activities and environment for women in science; the women faculty get together a couple of times each year to network and socialize. The policies at the college tend to be family-friendly in terms of stopping the tenure clock and parental leave. I believe that an institutional grant to provide a post-doc or summer money to kick-start research the year after childbirth would have enormous positive impact for keeping women on their research trajectory. I recognize that I owe my parents and my advisor's generation an enormous debt for paving the way for women in geology.

Apply Criteria to Seek Out Supportive Environments

Many of us learn the hard way, through bitter experience, to pick up on signals that suggest hostile environments or chilly climates that indicate potential problems with a position we are considering. The numerous anthologies, biographies, and autobiographies (Ambrose et al. 1997; Daniell 2006; Evans and Grant 2008; Mason and Ekman 2007; Monosson 2008) recounting the personal journeys of women scientists and engineers also provide indicators of problem situations from which readers can benefit. After a negative experience as a graduate student, followed by a positive postdoctoral experience, Sue knew what to look for when she went on the job market.

Biologist Sue Durant

Sue Durant believes her focus on research rather than institutional status has been the key to her success. Sue has observed that child care becomes a significant barrier for women scientists, although she herself does not have children. She has also seen evidence of other more subtle barriers such as those revealed in the MIT Report, where women obtain fewer resources in terms of space, start-up packages, support for and access to graduate students, and pay equity compared to their male peers.

After negative experiences colleagues and I had at prestigious research I institutions and large companies, I chose a position in a small, liberal arts college, where I perceived circumstances that would make them committed to me. I thought that someone would be watching out for me because I hold a Clare Booth Luce Professorship which I believe will make the institution feel accountable to the Luce Foundation. I also received a POWRE award from NSF. As a CBL Professor, I have attempted to attract other women to science by having women graduate students and holding summer science camps for girls.

When Sue entered graduate school, little research existed on the experiences of women scientists and engineers. Now a large body of literature has documented those experiences and the types of environments and situations in which women are more or less likely to succeed. Numbers of tenured women in the department, percentage of women graduate students completing the PhD, and transparent policies regarding tenure and promotion serve as indicators at the departmental level. At the broader, institutional level, presence of a strong women's studies program, an ADVANCE grant from NSF, an active committee on the status of women, and a suite of family-friendly policies including stop the tenure clock and parental leave, mark overall climate factors. When scientists and engineers become familiar with the research on women in science and engineering, they can use the information gleaned from the studies to avoid pitfalls in their own careers and those of their mentees. Some women scientists take this research a step further, applying it to test the potential climate for women when considering a position or institution.

Physicist Betsy Forest

After completing an undergraduate major in physics, Betsy entered graduate school in physics at a prestigious public university on the West Coast. In selecting an advisor who would be supportive when she started a family in graduate school, she applied the office test—students sleeping in the office/lab were a negative omen.

Clearly pregnant with her second child as she searched for a postdoc, she used people's reaction as another test that she applied to determine the suitability of a lab. This test also successfully placed her in a private institution in the Northeast with a supportive advisor during the two years of her postdoc.

When searching for tenure-track positions, I sought departments that did not require having continuous grants to fund research. Although my college does not have that requirement, the heavy teaching load, committee service, and lack of graduate students make it hard to build the research and publications needed for tenure, while balancing work and family.

Having a supportive spouse/partner, an encouraging family of origin, and a mentor who protects when appropriate and pushes at the right time, all can coalesce to facilitate a career. Some luck with entering the job market in a time of economic expansion rather than contraction, landing in a congenial department, and having an "easy" pregnancy and childbirth help significantly. But, the most important factors for a successful career over the long haul remain research productivity and publication.

Continue to Publish and Research to Remain Marketable

Computer Scientist Mary Frail

Mary Frail worked before she entered a junior college to major in computer science. After graduating from a public Southern university, she worked in industry as a programmer and software engineer. She continued to pursue her MS and PhD as she followed her husband around the country. A professor at a research I university gave her space and encouragement while she finished her PhD at another institution. Eager for stability, she continued to work with him as a postdoc.

> The receipt of a POWRE award allowed me to build my own career and distance myself from the faculty member. Under the POWRE grant, I published several articles on my own. These publications gave me the courage to get out of the trap of running his research laboratory and to obtain a tenure-track position where I could pursue my own research and build my own reputation.

Mary Ann Mason recounts how publishing a significant book facilitated her conversion from a part-time lecturer to a tenure-track position at the University of California–Berkeley (Mason and Ekman 2007, 85). A good track record in research and publication enables ascendancy through the professorial ranks at one institution. Combined with organizational and interpersonal skills, a good research record opens the door to administrative positions at that same place. Most important, it maintains the option of leaving at any time for a similar or better position.

The flexibility and freedom that emanate from the research productivity and potential marketability can't be underestimated. It enables saying and doing what one really thinks on important matters, even if others, including superiors, don't agree. It permits a matching offer for retention to improve salary and conditions at an institution where staying is desirable. Most significantly, it allows leaving a department, college, or institution where the situation has become untenable. Long-term national and international reputation in the profession evolves primarily from research and publication, so developing and maintaining them stand as the most crucial factors in the career.

These interviews and my personal experiences document the importance of having men mentors, as well as women, to provide support, encouragement, and guidance for women seeking a career in science. Some male mentors can provide access to a broader network of colleagues and contacts; some women mentors can provide the answer to that question about how to juggle breast-feeding with oversight of the lab. Knowing the literature on women in science helps to sort out the interventions from mentors that really support in a positive way. The substantial literature on mentoring (Dean 2009; Greene, Lewis, and Richmond 2008; Suiter 2006; Valian 1998) and initiatives such as ADVANCE have led to a growing consensus about the positive interventions and behaviors that should be avoided to facilitate the success of junior women scientists and engineers. As the next chapter documents, the data for senior scientists remains scant and support for senior women remains elusive.

Positive Interventions of Mentors to
Support Students, Postdocs, and Junior Faculty

1. Create opportunities for students, postdocs, and junior faculty to co-author or publish articles, chapters, and reviews. Passing on some of the numerous invitations that do little to help the career of an established scientist may provide experience, build confidence, and yield a publication for an emerging scientist.
2. Create opportunities for students, postdocs, and junior faculty to speak on panels with you or others at conferences and in other settings where they will receive exposure and critique of their work.

3. Create opportunities for students and postdocs to teach on their own. This provides them with experience that may give them an edge in the job market compared to others who have only taught a discussion section or laboratory under the supervision of a faculty member.

4. Allow and even encourage students, postdocs, and junior faculty to take a break and/or explore another topic when they experience severe frustration over a long period with their current research.

5. Demonstrate confidence in the ability of students, postdocs, and junior faculty to achieve ultimate success when they are experiencing a current difficulty with their teaching or research. Help them to place that current problem in perspective by discussing the ups and downs in the cycle of research and teaching.

6. Encourage students and postdocs to seek career opportunities that would benefit them and their long-term goals, even when losing them would cause a temporary setback in your own research.

7. Be willing to serve as an informal mentor and sounding board for all students, postdocs, and junior faculty. Be willing to ask them questions that lead them to consider their ultimate career goals and how much their current laboratory situation furthers them.

8. Provide postdocs and junior faculty with limited, appropriate service obligations.

9. Consider carefully whether comments, structured activities, or atmosphere of the laboratory or department assume men or masculinity as the norm. If so, work to change those assumptions so that all feel they will be welcome as professionals.

10. Create and provide opportunities for women students, postdocs, and faculty to interact extensively in male-dominated environments and networks that hold significant prestige and opportunities for important contacts.

11. Encourage women students, postdocs, and faculty to affiliate with women-focused groups such as Women in Science and Engineering (WiSE) and female-affiliated fields such as women's studies.

12. Provide visible signals in the laboratory, on the website, and in conversations, of family-friendly policies and support, recognizing that students, postdocs, and junior faculty seek signals of such supportive environments when interviewing.

Positive Choices and Interventions Women
Scientists and Engineers Can Make

1. Request and take up opportunities suggested by your mentor to publish, teach, and speak, even if they arise before you feel you are ready.

2. Persist in research and teaching even when things are not going well. Try to remember the ultimate goal and keep the current difficulties in perspective.

3. Seek women role models who are successful in the field and learn what helped them to succeed.

4. Be willing to move to further your career, even when it means disruption to your family and of a current work situation that is temporarily acceptable.

5. Know the long-term career goals you seek (for example, a tenure-track position) and evaluate how your current situation, including how long you remain, contributes to that long-term goal.

6. Seek and accept opportunities to interact in male-dominated environments significant for your chosen profession.

7. Seek affiliations with women in science and engineering, status of women committees, women's studies, or the women's caucus of your professional society to obtain support needed for your career.

8. Realize that having a spouse/partner who is supportive of your career is equally or more important than having a supportive mentor.

9. Recognize that extended family can support or undercut a career in significant ways.

10. Look for evidence of women-friendly and family-friendly policies, lactation stations, women's studies programs, and other institutional policies and practices that may facilitate your career when interviewing and considering whether to accept a position in a particular laboratory or institution.

%% 4 %%

New Filters for
Senior Women Scientists

Biologist Caroline Dogman has been at her research I public institu-tion in the Southeast for almost 25 years now. From her position as department chair, she has seen how receiving salary raises to counter offers from outside institutions works to the advantage of senior men at her institution.

> Yes. Targeted recruitment almost always focuses on men. I finally got our dean to acknowledge that the distinguished chairs and top sala-ries are all for men. There is good equity at other ranks, but virtu-ally no really top-level women in terms of pay—quality yes, pay no. Also, women at our university tend to stay put, so the loyalty tax has greater impact. My simple answer is that what is needed is a change in belief about the value of diverse personal perspectives to science.

The accumulating quantitative data on flat percentages of women sci-entists in academia, especially in fields such as computer science and engineering, and on obstacles and barriers, particularly in elite research universities (NAS 2007), combined with anecdotal and qualitative studies (Rosser and Daniels 2004) such as those described in earlier chapters, led NSF to consider funding approaches to encourage institutions to adopt policies and practices that would facilitate advancement of women sci-entists to senior positions. While continuing to fund the research of indi-vidual women scientists and engineers, the National Science Foundation recognized the importance of removing institutional and systemic bar-riers through its ADVANCE institutional transformation initiative (NSF 2005) to empower women to participate fully in science and technology.

Earlier research I conducted analyzed the responses of more than 450 women scientists and engineers to an email questionnaire regarding specific barriers that institutions and professional societies might remove through changes in policy and practice. The respondents had received either a NSF Professional Opportunities for Women in Research and Education (POWRE) award (Rosser 2001; Rosser and Lane 2002a) or a Clare Booth Luce (CBL) Professorship award (Rosser and Daniels 2004). I then conducted follow-up interviews with a subsample of 50 of the questionnaire respondents to better understand the qualitative context for the problems and potential solutions. The results of this research have been useful, particularly to institutions with ADVANCE grants, in identifying potential changes to remove barriers.

Since the overwhelming majority of the POWRE and CBL Professors are untenured, assistant professors, the barriers they identified are particularly problematic for younger women scientists and engineers at early stages of their academic careers. Anecdotal evidence from ADVANCE institutions, as well as the MIT Report (Hopkins 1999), suggests that more senior women scientists may face a different, equally problematic, set of barriers. I used the population of AWIS Fellows, more than 100 senior, distinguished scientists and engineers, the overwhelming majority of whom are women, elected by the Association for Women in Science (AWIS) for their contributions to science and technology and for supporting women in science and engineering, to explore perceived differences of barriers for junior and senior women scientists.

Population of AWIS Fellows

Launched in 1996 as part of the 25th anniversary celebration for AWIS, the Fellows Program aims to recognize and honor women and men who have demonstrated exemplary commitment to the achievement of equity for women in science, technology, engineering, and mathematics (STEM) . . . The criteria for nomination includes (sic):

1. Nominees can be AWIS members, but membership in AWIS is not required;
2. Nominees have made significant contributions to the promotion of women in STEM through scholarship, leadership, education, mentoring, advocacy, or service; and
3. Nominees have demonstrated commitment to issues of women in STEM and/or made significant contributions to the mission of AWIS (www.awis.org/network/fellows.html).

As suggested by the criteria, most AWIS Fellows have achieved considerable success in their own careers that has brought them to a position where they have enabled women in STEM at a level worthy of national recognition. The AWIS fellows include a significant number of university presidents, CEOs of major corporations, executive directors of professional societies, foundations, or non-profit organizations, as well as deans, department chairs, professors, government agency heads, and industrial research scientists.

Because I am an AWIS Fellow myself and a former member of the AWIS Executive Board, the Board gave me permission to administer the same email questionnaire that was previously given to the POWRE and CBL Professors (Rosser 2001), with particular emphasis on differences between junior and senior women, to the entire population of 109 AWIS Fellows elected between 1996 and 2005. The population of 109 AWIS Fellows elected during this decade included three individuals known to have died, 14 individuals for whom no or only an invalid (bounce-back) email address could be located, three retirees who indicated they no longer responded to questionnaires, and four members of Congress who were not sent the questionnaire. Eliminating these 24 individuals reduced the number to 85 that received the questionnaire. Since AWIS Fellows constitute a population of very successful individuals in science, their responses reflect the view from that perspective. Out of these 85 members, 46 responded (37 women and 9 men), resulting in a response rate of 54.1%. The demographic breakdown of the respondents by discipline was as follows: 19 biologists; seven physicists; eight social scientists, including policy; three mathematicians; three chemists; two humanists, including science writing and philosophy of science; two geoscientists; and two computer scientists and engineers.

Table 4.1 lists the categories into which the responses to question 1 by AWIS Fellows were divided. The first 17 categories had been used in previous studies with a similar questionnaire given to POWRE and CBL awardees (Rosser 2001; Rosser and Lane 2002a; Rosser and Zieseniss 2000). (See Rosser and Zieseniss 2000 for further methodological details.) The categories and data were discussed at a national conference by 30 social scientists, scientists, and engineers whose work focuses on women and science (Rosser 1999). The same codes and categories were applied to the responses from the AWIS Fellows, as they had been previously to the POWRE and CBL Professors. Although most respondents replied with more than one answer, some gave no answer. Nine new cate-

TABLE 4.1. Responses to Questions 1 and 2

Question: What are the most significant issues/challenges/opportunities facing junior or senior women scientists today as they plan their careers?

Categories	1997 % of responses	1998 % of responses	1999 % of responses	2000 % of responses	Current CBL Profs. % of responses	Past CBL Profs. % of responses	Total CBL Profs. % of responses	Junior AWIS Fellows % of responses	Senior AWIS Fellows % of responses
1. Balancing work with family responsibilities (children, elderly relatives, etc.)	62.7 (42/67)	72.3 (86/119)	77.6 (76/98)	71.4 (75/105)	73.2 (30/41)	87.5 (7/8)	75.5 (37/49)	60.9 (28/46)	10.9 (5/46)
2. Time management/balancing committee responsibilities with research and teaching	22.4 (15/67)	10.1 (12/119)	13.3 (13/98)	13.3 (14/105)	2.4 (1/41)	38.0 (3/8)	8.2 (4/49)	4.3 (2/46)	13.0 (6/46)
3. Low numbers of women, isolation and lack of camaraderie/mentoring	23.9 (16/67)	18.5 (22/119)	18.4 (18/98)	30.5 (33/105)	26.8 (11/41)	—	22.4 (11/49)	17.4 (8/46)	4.3 (2/46)
4. Gaining credibility/respectability from peers and administrators	22.4 (15/67)	17.6 (21/119)	19.4 (19/98)	21.9 (23/105)	9.8 (4/41)	12.5 (1/8)	10.2 (5/49)	21.7 (10/46)	23.9 (11/46)
5. "Two Career" problem (balance with spouse's career)	23.9 (16/67)	10.9 (13/119)	20.4 (20/98)	20 (21/105)	9.8 (4/41)	—	8.2 (4/49)	6.5 (3/46)	—
6. Lack of funding/inability to get funding	7.5 (5/67)	4.2 (5/119)	10.2 (10/98)	8.6 (9/105)	4.9 (2/41)	12.5 (1/8)	6.1 (3/49)	28.3 (13/46)	2.2 (1/46)
7. Job restrictions (location, salaries, etc.)	9.0 (6/67)	9.2 (11/119)	7.1 (7/98)	5.7 (6/105)	—	—	—	0 (0/46)	—
8. Networking	6.0 (4/67)	<1 (1/119)	0 (0/98)	4.8 (5/105)	2.4 (1/41)	—	2.0 (1/49)	2.2 (1/46)	—
9. Affirmative action backlash/discrimination	6.0 (4/67)	15.1 (18/119)	14.3 (14/98)	12.4 (13/105)	2.4 (1/41)	—	2.0 (1/49)	13.0 (6/46)	21.7 (10/46)
10. Positive: active recruitment of women/more opportunities	6.0 (4/67)	10.1 (12/119)	9.2 (9/98)	14.3 (15/105)	14.6 (6/41)	12.5 (1/8)	14.3 (7/49)	4.3 (2/46)	—
11. Establishing independence	3.0 (2/67)	0 (0/119)	6.1 (6/98)	2.9 (3/105)	—	—	—	4.3 (2/46)	—
12. Negative social images	3.0 (2/67)	3.4 (4/119)	2.0 (2/98)	<1 (1/105)	2.4 (1/41)	—	2.0 (1/49)	2.2 (1/46)	—

Categories	1997		1998		1999		2000		Current CBL Profs.		Past CBL Profs.		Total CBL Profs.		Junior AWIS Fellows		Senior AWIS Fellows	
	% of responses		% of responses		% of responses		% of responses		% of responses		% of responses		% of responses		% of responses		% of responses	
13. Trouble gaining access to nonacademic positions	1.5	(1/67)	1.7	(2/119)	1.0	(1/98)	1.0	(2/105)	—		—		—		0	(0/46)	—	—
14. Sexual harassment	1.5	(1/67)	<1	(1/119)	2.0	(2/98)	1.9	(2/105)	—		—		—		2.2	(1/46)	—	—
15. No answer	0	(0/67)	<1	(1/119)	1.0	(1/98)	1.9	(2/105)	—		—		—		4.3	(2/46)	13.0	(6/46)
16. Cut-throat competition	—		—		1.0	(1/98)	1.9	(2/105)	—		12.5	(1/8)	2.0	(1/49)	2.2	(1/46)	—	—
17. Gender bias in student evaluations	—		—		—		—		2.4	(1/41)	12.5	(1/8)	4.1	(2/49)	0	(0/46)	—	—
18. Murky career path	—		—		—		—		—		—		—		2.2	(1/46)	—	—
19. Politization of science	—		—		—		—		—		—		—		2.2	(1/46)	—	—
20. Leadership	—		—		—		—		—		—		—		—		21.7	(10/46)
21. Executive glass ceiling for women	—		—		—		—		—		—		—		—		21.7	(10/46)
22. Bitterness and/or burnout because of experiencing inequities/discrimination over time.	—		—		—		—		—		—		—		—		17.4	(8/46)
23. Not nominated for awards.	—		—		—		—		—		—		—		—		15.2	(7/46)
24. Men resent competition from them.	—		—		—		—		—		—		—		—		13.0	(6/46)
25. Must mentor junior women.	—		—		—		—		—		—		—		—		10.9	(5/46)
26. Lower salaries	—		—		—		—		—		—		—		—		6.5	(3/46)
27. different pressures	—		—		—		—		—		—		—		—		2.2	(1/46)
28. Same as for juniors except childbearing.	—		—		—		—		—		—		—		—		2.2	(1/46)

gories not evident from the POWRE and CBL responses emerged in coding the responses of AWIS Fellows. The survey data are categorical and therefore not appropriate for means testing.

> Question 1. What are the most significant issues/challenges/opportunities facing junior women scientists today as they plan their careers?

Table 4.1 documents that the responses of the AWIS Fellows to question 1 about junior women were very similar to those of the POWRE and CBL awardees. Balancing work with family responsibilities predominates as the overwhelming response (60.9%), with gaining credibility/respectability from peers and administrators (21.7%) and low numbers of women, isolation, and lack of camaraderie/mentoring (17.4%) receiving frequent responses. The junior status requires that most of these women struggle with gaining credibility in establishing their careers while they also seek to establish their families and personal lives. This leads to a juggling act between work and family, with little time for anything else. In fields such as computer science and engineering with few other women, the women scientists and engineers may feel especially isolated.

The interview with AWIS Fellow Harold Rubin underlines what he has seen from working in a variety of educational institutions, government agencies, and foundations regarding issues for women scientists.

AWIS Fellow Harold Rubin

Harold Rubin always felt he had an unusual career, particularly because he did not find the academic life to be fulfilling forever. Probably the seeds for that dissatisfaction were planted in graduate school; he attended a non-elite graduate school in the process of raising its national profile that produced one PhD in his field per year at the time he was there. He also began mid-year and was a religious minority in a religiously identified institution. His advisor served as department chair who pushed Harold to finish his degree quickly and obtain a position in a secular institution. Having completed all but the dissertation (ABD), Harold took a position in a comprehensive public institution in the same state. After finishing his PhD that year, while teaching a full load, he, his wife, and their two children moved to the Northeast to a private elite research institution where he had landed a postdoc.

At that institution, he not only honed his research skills, but gained a genuine appreciation for teamwork. He always had prominent women as mentors or role models. He went to another research institution for a year and then landed a faculty position at a research I public institution in the South. Although Harold enjoyed his time there on the faculty in social sciences, which included a very diverse faculty with regard to race and gender, he left academia for Washington, DC. In Washington, he has worked for a variety of government agencies and foundations, including the National Science Foundation (NSF), Office of Technology Assessment (OTA), Office of Science and Technology Policy (OSTP), and the Office of Management of Budget (OMB), in the area of science and technology policy. In most if not all of these positions, a female or man of color served as his mentor and/or supervisor. He has learned from and thrived from working with diverse teams. Harold finds this a bit different from the successful women scientists with whom he has talked, who appear to be inner-directed and tough minded.

I find that balancing career and family constitutes a generational or cohort issue that becomes especially problematic for dual-career couples. Unfortunately, it has been cast as a women's issue, instead of an issue that affects men, women, and society. Academia must take on this issue to catch up with industry. Demands on their time, especially for mentoring and committee work, become additional major issues for junior women faculty. I believe that if people did a better job of cross-gender mentoring, this would reduce the demand for women scientists and engineers to mentor other women.

I think that the issues for senior women differ from those facing junior women. More women need to ascend to positions of influence within the institution to help improve the policies, practices, and climate. Not enough women are rising through the ranks, and some are unwilling to move to other institutions, which provides a typical path of ascent. I also believe that the elite institutions will only consider a narrow subset for the pool of candidates from which they recruit. They are unwilling to develop their human resource pool in terms of diversity, so they end up stealing women and minorities from other institutions where they have already proven themselves. They refuse to take a chance on gems in the rough.

Tenure and promotion become the pivot points around which institutions can develop support structures to help level the playing field to retain women and minorities. Research performance is decisive in the tenure decision, so institutions must provide support in terms of day care, policies that are more supportive of children, such as stop the tenure clock without stigma, and active service, modified duties.

I also think that the reward structure of the institution needs to change to recognize other service such as mentoring and advising. Having people in key leadership positions, especially provost and president, who implement and enforce such changes becomes critical. Studies need to be done of how successful institutional transformation along these lines has occurred.

In my opinion, the current climate for women is bad and getting worse. Given that women constitute half the population, ignoring these disparities seems ridiculous. Women do well at the undergraduate level and then thin out at each stage of the pipeline. Clearly the culture has not changed rapidly enough; very few change agents exist.

In the current anti-affirmative action climate, the situation for racial/ethnic minorities is even worse than that for women. In academia, I believe that we need to consider who the other allies, such as financial aid, students, and programs that share similar goals to those of women in science are, and form coalitions with them to survive in this current hostile climate.

Just as Harold Rubin underlined in his interview, balancing career and family, gaining credibility and respectability, and low numbers stand out as major issues for women scientists (Rosser 2004). The other two most frequent responses of AWIS Fellows, "lack of funding/inability to get funding" (28.3%) and "discrimination" (13.0%), were also listed by the CBL and POWRE awardees relatively frequently, but not usually in the top five most frequent responses in most years. The frequent response of "lack of funding/inability to get funding" by AWIS Fellows may reflect the difference in timing between administration of the two questionnaires. The POWRE questionnaires were administered between 1998 and 2001; the CBL questionnaires were administered in 2002. In contrast, the AWIS email questionnaires were administered in fall 2005. During this time period, federal funding for scientific research had become increasingly tight, particularly with the flattening of the NIH budget and increase in earmarks (Brainard 2006). Awareness on the part of the senior individuals who constitute AWIS Fellows of the importance of funding for career success of junior people represents an alternative, complementary hypothesis. Statements such as "the difficult funding environment and the limited academic opportunities, especially in the biological sciences" and "the paucity of long-term research funding especially for recent graduates" exemplify the concerns of senior leaders for their junior colleagues and suggest that the current state of tight federal funding is much on the minds of senior scientists. The recession that began in 2008 has further exacerbated these fears, despite the increases in NIH and NSF budgets provided by the Stimulus Funding. With layoffs and hiring freezes, obtaining a stable position becomes a major challenge for postdocs and new PhD's (Schrecker 2009).

The interview with AWIS Fellow Nicole Shepherd outlines how her own life and educational story make her worry particularly about the impact of cutbacks in funding on public institutions and on the careers of young scientists.

AWIS Fellow Nicole Shepherd

Nicole Shepherd grew up and received her education, including her PhD, in Europe. Certain aspects of her educational environment influenced her beyond science. For example, she believes in public universities because her education was free; since her parents would not have paid for her to attend the university, she would not be a scientist today had her education not been free. Also, since she began to study to become a veterinarian and then switched to biology, she understands the issues of applied vs. basic sciences. After she received her PhD, she was told there was no way she could have a career in academia. She received a postdoc to go to the United States to a major research institution; her advisor there brought her into the U.S. system, taught her how to obtain grants, and helped her obtain an academic position. Because at that time she was not very self-directed, she appreciates the importance of mentors who take a proactive role, supporting and encouraging their graduate students and postdocs.

> I believe that the whole child care issue and balancing career and family is a red herring and dangerous issue that will get women scientists nowhere. More than half of women scientists either don't have children or aren't married; young male faculty also wish to spend time with their families. I believe that we need to work with the reality of different life histories.

I see child care as only one facet of a bigger problem. Today academia is more and more regulated because of administrative bloat; this is killing scientists and making science very unattractive as a career for younger people. Pushed to bring in at least $1 million in federal grants and produce three publications per year, the young women hate their lives and are unsure they want to remain in the system and achieve tenure. With switches in federal funding priorities, many have lost their grants and ability to do their research; soon their creativity dissipates. They see the additional pressure on the senior people and want out; in addition they realize that some bitter senior faculty set unrealistic standards that they have never met themselves, for junior people. This becomes a genuine problem since if we don't take care of the junior faculty, there will be no senior faculty. Currently very few American-born graduate students are going into science; they see the situation of the faculty and become turned off to science. The Chinese and Indian students currently trained here are returning home, where scientists are respected and treated well. In the United States the public now cuts and refuses to fund higher education. I believe this results in the best and brightest no longer choosing science and academia and makes the current faculty also feel disrespected and unhappy. Unless this situation is reversed, I think that in a decade the American research enterprise will not continue.

In addition to concerns about funding, the time difference in when the questionnaire was administered may also account for the increased response of "discrimination" by the AWIS Fellows, since the time of questionnaire administration coincided with an increasingly politically conservative era. Most of the POWRE questionnaires were administered during the Clinton administration; in contrast, the AWIS questionnaires were administered during the first half of the second term of the Bush administration. Their own awareness of discrimination because of their seniority and leadership positions provides an alternative, complementary hypothesis for why the AWIS Fellows more frequently gave discrimination as a response.

Many of the POWRE and CBL responses less frequently given also were cited infrequently by AWIS Fellows. Two new responses, "murky career path" and "politization of science," not mentioned by either

POWRE or CBL awardees, were each mentioned by one AWIS Fellow respondent. Because most responses from AWIS Fellows overlapped considerably with those given by POWRE and CBL awardees and published previously (Rosser and Daniels 2004; Rosser 2001; 2004; Rosser and Lane 2002b; Rosser and Zieseniss 2000), I will not provide sample quotations of these.

> Question 2. Do you think that senior women scientists and engineers face a different set of issues/challenges/opportunities than their junior colleagues?

Table 4.1 also documents the responses of AWIS Fellows (Senior AWIS Fellows) to Question 2. "Gaining credibility/respectability from peers and administrators," "discrimination," "leadership," "executive glass ceiling," and "bitterness or burnout" were cited most frequently. Only one of the top five most frequently cited issues for senior women, "gaining credibility/respectability from peers and administrators" (23.9%), overlaps with the top responses for junior women, as exemplified in this quotation:

> Yes, there is substantial pay discrimination at senior levels as well as space, recognition, and other perks. There is still a glass ceiling in top institutions and in many disciplinary organizations.

"Discrimination," one of the second most frequently cited issues for senior women (21.7%), is relatively frequently cited for junior women. "Balancing career and family" (10.9%), "time management" (13.0%), "low numbers of women/isolation" (4.3%), and "lack of funding" (2.2%) constitute other overlap issues also cited for senior women, but typically not as frequently as for junior women.

"Leadership" (21.7%), "executive glass ceiling" (21.7%), "bitterness or burnout" (17.4%), "not nominated for awards" (15.2%), and "men resent competition from them" (13%) represent issues for senior women, never mentioned for junior women. Other issues mentioned by more than one individual for senior women, not discussed for junior women, included "must mentor junior women" (10.9%) and "lower salaries" (6.5%).

The following quotation illustrates leadership as an issue, mentioned by 21.7% for senior women but not seen as a problem confronting junior women:

Senior women (and men) also face situations in which leadership roles are offered to/thrust upon them, sapping their time and energy. For women, this may make a bigger difference if they also are doing more teaching or more home involvement. I think also that as women get older and their labs larger or more established, and/or if they are put in positions of leadership and authority, they are more likely to encounter resentment (among men and other women) than might happen when they are younger.

I will examine these tensions over whether or not to seek leadership roles extensively in the next chapter. Here I only underline the position of the issue as the barrier cited second most frequently for senior women. Resentment can cause women to become bitter and burn out, especially when they experience discrimination because of age as well as sex.

In contrast with their male counterparts, women face limitations of both sexism and ageism:

Yes, we hit the glass ceiling already and many cannot make changes and break out.—Ageism hits just when sexism is coming down.

As the work of several researchers (Zuckerman, Cole, and Bruer 1991; Hall and Sandler 1982; Xie and Schauman 2003) has documented, micro-inequities over a lengthy career take their toll in a variety of ways. For some, it affects relationships with others, which can lead to anger as well as decreased self-confidence:

Over time, the accumulation of past inequities becomes a very difficult burden and affects relationships with others and sense of self.

Other women scientists, rather than becoming angry, find themselves marginalized by their male colleagues:

Yes, at some point they can become marginalized by senior male colleagues, who may see them as competitive.

Male colleagues may treat junior women differently than they treat colleagues their own age. Powerful, senior males may see junior women as daughters whom they should mentor:

Junior women are seen as having exciting potential and are them-selves often very upbeat, while senior women get beaten down by facing the same prejudices over long periods of time. As they get dis-couraged, they are often discounted and sometimes ignored.

Sadly, the role of mentoring junior women to fill the pipeline may rep-resent just one more burden that leads to burnout for senior women:

Senior women also face the challenges of mentoring junior women whose issues may not be the same as ours.

Ultimately the senior women get burned out and discouraged:

Yes!! I have many senior women colleagues who are constantly asking me to get AWIS and other women in science groups to think seri-ously about burnout!

Although anger, marginalization, and burnout may characterize the rela-tionships of senior women with their departments and broader profes-sion, their own laboratories often prove a positive locus for leadership, control, and competence. Junior women must first pass through a series of hurdles and stages of becoming established to create their own positive laboratory environment. Once they become senior, their laboratory can become a haven for themselves and other women scientists.

Question 3. How does the laboratory climate (or its equivalent in your subdiscipline) impact upon the careers of junior women scientists?

Table 4.2 documents the responses of the AWIS Fellows about junior women scientists: "hostile environment/intimidating" (19.6%), "boys' club atmosphere" (13.0%), and "establishing respectability/credibility" (10.9%). The following quotation illustrates how the old boys' network makes it more difficult for women to establish credibility/respectability:

The old-boys' network makes it easier for men to get grants, to get their papers accepted in high-impact journals, and thus to sur-vive. Without several grants at the same time, junior women sci-entists cannot remain in the research universities and the cycle is perpetuated.

Table 4.2. Responses to Questions 3 and 4

Question: How does the laboratory climate (or its equivalent in your subdiscipline) impact upon the careers of women (junior or senior) scientists?

Categories	1997 % of responses	1998 % of responses	1999 % of responses	2000 % of responses	Current CBL Profs. % of responses	Past CBL Profs. % of responses	Total CBL Profs. % of responses	Junior AWIS Fellows % of responses	Senior AWIS Fellows % of responses
1. Don't know/Question unclear	16.4 (11/67)	4.2 (5/119)	7.1 (7/98)	5.7 (6/105)	12.2 (5/41)	12.5 (1/8)	12.2 (6/49)	0.0 (0/46)	2.2 (1/46)
2. Balancing career and family/ time away from home	13.4 (9/67)	19.3 (23/119)	16.3 (16/98)	13.3 (14/105)	26.8 (11/41)	12.5 (1/8)	24.5 (12/49)	8.7 (4/46)	— —
3. Have not experienced problems	11.9 (8/67)	16.8 (20/119)	10.2 (10/98)	9.5 (10/105)	2.4 (1/41)	— —	2.0 (1/49)	8.7 (4/46)	— —
4. Not in lab atmosphere/can't answer	11.9 (8/67)	5.9 (7/119)	1.0 (1/98)	8.6 (9/105)	2.4 (1/41)	25.0 (2/8)	6.1 (3/49)	28.3 (13/46)	21.7 (10/46)
5. Lack of camaraderie/communications and isolation	9.0 (6/67)	11.8 (14/119)	9.2 (9/98)	14.3 (15/105)	12.2 (5/41)	12.5 (1/8)	12.2 (6/49)	2.2 (1/46)	4.3 (2/46)
6. "Boys club" atmosphere	9.0 (6/67)	9.2 (11/119)	18.4 (18/98)	9.5 (10/105)	12.2 (5/41)	— —	10.2 (5/49)	13.0 (6/46)	— —
7. Hostile environment/intimidating/lack of authority	9.0 (6/67)	14.3 (17/119)	15.3 (15/98)	8.6 (9/105)	19.5 (8/41)	12.5 (1/8)	18.4 (9/49)	19.6 (9/46)	2.2 (1/46)
8. Establishing respectability/ credibility	9.0 (6/67)	10.9 (13/119)	10.2 (10/98)	3.8 (4/105)	— —	25.0 (2/8)	4.1 (2/49)	10.9 (5/46)	— —
9. No answer	7.5 (5/67)	6.7 (8/119)	5.1 (5/98)	<1 (1/105)	— —	— —	— —	0.0 (0/46)	— —
10. Positive impact	6.0 (4/67)	10.1 (12/119)	6.1 (6/98)	11.4 (12/105)	2.4 (1/41)	— —	2.0 (1/49)	2.2 (1/46)	— —
11. Lack of numbering/net-working	4.5 (3/67)	6.7 (8/119)	12.2 (12/98)	4.8 (5/105)	2.4 (1/41)	— —	2.0 (1/49)	0.0 (0/46)	— —
12. General problem with time management	4.5 (3/67)	1.7 (2/119)	5.1 (5/98)	3.8 (4/105)	— —	25.0 (2/8)	4.1 (2/49)	2.2 (1/46)	— —
13. Safety concerns/presence of toxic substances (health concerns)	3.0 (2/67)	0 (0/119)	4.1 (4/98)	1.9 (2/105)	2.4 (1/41)	— —	2.0 (1/49)	0.0 (0/46)	— —
14. Benefit by working with peers	3.0 (2/67)	2.5 (3/119)	3.1 (3/98)	5.7 (6/105)	14.6 (6/41)	25 (2/8)	16.3 (8/49)	0.0 (0/46)	— —
15. Problem of wanting research independence	3.0 (2/67)	0 (0/119)	1.0 (1/98)	<1 (1/105)	— —	— —	— —	2.2 (1/46)	— —

Categories	1997	1998	1999	2000	Current CBL Profs.	Past CBL Profs.	Total CBL Profs.	Junior AWIS Fellows	Senior AWIS Fellows
	% of responses	% of responses	% of responses	% of responses	% of responses	% of responses	% of responses	% of responses	% of responses
16. Lack of funding	1.5 (1/67)	<1 (1/119)	5.1 (5/98)	<1 (1/105)	—	—	—	6.5 (3/46)	— —
17. Benefit from time flexibility/determine own lab hours	3.0 (2/67)	1.7 (2/119)	3.1 (3/98)	1.9 (2/105)	2.4 (1/41)	—	2.0 (1/49)	0.0 (0/46)	— —
18. Did not answer	0 (0/67)	0 (0/119)	3.1 (3/98)	0 (0/105)	—	—	—	6.5 (3/46)	10.9 (5/46)
19. Department doesn't understand basic issues	—	—	—	<1 (1/105)	—	—	—	4.3 (2/46)	—
20. Cultural/national stereotypes for women	—	—	—	6.7 (7/105)	—	—	—	0.0 (0/46)	—
21. Space	—	—	1.0 (1/98)	0 (0/105)	—	—	—	0.0 (0/46)	—
22. Better bathroom facilities	—	—	—	<1 (1/105)	—	—	—	0.0 (0/46)	—
23. Subtle discrimination	—	—	—	—	—	—	—	2.2 (1/46)	—
24. Very competitive	—	—	—	—	—	—	—	4.3 (2/46)	—
25. Better for senior women; they're in charge	—	—	—	—	—	—	—	—	17.4 (8/46)
26. Same as for juniors	—	—	—	—	—	—	—	—	8.7 (4/46)
27. Less of an issue; senior women learned to cope.	—	—	—	—	—	—	—	—	8.7 (4/46)
28. Burnout over time due to hostility	—	—	—	—	—	—	—	—	8.7 (4/46)
29. Males threatened by leadership of a woman.	—	—	—	—	—	—	—	—	6.5 (3/46)
30. Squeezed out of labs; pressured to retire	—	—	—	—	—	—	---	---	4.3 (2/46)
31. Glass ceiling	---	---	---	---	---	---	---	---	2.2 (1/46)
32. Viewed as more threatening	---	---	---	---	---	---	---	---	2.2 (1/46)
33. Fewer opportunities for field work.	---	---	---	---	---	---	---	---	2.2 (1/46)

All of these issues had been mentioned relatively frequently by the junior awardees as issues, although "balancing career and family" and "have not experienced problems" both remained salient and were cited more frequently by junior women.

The only other issues for junior women cited by more than one senior scientist, other than "did not answer," were "lack of funding" (6.5%), "department doesn't understand basic issues" (4.3%), and "very competitive" (4.3%). Of these, only "very competitive" had not been cited by junior women scientists.

The following quotation illustrates the concerns of senior scientists about severe competition:

> The evidence suggests that the competitive climate in labs, departments, fields, etc. inevitably has more adverse effects on women because of their generally more cooperative approach to life. Some women do as well as men in a competitive environment, and most women will do well if supported by others. Often support is lacking for women, especially if they are a token, or a minority in the situation.

One respondent more directly explicates the erosion of self-confidence women experience under the stress of competition to obtain grants:

> It is heavily male dominated with very few exceptions, and the increasing grant pressures are much less well tolerated by the women scientists whose self-confidence almost always seems to create doubts of their ability to persist.

In sum, the senior scientists identified very similar laboratory climate issues for junior women as had the junior scientists.

The following quotation suggests that the issues in some fields with fewer women such as computer science and engineering may be especially problematic:

> There is no question that the "all-nighters with Coke and Twinkies" culture of computing has a very negative impact on younger women. Fortunately that mostly disappears after graduate school.

In fields where few women remain isolated, they may constantly face a culture that pits their professional life in opposition to their family life.

Unrealistic expectations to remain all night in the laboratory exacerbate feelings of isolation and not belonging for many women, particularly when they fear raising issues surrounding the problems of finding child care at night and worries about personal safety when they leave the lab in the middle of the night.

Question 4. How does the laboratory climate (or its equivalent in your subdiscipline) impact the careers of senior women scientists?

Almost no overlap occurred between the issues surrounding the impact the laboratory climate (or its equivalent in the subdiscipline) has on the careers of senior women scientists and engineers compared to junior women (table 4.2, Senior AWIS Fellows). Putting aside responses of "not in lab atmosphere/can't answer," "don't know," and "did not answer," only two responses overlapped. Both "lack of camaraderie/communications, and isolation" (4.3%) and "establishing credibility/respectability" (2.2%) were mentioned infrequently as problems for senior women. However, it should be noted that 8.7% cited the issues for senior women as the "same as those for juniors."

If the junior women survive the hurdles of negotiation, start-up, and successfully establishing laboratories so that they obtain tenure and promotion, life in the laboratory becomes a source of strength for senior women. A new, non-overlapping set of categories then describes the laboratory climate for senior women. "Better for senior women/they're in charge" (17.4%) and "less of an issue because senior women have learned to cope" (8.7%) suggest that women who make it to the senior level have found a way to survive:

Currently the senior women scientists who have managed to remain in academe ("a survival of the fittest" and/or "survival of the most politically astute") often have the support of a good network, making the laboratory climate less stressful than that of their junior colleagues.

Being in charge means women control their own labs:

No, because often senior women are "in charge" and therefore more removed from working directly in the lab. We are writing proposals, serving on reviews, managing groups, etc. Our challenge is to ensure that there is a supportive climate in the lab for the younger researchers.

As suggested in the quotation above and the one below, senior women can provide a positive atmosphere for those under their leadership:

> Yes, it is much different, mainly because the senior women are running their own lab groups and are doing so in a collaborative style.

They can teach some of their coping strategies to junior colleagues:

> It affects all, but senior women have usually learned to cope in some way. Finding explicit strategies for dealing with the climate is important. Senior women (and senior men!) should take responsibility for mentoring junior women to be effective in the climate.

Although life in the lab is better for senior women, over time, different pressures emerge from maintaining a research lab. "Burnout over time due to hostility" (8.7%), "males threatened by leadership of a woman" (6.5%), and "squeezed out of their lab and pressured to retire" (4.3%) were all cited by more than one individual. Although senior women have learned to survive and attempt to provide a supportive climate for their younger colleagues, this often takes its toll:

> Yes—you become exhausted from it over years and have less energy to fight it off.

Senior male colleagues, especially those from some cultures, resent a successful woman scientist:

> For senior women there is sometimes a problem if male members of their group resent taking orders from women. I have had a Japanese scientist refuse to work in my group.

Not all junior men like having a female laboratory head:

> Maybe also for ambitious young men, they are less comfortable with a woman PI and also less concerned about her career needs over their own.

Some women leave the field under pressure:

There may be fewer opportunities for senior women scientists and engineers to do field work than their male counterparts (combination of sexism and ageism). Senior women might be squeezed out of their laboratories or pressured to retire sooner than senior men.

No one factor explains the attrition of women scientists. Instead, the pattern becomes complex, because it is shaped by practices and colleagues' behavior, as well as the individual herself. The accumulation of micro-inequities over a long career results in increasing disparities found with rank and leadership position. This points to the necessity for changing institutional policies and practices rather than focusing on each individual woman scientist.

> Question 5. In your opinion, what changes in institutional policies and practices are most useful for facilitating careers of academic women scientists or engineers at the junior level?

Mentoring for junior faculty and a series of family-friendly policies emerged as the major changes (see table 4.3). AWIS Fellows demonstrated eloquence in identifying problems for junior and senior women both in their overall careers and in the laboratory environment. The Fellows also had thoughts about the changes in institutional policies and practices that would be most useful for facilitating the careers of academic women scientists and engineers, particularly at the junior level.

"Mentoring for junior faculty" emerged as the response most frequently given by senior scientists (41.3%) as the institutional policy/practice most useful for facilitating the careers of junior academic women scientists or engineers:

> Intense, active, continuing mentoring and establishment of support groups (breakfast, lunch or dinner on a regular basis—i.e., weekly or biweekly, gatherings) where women feel comfortable airing their concerns, gripes, fears, questions, to get reassurance, information, advice . . . from their peers.

Another set of important policies and practices cited second most frequently centered on family-friendly issues such as "family-friendly policies" (30.4%), including "extension of the tenure clock for childbearing/adoption" (26.1%) and "career partner positions" (13%):

TABLE 4.3. Responses to Question 5.

Question 5: In your opinion, what changes in institutional policies and practices are most useful for facilitating careers of academic women scientists or engineers at the junior level?

Categories	% of responses	
1. Mentoring for Junior faculty	41.3	(19/46)
2. Family friendly policies	30.4	(14/46)
3. Daycare	28.3	(13/46)
4. Opt-out policies available to everyone	28.3	(13/46)
5. Extension of tenure clock	26.1	(12/46)
6. Train faculty and administrators for nondiscrimination	15.2	(7/46)
7. Monitor infrastructure issues -- start-up, salaries, space	13.0	(6/46)
8. Career partner positions	13.0	(6/46)
9. No response	13.0	(6/46)
10. Transparency of expectations, especially for tenure and promotion	10.9	(5/46)
11. Network/support group for women	8.7	(4/46)
12. Don't overload with excess of committee work	6.5	(3/46)
13. Seed money for women	6.5	(3/46)
14. Workshops on negotiation	4.3	(2/46)
15. Availability of Federal money	4.3	(2/46)
16. Best practices in recruitment	4.3	(2/46)
17. Sick daycare	4.3	(2/46)
18. More women on search, admissions and tenure committees	4.3	(2/46)
19. Woman president, provost	4.3	(2/46)
20. Hire more senior women	4.3	(2/46)
21. Access to graduate students	4.3	(2/46)
22. Establish rainy day fund - unanticipated emergencies	4.3	(2/46)
23. Change 24/7 expectations for academics in science	4.3	(2/46)
24. Value service more	4.3	(2/46)
25. Train graduate students/post-docs in career management	4.3	(2/46)
26. Rethink tenure	2.2	(1/46)
27. Encourage post-docs to aim high	2.2	(1/46)
28. Incentives to value diversity	2.2	(1/46)
29. Train promotion and tenure committees	2.2	(1/46)
30. Leadership training	2.2	(1/46)
31. Counselor for career issues	2.2	(1/46)
32. Awards/recognition	2.2	(1/46)
33. Positive media portrayal of women	2.2	(1/46)
34. Stop using graduate students and post-docs as underpaid teachers/technicians.	2.2	(1/46)

Improved family-friendly policies—stopping the tenure clock, maternity/adoption leave, elder care leave. Career partner positions, created in a way that makes partners welcome additions to their host departments, rather than unwelcome intruders.

Most viewed "day care" (28.3%) as the critical family-friendly policy:

Day care, day care, day care.

Respondents recognized particular problems posed by sick children (4.3%):

Somehow provide access to child care even when a child has a cold.

Rather than the stigma of having to request that the policy be applied, respondents preferred "opt-out policies available to everyone" (28.3%):

Being sure that policies designed to help women are "opt out" rather than "opt in" policies—that is, available to everyone so that there is no stigma (real or imagined) attached to choosing to take advantage of, say, a one-year extension prior to the tenure decision.

In fact, given the variety of facets and methods of expressing these issues, family-friendly issues, when grouped together, could be seen as highest priority for institutional policies for junior women.

AWIS Fellow Terri Mysbad, a researcher at a think-tank, describes the intertwining of tenure-clock, childbearing, and institutional policies.

Researcher Terri Mysbad

Terri Mysbad, like so many women, had a rather strange career path. She began in English literature and then moved to education and educational research. Post-PhD, she has only worked at two places. Both of these continue to be top social science research enterprises. At her first job in the metropolitan New York area, she worked very hard, including weekends and evenings. Although the environment was not good for her as a Latina, she put her nose to the grindstone and learned how to get funding. Her mentor was a tough woman who provided honest, almost brutal critiques of Terri's work that taught her how to succeed. This positioned her well so that she could leave and find an excellent position in Washington, DC, where she wanted to be. In her new position, she again worked hard and focused on building a reputation and doing work she enjoyed, not on having grandiose plans.

Throughout her career she consciously has attempted to mentor women and minorities. Others asked how she managed to always have an excellent group that included all women, at least 50% of whom are women of color. Where did she find them? She always says if you're committed, you can find them. Her group has the second highest success rate out of 500 in terms of bringing in funding. When the immediate boss did not recognize and reward their success, Terri went to the president of the research institute. She and her group provided data that demonstrated their success. The president listened and rewards them accordingly; she now has access to the president and meets with him directly. Terri believes it's important to excel and to defend yourself and your group.

Balancing career and home/personal life probably stands out as the most salient issue for women, in my opinion. Particularly when beginning a career, putting in a certain amount of time becomes crucial. Somehow men seem to get let off the hook in dealing with the children. I wonder where the fathers are? Men need to do their part, such as taking time off when children become ill, just as women are expected to do.

As women become senior, the family issues usually diminish. Sexism then starts to rear its head, since men do not wish to give women room at the higher levels. Some men, who do not like women to hold equal positions or positions of authority, behave in very nasty ways to women, and seem to undermine them. Senior men often use junior women to do their work; they then translate this further to senior women whom they expect to do the heavy lifting.

I feel that tenure constitutes a major problem for women in academia. The time limit for obtaining tenure tends to coincide with the childbearing years, unless women have had their children earlier. Stopping the tenure clock may disadvantage women, unless the tenure committees have been trained to understand bias. The lack of childcare on campus also complicates childbearing for women in academia.

I believe that men are not inclined to move over, make room, and accept women as equals. Networking and knowing the right people become critical for success. Institutions and senior individuals need to mentor women and inform them as to how to put themselves forward. In order to succeed, women must be aggressive and ask. This runs contrary to most women's notions that they will get what they deserve if they're good. Most women tend to be modest and not publicize their successes. Simultaneously, promoting women too early, before they are ready to assume additional or administrative positions, can be problematic. Mentoring for appropriate positions and expectations helps prevent women from having their careers derailed.

In my area of social science research and within the world of nonprofit organizations, I find that women experience a favorable climate. Because of the topic of the research I do, people in the field are equity conscious; a number of women also hold vice-presidential level positions in my field. I believe that less racial/ethnic equity than gender equity exists in this arena. Some hold lowered expectations for minorities and are willing to overlook bad performance. This contrasts with the climate at the research institution where I began my career, which was both racist and sexist; in fact, the minorities who succeeded there were those who played along with the stereotype of their race/ethnicity.

Just as Terri found it important to have direct access to the president of her organization, senior scientists understood the significant role top administrators play. A third set of issues that emerged from senior scientists might be described as practices/policies and directives for administrators. "Train faculty and administrators for non-discrimination" at various levels (15.2%):

sensitizing administrators about the realities of practices that would produce adverse vs. positive effects on outcomes with tenure, grant productivity, research productivity more generally, etc.

The importance of transparency and monitoring (13%) on a continuing basis were seen as crucial:

Infrastructure that monitors whether there is equal (or equitable) treatment (e.g., start-up, salaries, time to promotion), and that does not depend on a case-by-case negotiation.

Respondents also cited "transparency of expectations, especially for tenure and promotion" (10.9%), set up a "network/support group for women" (8.7%), "don't overload with excess committee work" (6.5%), provide "seed money for women" (6.5%), and "workshops on negotiation" (4.3%), use "best practices in recruitment" (4.3%), place "more women on search, admissions and tenure committees" (4.3%), "hire more senior women" (4.3%), including a "woman president and provost" (4.3%), insure "access to graduate students" (4.3%), "establish a rainy day fund for unanticipated emergencies" (4.3%), and "value service more" (4.3%).

Several respondents underlined the significance of leadership from the top as the key to implementing these policies and practices. A few other issues mentioned by more than one individual focused more on changes in practices that need to occur on the national level or in the culture of the profession. "Availability of federal money" (4.3%) and "training grad students/postdocs in career management" (4.3%) exemplify these issues that need to be addressed by the profession as a whole rather than solely at the institutional level:

> Academic institutions and other workplaces that employ scientists need to reach out more actively to recruit female scientists and engineers. Some junior female professors are overloaded with committee work, making it more difficult for them to accomplish the research and teaching needed to attain tenure. Stopping this often unintended practice would be helpful.

In short, senior scientists articulated policies for individual faculty, institutions, and the profession. Taken together, family-friendly policies, mentoring for junior faculty, coupled with training for non-discrimination and biases, followed by monitoring to insure the training is carried out, would improve the institutional climate for junior women.

> Question 6. Do you think that other changes in institutional policies and practices would be more useful for facilitating careers of senior academic women scientists and engineers?

Fewer suggestions emerged for institutional policies and practices to facilitate the careers of senior academic women scientists (see table 4.4), in contrast to the institutional policies the senior scientists outlined to improve the lot for their junior colleagues. Two of the top five responses were "no or inappropriate response" (21.7%) and "can't think of anything" (8.7%), although some (4.3%) indicated the practices are the "same as for junior women." At least two people explicitly suggested some of the same

TABLE 4.4. Responses to Question 6.
Question 6: Do you think that other changes in institutional policies and practices would be more useful for facilitating careers of senior academic women scientists and engineers?

Categories	% of responses	
1. Monitor equity in space, salaries, travel, students etc	23.9	(11/46)
2. No response or inappropriate	21.7	(10/46)
3. Training for leadership	15.2	(7/46)
4. Reward service	10.9	(5/46)
5. Can't think of anything	10.9	(5/46)
6. Commitment to women from top administration— not the Larry Summers approach	8.7	(4/46)
7. Provide male colleagues a safe way to discuss their gender biases and learn how to overcome them	8.7	(4/46)
8. Have women in highest levels of power	6.5	(3/46)
9. Don't base salary on outside offers	6.5	(3/46)
10. Transition to retirement roles	4.3	(2/46)
11. Ways to overcome isolation such as networking	4.3	(2/46)
12. Recognition that diversity improves creativity and research	4.3	(2/46)
13. Targeted recruitment for senior women	4.3	(2/46)
14. Same as for junior	4.3	(2/46)
15. Awards and honors not based on old boys' network	4.3	(2/46)
16. Get rid of all age limits	2.2	(1/46)
17. Granting agencies need to hold institutions accountable for equity	2.2	(1/46)
18. Making sure women are in key decision-making positions	2.2	(1/46)
19. Eldercare	2.2	(1/46)
20. Committee to examine situation of senior women	2.2	(1/46)
21. Bridge/seed funding	2.2	(1/46)
22. Value human impact and impact on community	2.2	(1/46)
23. Talent-scouting	2.2	(1/46)

practices as for junior people, but with a slight twist, including "networking and ways to overcome isolation" (4.3%) and "awards and honors not based on old boys' network" (4.3%).

AWIS Fellow Sue Tan discusses how traditional disciplinary attitudes become translated into institutional policies that limit rewards for senior women.

Mathematician Sue Tan

Sue Tan grew up in a small town in the Midwest. No one ever suggested to her while she was in either high school or undergraduate school that women could not do math or science. She majored in math at the small liberal arts college she attended. Her study of German also led her to apply for a Fulbright, opening up international experiences to her, which have remained important throughout her career.

In graduate school she experienced some discrimination. For example, when her professor learned she had an NSF Fellowship, he said that she was taking the place of a man. The dean of the graduate school also said that he believed women could not do mathematics.

Married after graduate school to a supportive husband on the faculty of a research I public institution on the West Coast, Sue taught in the four-year state institution. When she learned that the publications had been removed from her file before it went forward, she appealed her denial of tenure and promotion to the union. The union took the case to the Chancellor of the System which resulted in the president of her institution being fired and her receiving a promotion. It also led to her becoming involved in the union on an active basis.

> I believe that accommodations for junior women become a complex issue. Child care, paid leaves for pregnancy, and stop the tenure clock, if viewed as "special benefits," can lead people to expect more from women; in countries such as Sweden where these benefits exist, very few women are in math and science. In contrast, child care has been helpful and can be sold as an issue benefiting both men and women.
>
> I find that senior women continue to face hide-bound attitudes in the profession. Harvard, Chicago, Yale, and other similar institutions still claim that they cannot find women who are good enough for the math department. Women still are not getting the senior plum positions, nominations for prestigious awards, or travel and other perks. The men seem to be more pushy.
>
> Today, the first jobs that junior women receive are OK; they have accommodations that the senior women didn't have. Junior women are no longer put on every committee; now this seems to be a phenomenon occurring to senior women. Recognition, the best salaries, and extra benefits remain a problem for senior women.

I think that the field of mathematics still suffers from the young boy genius expectation that if you haven't made a major contribution by age 25, you are washed up. This tends to work against women. Many women in mathematics have started in peripheral fields, such as math biology, chaos, wavelets, or learning theory. Statistics and other applied fields have been more hospitable to women; applied work with people in other disciplines also builds on women's collaborative strengths which many of their male mathematician counterparts lack. The government agencies have provided an alternative career outlet for women in applied mathematics and statistics.

The work of Barbara Reskin on job queuing and gender (Reskin and Roos 1990) provides an explanation for why senior women experience marginalization from their male colleagues who see them as competitive and push them into the peripheral fields, the less rewarding and more time-consuming aspects of the jobs. As women enter the previously male-dominated professions of science and engineering, the men will engage in behaviors to ensure that they retain the higher rewards and best positions available in the profession.

Supporting Sue Tan's interview impressions that senior women do not have access to the same resources and perks as their male peers, the most frequent response to the questionnaire by senior scientists, "monitor equity in space, salaries, travel, graduate students, etc." (23.9%), echoed the findings of the MIT Report (Hopkins 1999) that disparities between men and women in these arenas rank as major issues for senior women:

> Vigilance on the part of senior managers and, where applicable, Boards, to the negative effects of stereotyping, and monitoring of the rates of advancement for women compared with these rates for men.

In addition to the commitment of top leadership, "training for leadership" (15.2%) ranked as an important suggestion for advancement:

> Leadership training—specific guidance to make the transition to chairs, deans, management of time, etc.

"Reward service" (10.9%), "providing male faculty and administrators a safe way to discuss their gender biases and learn how to overcome them" (8.7%), "have women in the highest levels of power" (6.5%), and "don't base salary raises on obtaining outside offers" (6.5%), each were mentioned by several people. At least two people recommend "targeted recruitment for senior women" (4.3%) and "recognition that diversity improves creativity and research" (4.3%):

The positive benefits of diversity for science itself, rather than an emphasis on numbers, may be the most creative approach to argue for the need for women in science at the senior levels. Discoveries in science made by individuals who took a different approach or saw an old problem in a new way are appealing. Most scientists become excited when they understand the benefits in terms of focus on different issues and problems, new approaches, and differing interpretations and conclusions drawn from data to science that accrue from diverse leadership.

The responses of senior scientists to question 6 about changes in institutional policies and practices that would be more useful for facilitating careers of senior academic women scientists underline two of the reasons why I undertook this survey of issues for senior women. First, combining the numbers of individuals saying "they can't think of anything" (5/46) with "no response" or a response inappropriate to the question (10/46) sums to almost one-third (15/46) of respondents. Since these 15 individuals did not give multiple responses, all other responses came from the remaining 31 individuals, reinforcing that the issues for senior women remain understudied. Indeed, the response of one individual to the question was as follows:

> I think we need to know more about what senior women scientists feel is important—is it lab space, release time, more postdocs, higher salary, a chance for an administrative assignment, etc. Do we know this?

Second, relatively little overlap exists between the policies and practices suggested for senior and junior women, probably because as documented by responses to questions 2 and 4, the issues for the two groups do not overlap very much. The responses suggest that although "gaining credibility, respectability" persists as an issue for women as they advance from the junior to the senior level, as do "balancing career and family" and "time management" to some extent, most of the issues for junior and senior women do not overlap.

On the whole, the laboratory climate does not seem to be as problematic for senior women as it does for their junior counterparts. Attaining the status of "senior" suggests that these women have learned how to cope well enough to survive, if not thrive. Although some male colleagues and students may be threatened by their leadership in the department, university, and broader profession, at least senior women are in charge in their own labs.

A cautionary note is that the population who responded to this questionnaire may have been biased toward this "survivorship" response. The respondents to this questionnaire were drawn from the 109 AWIS Fellows, who received the award because of their success in science and commitment to promotion of women scientists. The questionnaire did not solicit information from this group to assess how many of them had children, families, and working partners. Such information would have helped to enhance the context and perspective for their responses. These results also provide little insight about the women who haven't achieved such a level of success. Do these women have the same barriers to overcome? Do they face different, even more daunting obstacles? Since lack of momentum in one's career can become an increasing barrier over time, what is the situation for women who never reach senior, leadership positions?

Many of the recent institutional changes adopted by both prestigious private institutions (Bartlett 2005; Fogg 2005; 2006; Pope 2005) and institutions funded through the NSF ADVANCE program (Stewart, Malley, and LaVaque-Manty 2007) heralded as significant for attracting and retaining women in science focus on family-friendly policies and/or changes in promotion and tenure clocks or practices. Both represent significant issues, particularly for junior women.

On one level, this focus on junior women remains critical, particularly in light of a study conducted at Penn State documenting the significant difference in the percentage of women faculty (48%) achieving tenure at ten top research institutions relative to their male peers (56%) (Wilson 2006). If institutions do not evolve policies to attract and retain junior women, especially in STEM, there will be no issues for senior women, since there will be few or no senior women.

Attention also needs to be given to the environment for senior women. These women represent a group of successful scientists who have survived and thrived, despite obstacles and barriers that deterred others. They have made significant contributions to STEM, the institution, and the broader profession. Yet, as the MIT Report documented, these very successful women scientists and engineers do not have the same access to space, awards, students, and perks as their male peers. An initial impetus for ADVANCE also came from the recognition of a glass ceiling (Rosser and Zieseniss 1998) and problems for senior women, including in the life sciences which have a substantial percentage of women.

The MIT Report (Hopkins 1999), ADVANCE, the reaction (Finder, Healy, and Zernike 2006) to the remarks of Harvard President Larry Summers (Summers 2005a), and the reports from the National Academies (2006, 2009) continue to center attention on issues facing women in STEM. A closer examination reveals that most of the studies, attention, and proposed institutional solutions address issues for junior women.

The results of the email questionnaire to AWIS Fellows (a group of successful senior scientists and leaders in STEM) begins to tease apart overlap and differences in issues and institutional policy and practice improvements facing junior compared to senior women scientists. The responses of these senior scientists agreed substantially with those of CBL and POWRE awardees (largely junior women) who had responded to questions 1 and 3 in a previous questionnaire (Rosser and Daniels 2004) about issues facing junior women scientists and engineers. In contrast, the AWIS Fellows identified a very different set of issues for senior women that largely did not overlap with those for junior women. The different issues require the need for different institutional responses. Although AWIS Fellows suggested some possible institutional solutions, the relative dearth of suggestions for institutional responses for senior women suggests a need for more studies to elaborate further on the situation of senior women.

Institutions may be responding to issues raised by junior women scientists in some ways to change structures to remove barriers to establishing their careers in traditional academic sciences. As the next chapter reveals, senior women administrators may constitute a powerful way to facilitate removal of barriers and promote institutional transformation.

Recommendations for Institutions for Junior Women Scientists and Engineers

Improving the Hiring Process

1. Train faculty and administrators so that they understand how not to discriminate during the hiring process.
2. Monitor issues surrounding start-up packages, salaries, and space to insure equity between men and women candidates.

3. Have a well-defined and articulated policy that promotes dual-career hires.
4. Provide workshops for department chairs and deans to insure that they understand why women may ask for less during negotiation and how this can ultimately delay their careers.
5. Emphasize best practices in recruitment.
6. Appoint more women to search, admissions, and tenure committees.
7. Hire more senior women.

Developing a Series of Family-Friendly Policies

1. Articulate a series of family-friendly policies that are published on websites and disseminated widely.
2. Provide on-campus day care for faculty, staff, and students.
3. Include a provision and/or facility for sick day care.
4. Develop a policy for extension of the tenure clock for probationary faculty available at the time of childbirth, adoption, or other major life-changing events.
5. Consider carefully whether, and educate the campus as to why, the policies are opt-out and available to all.
6. Establish a rainy day fund for unanticipated emergencies such as child care expenses while traveling to a conference.

Facilitating Tenure and Promotion

1. Provide both a formal mentoring program and informal mechanisms to insure mentoring for junior faculty.
2. Establish a network or support group for women scientists and engineers, particularly including those in fields where women are isolated.
3. Make the expectations for tenure and promotion transparent.
4. Do not overload junior women with excessive committee work.
5. Provide seed money for pilot data to establish a new research project.
6. Develop mechanisms to insure that junior faculty have access to graduate students.
7. Consider whether service should be valued more, particularly in promotion to full professor.

Recommendations to be Addressed by Both the Profession and Institutions to Facilitate Success for Junior Scientists and Engineers

1. Increase the availability of federal money for research.
2. Change the expectation that a successful academic scientist must spend 24/7 in the lab.
3. Provide formal training for graduate students and postdocs in career management.
4. Encourage the hiring of more women presidents and provosts.

Recommendations for Institutions for Senior Women Scientists and Engineers

1. Monitor space, salaries, travel funds, and graduate students to insure equity between men and women faculty.
2. Reward service.
3. Provide a safe way for male colleagues to discuss their gender biases and learn how to overcome them.
4. Have individuals in top leadership positions with a demonstrated commitment to advancing women.
5. Have women at the highest levels of power and in key decision-making positions in the institution.
6. Do not make responses to outside offers the primary means to increase salaries.
7. Provide some mechanisms such as working part-time as a transition to retirement.
8. Provide networking and other means to overcome isolation.
9. Recognize that diversity improves creativity and research.
10. Establish targeted recruitment for senior women.
11. Insure that the old boys' network does not control the distribution of awards and honors.
12. Provide bridge and/or seed funding as a transition between research projects.
13. Establish a committee to examine the situation of senior women.
14. Include eldercare among family-friendly policies.

Recommendations for Both Institutions and the Profession to Address for Senior Women

1. Remove all age limits for funding and administrative positions.
2. Require granting agencies to hold institutions that receive awards accountable for equity at all levels throughout the institution from students through faculty to administration.
3. Incorporate the value of the impact of the science and scientist upon the community as part of the prestige and recognition received.

5

Advancing Women Scientists
to Senior Leadership Positions

This year, for the first time in Harvey Mudd College's 55-year history, our first-year class is comprised of more women than men: 52 percent women in the first-year class at a college of engineering, science and math. . . . A strategic planning process in 2006 with the arrival of our new and dynamic president, Maria Klawe, confirmed our commitment to "excellence and diversity at all levels" but also challenged the College to enhance its commitment to "educating the whole person". . . So after years of hovering around 25–30 percent women at the College how did we enroll a first-year class that is 52 percent women? By lowering our standards? Not at all. With large increases in our applicant pool over the past several years, we had more talented women from which to choose . . . Thirty-five percent of our faculty is women, a sizeable percentage of a technical school. Our president is a woman, as is our student body president. Each of these women is in her position not because she is a woman but because she is talented and inspiring. Our retention and graduation rates have also improved since more women have enrolled.

—Briggs 2010

Let me add that policies and practices are good—but there is no substitute for commitment from the top.

—AWIS Fellow 2006

As long as Larry Summers and his ilk are top brass, women have it tough.

—AWIS Fellow describing the negative impact
on senior women of male leaders such as
former Harvard President Larry Summers

Having women in leadership positions in academic administration may constitute one of the most effective ways to remove institutional barriers and change the environment for senior women in general at the university and for senior women scientists in particular. One senior woman scientist voiced the explicit response to the question of how to obtain the required changes in leadership: "A few years ago, I asked this question of Dr. Shirley Tilghman, President of Princeton University, at a meeting on women in science at Yale. She replied, 'First you change the president, then you change the deans, and then you change the department chairs" (Rosser 2006, 285).

ADVANCE, the NSF-funded program for institutional transformation to attract and retain more women scientists and engineers, also underlines the importance of commitment from the top and leadership: "Since 2001, ADVANCE Institutional Transformation awardees have developed an understanding of the steps needed to create a more equitable environment for women faculty . . . In order to be successful and sustainable, these activities should involve the institutional leadership, mid-level administrators, and faculty" (NSF 2011, 8). A major theme of ADVANCE focuses on advancing women to senior leadership positions such as professor, chair, dean, and beyond: "For many decades, an increasing number of women have obtained STEM doctoral degrees, yet women continue to be significantly underrepresented in almost all STEM academic positions. The degree of underrepresentation varies among STEM disciplines, although women's advancement to senior ranks and leadership is an issue in all fields" (NSF 2011, 2). Although ADVANCE emphasizes moving up the ranks, in contrast to President Tilghman's approach of starting with the top, both recognize the importance of having women in top leadership positions.

Women Presidents and Chancellors of Elite Research Institutions

In 2009, the American Council of Education reported from its most recent statistics (2007) that women constitute 23 percent of college and university presidents. That represents a marked increase over 20 years from the 9.5 percent of women presidents in 1986 (ACE 2009). Very significantly, over half of the elite private institutions in the Ivy League are headed by a woman: Brown—Ruth Simmons; Harvard—Drew Gilpin Faust; University of Pennsylvania—Amy Gutmann; and Princeton—Shirley Tilghman. In keeping with the Ivy League tradition where most of the male presidents, with the exception of the two physicians that head Cornell and Dartmouth, have disciplinary backgrounds other than science and engineering, only Shirley Tilghman of the Ivy League presidents is a scientist. Susan Hockfield serves as President of Massachusetts Institute of Technology (MIT), the most prestigious technological institution. African American engineer Shirley Jackson serves as head of Rensselaer Polytechnic Institute (RPI).

In 2010–2011, women also led many of the most prestigious public institutions in the Big 10 and the University of California System. Five women headed the Big 10 institutions: Iowa—Sally Mason; Michigan— Mary Sue Coleman; Michigan State—Lou Anna Simon; Purdue—France Cordova; and Wisconsin—Biddy Martin (until summer, 2011, when she resigned to become President of Amherst). Three of the five women leaders and two of the five men Big 10 leaders hold terminal degrees in the natural or physical sciences. Women serve as chancellor of three of the ten UC campuses: Davis—Linda Katehi; San Diego—Marye Anne Fox; and San Francisco—Sue Desmond-Hellman. All ten chancellors, including all three women, of the UC system campuses are scientists, engineers, or physicians.

Why do so many women scientists and engineers head public research I institutions? Clearly the skills and experiences that have made these women outstanding scientists and engineers overlap significantly with those required of successful presidents, particularly of public institutions. Successful scientists with a large laboratory and lengthy track record in research have learned to project, plan for, and manage large budgets. In addition to substantial expensive equipment and facilities, such scientists support a large number of individuals in their laboratory at a variety of levels, ranging from undergraduate and graduate students, through technicians and postdoctoral fellows. Typically, their laboratory teams will be working on a number of different projects that relate to an overall theme but may not be that closely related to each other. Depending upon the field, the projects are likely to be on different timelines and funded by grants and/or contracts from a number of different foundations, agencies, and even industry. In order to obtain funding for the laboratory, the scientists not only follow the funding trends at the national level by keeping closely in contact with trends in Washington, DC and at the state or corporate level, where appropriate, but probably help to establish the priorities and agenda for funding science and technology through relationships with program officers at federal funding agencies such as the National Science Foundation (NSF), National Institutes of Health (NIH), or whatever federal agency funds research in their area of expertise. Liaisons with congressional staff and leadership in professional societies foster their ability to impact the national agenda for science and technology. These contacts increase the likelihood that the grants they write will be successful because they mesh with the national priorities and agenda for scientific research.

Managing the laboratory includes more than managing the budgets, insuring state of the art equipment and facilities, and providing overall leadership for the projects and their future. Scientists in charge of large laboratories spend a significant proportion of time managing people. In addition to hiring, firing, negotiating equipment needs and space, and providing appropriate advice about both the science they are doing and their individual careers to people ranging from undergraduates to postdocs, they must make certain that the laboratory teams function efficiently and effectively to complete projects on time. This includes knowing who holds the skill set and creativity to function best for that particular project in a particular role on the team.

The scientist also provides leadership for collaborations with other laboratories both inside the university and with a variety of institutions and individuals nationally and globally. Understanding which collaborations will be mutually beneficial and should be pursued to forward the agenda of her laboratory, compared to those that might cost the laboratory opportunities or send it off on a tangent that would not be useful for the future, represents a significant leadership challenge she has learned to manage.

The skills of managing large numbers of collaborations, people, facilities, equipment, and budgets mastered by successful scientists translate well to many of the major responsibilities faced by presidents of research I institutions, especially public universities. Presidents of major universities devote much of their time to obtaining resources for their institutions. This involves working with the state legislature and possibly the governor to convince them of the importance of public higher education and its economic contribution to the state's future at a time of dwindling public support and competing demands for decreased tax revenues. It includes knowledge of trends, relationships with a variety of individuals in Washington, DC, and a profile at the national level to insure that their institution obtains its share of federal grants, stimulus dollars, and earmarks. It extends to fostering mutually beneficial relationships with appropriate industries vital to the state and nation to obtain donations and contracts for research, facilitate technology transfer, and acquire scholarships, internships, and jobs for students.

After obtaining resources, a president must demonstrate that she has used them wisely to improve the institution in ways that will enhance the future of the state. In addition to buildings completed on time and within budget that enhance the community by providing venues for performing arts, incubators for start-up companies, or state-of-the-art medical facilities, the quality of people at the institution serves as the major indicator of how the president serves the state. Knowing how to hire, retain, and facilitate opportunities for top faculty who receive major grants and awards that lead to discoveries recognized for their significance nationally, staff who enjoy working at the university while contributing to their local community, and students who are sought by industry inside and outside the state upon graduation, signal a top-notch, well-run institution.

Movement Back and Forth among Sectors

In heading a university, the president uses many of the skills managing budgets, facilities, and people that she honed successfully to run her laboratory on the larger institution-wide scale. Cutting-edge science currently involves partnerships and connections among academia, government, and industry. Top scientific leaders are often tapped to head government agencies. For example, under President Clinton, Donna Shalala, then chancellor of the University of Wisconsin and currently president of the University of Miami, became the Secretary of Health and Human Services; Lawrence Summers served as Secretary of the Treasury. After his stint as president of Harvard, Summers went back to Washington for two years, as director of the National Economic Council in the Obama administration. The Obama administration includes many academics, such as Robert Gates, Secretary of Defense, former Head of Texas A&M; Elena Kagan, Solicitor General before her appointment as Supreme Court Justice, former dean of Harvard Law; Steven Chu, Secretary of Energy, professor of Physics at UC–Berkeley; and Christina Romer, chair of the Council of Economic Advisors until late 2010, professor of Economics at UC–Berkeley. As outlined in the next chapter on gender and patenting, many scientists also move back and forth between industry and academia, often serving simultaneously on corporate boards, particularly of start-ups, while a faculty member.

This movement back and forth among academia, government, and industry provides individuals with contacts and networks, knowledge of interrelationships among the private and public sectors, and opportunities to hone their administrative skills in ways that prepare them to become a university president. President Jane Ramirez has had a career path that includes experiences outside of academia that prepared and facilitated her transition to the position she holds today as president of a public research university:

> After receiving my PhD, I spent a decade at one of the national labs as a staff scientist before becoming the chair of the department at a major research I public institution. After four years as department chair, I accepted the offer to go to Washington, DC as chief scientist of a major federal agency. Three years later, I went to a public research institution on the West Coast as Vice Chancellor for Research. After six years in that position, I became the president of another public institution. Now I serve as president of a large, public research I university in the Midwest.

> Although many people have helped me along the way, suggesting that I apply for this or that, recommending that I serve on a special committee, or nominating me for certain positions, I had no real mentor. Instead I was guided by my own compass. My family of origin supported me; they helped me to go away. My spouse has been very helpful. I delayed childbearing until my career was established, giving birth to our first child at 38 and the second at 40. I have also had the good fortune of being healthy and holding a positive outlook on life. The latter is particularly important, as each career has a low point; it's important to be able to just "get over it."

> Although I had mostly good experiences as a younger scientist, I know that many junior women face biases in the workplace and lack of supportive environments. Many young women face struggles over spousal situations, either lack of support from the spouse or failure to find a suitable dual-career situation. Childcare, which our society in general, and academia in particular, has not come very far in dealing with well, can create considerable anxiety for many young women. Academia needs to consider policies and practices that will allow it to compete more favorably in the marketplace to recruit and retain younger women in science and engineering.

If senior women have a family, then balancing with career continues to matter. If the woman delayed childbearing until her career was established, then she faces some of the same issues as junior women. Eldercare also becomes an issue that leads to considerable time and worry faced by many senior women. Again, a supportive spouse becomes critical; successfully dealing with these issues requires a team.

Despite the challenges of free thinking, I find that faculty are quite conservative. The monastic origins of the academy may help to explain this conservatism. In addition, many faculty harbor their own prejudices that may work against the best interests of the institution as a whole. For example, many senior faculty think: Why should I retire? Junior faculty think: Why should I put in long hours? Because the struggles in the academy tend to be focused around power and prestige, rather than money, often prejudices and biases distort decisions. Often a department fails to hire the best people because the faculty currently in the department feel threatened by the notion that the new people might be better than they are; thus the department does not pursue its own best interests. In a similar fashion, they may isolate and exclude senior women, while saying that they are trying to attract and retain women.

Academia needs to consider why it may no longer be attracting the best and brightest to the profession. Law, medicine, and business appear more attractive to women. Science and engineering in particular attract few individuals in the United States now, and these fields especially do not appeal to women. Compared to other fields, science and engineering hold the reputation of being difficult, isolating, less nurturing, with fewer tangible and intangible rewards.

In most fields such as business or law, the reward structure revolves around money and bonuses. In the academy, recognition serves as the basis for rewards. Not enough awards exist for senior people to keep up morale. This dearth of rewards becomes especially problematic for women, since nomination for awards tends to depend upon the old boys' network and professional societies. Since women have not traditionally been a part of these networks and given biases in the academy, women tend not to receive the awards. Both more, diverse awards and new ways to award senior women need to be explored.

Significance of Mentors

Although Jane Ramirez indicated that she did not have a particular mentor, she recognized the importance of women being nominated for awards and prizes. Such nominations and recognitions not only become critical for advancement, but serve as one of the more important ways for a mentor to smooth the way for mentees to advance. A mentor or network of powerful mentors may help facilitate this movement back and forth among the different sectors, recommending the mentee for key positions and advising her when not to accept certain opportunities. Particularly for a woman scientist, a powerful male mentor may be critical for helping her to reach the top. Although senior women may face tensions over whether or not to seek leadership roles, as a senior woman scientist noted, they may ultimately encounter a glass ceiling:

> Yes, I think that senior women scientists and engineers may experience a "glass ceiling" that precludes their advancing in their careers beyond a certain level. I think that this is due to sexism, purely and simply, and that this sexism is fueled by men's fear of competition.

A senior woman director of a professional society suggests the importance of mentors in deciding who breaks the ceiling to attain the very top leadership roles:

> Yes, the glass executive ceiling. At the very top, only a few women get chosen and these because they have mentors and supporters—the extreme case being Condi Rice and her patron George W. Bush.

In an earlier article (Rosser 2007), I discussed the relative similarity or uniformity of the men's curriculum vitae (CV) compared to those of women faculty, which became evident to me after serving in administrative positions as dean and now provost that enable me to see hundreds of curriculum vitae each year. In that article focused on tenure and promotion, I wrote the following:

> Of course, the CVs of men varied in their content in terms of research and teaching focus and included some variety and variance in numbers and quality of publications, teaching evaluations, and service.

Although an occasional outlier among the male CVs stood out as especially strong or unusually weak, most of the men fit a bell curve without too much variation from the mean.

In contrast, the CVs of the women showed much more variation and could be described most accurately as a bimodal distribution. Many women substantially outperformed both their male and female peers in at least one, and often all areas of teaching, research, and service. Other women remained at the other tail of the distribution, lagging considerably behind both their male and female colleagues. (Rosser 2007, 191–92)

After discussing the impact on chances for promotion and tenure, I went on to speculate as to why the men appeared to be getting and responding fairly uniformly to the messages about expectations for promotion and tenure, while the women did not. After eliminating differences in background training upon hiring, start-up packages, and discrimination, I posited mentoring as a possible reason for the gender differences:

Differences in mentoring received by men and women faculty came to mind as a possible explanation, since receiving and comprehending messages about expectations appeared to characterize the difference. Somehow, most men seemed to get it and many women appeared not to get it, either wildly exceeding or falling quite short of the norm. (Rosser 2007, 192)

Based on this explanation, a focus on mentoring, particularly for tenure and promotion, became a major tenet of our NSF ADVANCE grant for institutional transformation at Georgia Tech. It included a component that insured that male leaders would mentor and interact with junior women faculty (Rosser and Chameau 2006).

Perhaps having senior male mentors can be equally or even more critical for women considering leadership positions in administration than they are for guiding women faculty to navigate tenure and promotion successfully. Male mentors may have access to networks, contacts, and even information through their service on boards, professional societies, and committees that may not be available to many women.

In my own career, I discovered that an appointment to a powerful national committee by a senior male colleague opened new opportunities for me. Like most women who had been a full professor for many years, as well as having served as a chair and then a dean, I had contributed substantial service on national committees. Several of these, including committees of the National Academy of Sciences, National Academy of Engineering, panels for the National Institutes of Health, and National Science Foundation, as well as numerous special committees and subcommittees, included university presidents and provosts, corporate CEOs, heads of government agencies, along with an occasional legislator or senator. Despite the considerable prestige of many of these committees, I knew that my research and expertise in gender in science, health, and technology provided the major reason for why I was asked to serve. My reputation for doing my homework, meeting deadlines, and approaching issues in a collegial manner, coupled with my being a woman dean at a technological institution, also contributed to the draw.

After all of this service, suggesting that I was not eager for another committee was a definite understatement. However, when the vice president for research asked whether I would serve as the sole representative of our institution on the search committee for the director of a new think-tank being created by a consortium of powerful universities, I was intrigued. Keenly aware that he, the provost, or perhaps the president himself, held the institutional position from which representatives on the committee were more likely to come, I asked the obvious question: "Why me?" The vice president for research said that he wanted to provide me (and my college) with this visible national opportunity.

As I served on the committee with the other members, mostly vice presidents and provosts, I recognized that the expertise gleaned from my years of administrative experience provided knowledge of public policy, higher education, and my institution's interests that these individuals also had. These experiences enabled us all to perform and represent our institutions well on the committee. Most also had research expertise that was valuable in making the decisions needed in the committee; my research expertise in women in science and engineering also provided me with additional skill for the task.

About three months after the committee completed its work, I began to receive nominations for positions of provost, vice president for research, and even president, at numerous institutions, some of them also prestigious research universities. I do not know who nominated me. I suspect one or more individuals from this search committee deserve the credit for the sudden uptick of interest in me as an administrator, given the timing, since I usually received only about five such nominations in one year rather than in one month.

Happy in my current position, I wasn't at all certain whether I was interested in pursuing another administrative position. However, I was grateful to our vice president for research for introducing me to these new networks and for showing confidence in me.

Since so many of the skills of successful scientists overlap those of top administrators, why don't more women scientists and engineers climb the administrative ladder in academia? In his interview cited in the prologue, Ned Bluesky noted that personal interactions differ between men and women:

> Obviously, this constitutes a gross generalization with many exceptions. However, I find men, on the average, more willing to put themselves forward. Since women tend to interact more with other women, they tend to be disadvantaged in the professional world because they are uncomfortable promoting themselves. Thus, they end up with the conditions enumerated in the MIT Report of smaller offices, less money, and fewer graduate students. Because many little decisions in academia remain secret, multiple opportunities exist to accumulate disadvantage.
>
> A related phenomenon results when women do not move up to senior administrative positions. Such positions do require going out into the political fray and subjecting oneself to other things. I have observed that many women are not willing to do that.

Basis of Fears about Administration

What are the negative consequences that women scientists fear from going into the political fray and subjecting themselves to other things? What have they observed from other women who have made the transition to higher administration that gives them pause?

Some women have gone into administration too early in their academic careers. Often they were pushed by mentors and/or other administrators who saw their potential and were eager to promote more women into positions in administration. Being lured into administration before reaching the rank of full professor and becoming established as a successful scientist cuts short the career as a scientist. Academic administration, even at the level of associate department chair, associate dean, or associate provost, demands significant attention that leaves little time to devote the hours in the laboratory needed to continue to build a successful scientific career. Most individuals who go into administration while still associate professors find that they are unable to complete the research required for promotion to full professor while in the administration. Ironically, because they have not yet obtained full rank, these same individuals often find that the path to higher administrative positions is also closed to them. Most research I institutions will not consider individuals who are not full professors for the powerful academic administrative positions of dean, provost, vice president for research, or president.

The interview of Sandy Ryan emphasizes how serving in administrative positions while an associate professor prevented her reaching full rank. Just as coming up for tenure too early can cause problems, being lured into administration too early can inhibit advancement to full rank. Because of the dearth of women in science, technology, engineering, and mathematics, women are more likely than their male counterparts to receive encouragement to enter administration before becoming a full professor. Since racial/ethnic minorities also receive similar encouragement, women of color stand as particularly vulnerable to getting sidetracked into administration before becoming full professors. Ultimately, this decision to enter administration prematurely not only impedes research advancement but it also places a ceiling on the level of administrative position that the woman can attain. Although excellent administrators, these individuals typically remain associate deans, associate department chairs, or associate provosts. The rank of full professor, in addition to considerable administrative experience, becomes a prerequisite for higher level positions in academia such as dean, provost, vice president for research, and president.

Geologist Sandy Ryan

Immediately upon receiving my PhD, without taking a postdoc, I took a faculty position at a major state university in the mid-South. I remain at the same institution today. Although the dean and upper administration have always been supportive, over the years my department has proved a mixed bag. Some of the older faculty, including past chairs, remained traditional and sexist, assuming that I must be more interested in marriage than field geology. At one point, I considered taking a job offered by industry. Instead, I tried my hand at administration, serving as undergraduate director, graduate director, and eventually as associate dean for seven years. Although I enjoyed administration, I feel that it retarded my research career, with the result that I remain an associate professor.

Currently, I've used POWRE to refocus and reinvigorate my research program. The NSF POWRE award not only allowed me to redirect my work and to develop a track record in a different area, it also gained me new respect from colleagues. The boost from the NSF funding and my support of two graduate students and one undergraduate are viewed positively by my colleagues. I believe that they will endorse me when I come up for promotion to full professor in a couple of years.

Administration appeals to many women who enjoy interacting with people and applying their problem-solving skills developed as a scientist in another venue. Although administration often draws those women who seek to escape a chilly departmental climate, as Sandy did, getting one's research back on track for promotion to full professor can be difficult after several years in administration.

Sandy Ryan perceived that her colleagues may have different criteria for her than for some of the men in her department and that she would have to work harder to prove herself. Being judged more harshly than male colleagues seems to apply also to women in administration. One senior woman discusses this harsh judgment, as well as women's issues with negotiation in her interview.

College Program Head Joanne Maynard

I followed a different route from the typical academic. I'm not on the tenure track, although I have always taught. I began my career in the 1970s working for the federal government, an invaluable experience that acquainted me with the federal scene, how to develop a program, and how to obtain funding. In the wake of the Equal Opportunity legislation, corporations began to look at hiring executive women. A data corporation hired me to run their quality assurance program, making me the only female executive at the high mid-level in the corporation. Although I learned a great deal, I felt very isolated.

After five years in the corporate world, I returned to Washington and began a consulting firm focused on contracts and grants with higher education, community colleges, and computer education.

Because of personal and health issues, I returned to the West Coast. After working on contracts with a major technology corporation, I took a state level appointment with the technology board. After this, I went into marketing and communication in the mid-1980s as the high-tech firms emerged. In addition to the CEOs, I got to know the dean of engineering at my local research I university. He hired me to attract and retain more women in engineering. After successfully establishing the women in engineering program, I realized I missed teaching. Now for the last 10 to 15 years, I have done what I love to do—teaching, writing proposals, and running programs. However, I'm not tenure-track and am 80% soft money. I have to keep on the go to maintain my staff.

I believe that the over-riding issue for junior women is that they do not know how to negotiate a compensation package with appropriate lab space, resident assistants, equipment, and release of classes. They do not know how to negotiate so that what they need is in their offer letter. They often end up having a delay of a couple of years to implement their research agenda, which places them behind, relative to their male counterparts; this results in a string of potential negative impacts. The negotiation issue exemplifies one of several areas in which I think junior women could profit from structured mentoring and professional development. Another key area includes learning how to feel out the senior people in the department, while establishing independence, without burning bridges. Women need to understand that they may need some of these senior folks in the future.

I agree that the issues for senior women do differ somewhat from those of junior women, although both need to be in departments that want women in order to thrive. The areas such as mechanical engineering and physics that remain dominated by white males present even more barriers for women than the biosciences.

Balancing career and family can continue to be a huge area for senior women. Often these women don't want to take on positions of leadership until the family has cleared out; frequently by the time the kids are gone, eldercare sets in. Women also struggle with their marriages/partnerships. This can turn into devastation if the partner also is in the same research area; a break-up can simultaneously destroy the personal and professional life.

At my current institution, the leadership pushes for women to advance. Many women now occupy positions as dean and vice president. I have observed, however, that women in these administrative positions appear to be judged more harshly, and perhaps different criteria apply to them. Women with women partners receive particularly harsh scrutiny.

I believe that engineering and the sciences have begun to value the contributions of the social sciences in general, and women in particular. Certain disciplines, such as nanotechnology, have virtually no women and no role models. This makes it difficult for the young women to consider going into those areas, especially since the informal networks exclude them.

Observation of the harsh judgment of other women in administration may stand as a powerful deterrent to women considering whether to leave the laboratory where they have been successful to hold an administrative position that may be fraught with difficulties. A few very high profile cases of successful women scientists and engineers who ran into extreme difficulties when they became chancellors or presidents reinforce this fear.

On Sunday morning, June 25, 2006, a colleague sent me an article, "U.C. Santa Cruz Chancellor Jumps to her Death in S.F." from the *San Francisco Chronicle* about a friend and colleague:

> UC Santa Cruz Chancellor Denice Denton, apparently despondent over work and personal issues, died Saturday after she jumped from the roof of a 42-story San Francisco apartment building, police said. Denton's partner, Gretchen Kalonji, has an apartment in the building, property records show.
>
> Denton, a well-regarded engineer, had been named this spring in a series of articles examining UC management compensation. She had been criticized for an expensive university-funded renovation on her campus home, and for obtaining a UC administrative job for Kalonji. (http://sfgate.com/2006/0624)

Suddenly, a flood of memories interrupted my finishing the article. Conferences, grants, and publications about women, science, and engineering had brought Denice and me together many times over the last decade: The meeting in Montreal on retaining women in engineering where we had first met, the Women's Engineering Program Advocates Network (WEPAN) workshop in DC, the numerous ADVANCE principal investigator meetings, many AAAS meetings, the January 14, 2005 Conference at Harvard where Larry Summers delivered his now infamous remarks, and the meeting at the National Academies in December 2005.

Several times during the 18 months before her death when I'd been in the Bay Area visiting my daughters, I had read some of the coverage in the *San Francisco Chronicle* of the situation she faced at Santa Cruz after she became chancellor. The tenacity and frequency with which the paper repeated the litany of details about her compensation, the hiring of her partner in the UC System Office, and the renovations to the chancellor's home, including the dog run, were evident, since they chose to include them in articles uncovering compensation abuses focused on other UC leaders, particularly women.

The coverage of her death in the San Jose *Mercury News* revealed that the protests had continued during 2006, becoming increasingly nasty and encroaching:

> She had been recently ridiculed by area cartoonists. And on campus, she had been the target of many protests, students said, with protesters rallying against everything from employee wages on campus to workplace conditions in foreign countries where UC apparel is made.
>
> Denton had called campus police a few times after protesters camped out on the grounds around her house, said Santa Cruz City Councilman Mike Rotkin, a lecturer at the school. She asked for increased security after someone threw a parking barricade through a picture window at her university home.
>
> "I don't think she was worried or afraid about a particular person," he said, "but I think she felt personally threatened by it."
>
> After one recent event in which students surrounded her car and performed a five-minute play in support of workers and students of color, she seemed to grow increasingly fearful, said Josh Sonnenfeld, a student organizer.
>
> "She or the university hired a security guard to be outside her campus home 24/7. She hired a bodyguard-type figure to go around with her everywhere," he said. (MercuryNews.com/06/25/2006)

The author of nearly 100 scholarly journal articles, book chapters, and conference papers, Denice Denton had earned her BS, MS, and PhD degrees in Electrical Engineering at the Massachusetts Institute of Technology. Her research was in microelectromechanical systems (MEMS) as an enabling technology, particularly in life sciences applications. She also worked in the arena of transformational change in higher education.

She began her academic career at the University of Wisconsin–Madison in 1987, leaving as professor in the Departments of Electrical and Computer Engineering and Chemistry to become dean of the College of Engineering and professor of Electrical Engineering at the University of Washington (UW), the first woman to hold such a position at an NRC-designated research I university. Denice became the ninth chancellor of the University of California, Santa Cruz on February 14, 2005.

In addition to numerous prestigious engineering and science awards, she earned an international reputation for effective advocacy supporting access to science, math, and engineering opportunities for women and minorities. In May 2004, Denton was among nine scholars honored by the White House with a Presidential Award for Excellence in Science, Mathematics, and Engineering Mentoring, recognizing her role as a major leader in enhancing diversity in science and engineering. She had been selected to receive the Maria Mitchell Women in Science Award for 2006, a prestigious national recognition of exceptional work that advances opportunities in the sciences for women and girls.

Given her stellar background and reputation, the very harsh treatment that Denice Denton received as chancellor holds a message of deterrence for many women scientists and engineers considering whether to move into a top leadership position. They wonder, if this could happen to someone as outstanding as Denice, what could happen to me? Why should I risk the career I've built as a scientist where everything seems to be going relatively well to face the unknown perils that might await me in administration?

Positive Reasons for Women Scientists to Become Administrators

In contrast to these negative fears, a positive reason that some women scientists do not accept senior administrative positions stems from their love of science. They recognize that top administrative positions such as vice president for research, provost, and president are more than full-time jobs that will require them to give up their laboratory and a successful scientific career. They question whether they can make a greater contribution by remaining in the laboratory to discover more about the area in which they hold world-class expertise or whether they can have a greater impact by moving into institutional leadership, where they can set the agenda and priorities for education and research for the future.

When she received the Nobel Prize in Physiology or Medicine in 2009, Elizabeth Blackburn addressed the importance of doing what makes it more feasible for women to be in science and do the science they like in her telephone interview on October 5:

ADAM SMITH: I just wanted to ask you one last thing which was that it's been commented previously that telomerase and telomere research is a field which has, happily, a large number of women working in it. Do you agree with that and is that something that...

ELIZABETH BLACKBURN: Well, yes, and, I'll turn your comment around and say it's fairly close to the biological ratio of men and women. It's all the other fields that are aberrant.

AS: Absolutely, yes.

EB: So, this is the normal field, right? Because it is a much more even distribution between men and women, absolutely. No, I can't compare with other fields that are aberrant.

AS: Yes, but is it something you think you have actively worked on promoting, to make it like that?

EB: You know, I've only actively promoted what we always hope is good science. And, then it's not as if one would favor a woman researcher in the area over a man researcher in the area. But, women have come into this field perhaps because in the molecular days of the field, that is the kind of things that I've been doing and that Carol . . . we were women, we tended to have women students and postdocs, which was not 100 percent. They tended to be 50-50, men and women, which is already a little higher than the usual ratios. And so there's a sort of self-perpetuating aspect to that. Because there's nothing particularly about the science per se which has any, sort of gender-like quality to it. You know what I'm saying? I think we're looking very much at sort of sociological phenomena here.

A: Yes, but one might hope that since it's seen to be possible in this field it could be possible in all fields.

EB: You really do hope that when people see something like this working, that this could be seen as, that this would be, the norm. And the different ratios of men and women researchers in other fields would be the aberrancy. That's what I'd like to see, because you want women to have access to science because it's such a wonderful thing to do. Anything that makes it more feasible for women to be in science and do the science they like, that's good. (Nobelprize.org 2009)

Considerable research (Miller et al. 2000; Cheryan et al. 2009) has documented that helping others motivates women in particular to choose careers in science and engineering. Compared to their peer male scientists, more women scientists underline that they wanted to help living beings—animals, the environment, and particularly people—and that they view science as the best way to provide the dramatic help needed. In making the decision between continuing to head the laboratory or moving into university administration, the issues of helping more and having the greatest impact, factor heavily in the decision for some women. A former dean and currently a vice president for research, Mary Wyatt felt that she could help women stay in science and move ahead by helping them deal with their anger.

Vice President for Research Mary Wyatt

I grew up in the UK. A teacher at the all-girls high school I attended encouraged me and made me realize the importance of going on to a top university. One of the women teachers encouraged me to start thinking about possible careers, including research in biology. This was particularly important for me, since I was the first in my family to go to college and no one from my family would have considered research in biology as a possible career.

My undergraduate educational environment was supportive. Interacting one on one with a particular faculty member increased my enthusiasm for research and made me want to go on to graduate school. In graduate school, I had to choose between two individuals who worked in the area in which I was interested to serve as my PhD advisor. One, quite well-known, had really inspired me as an undergraduate. I decided to work with the less well-known individual. In retrospect, I realize that this decision proved especially wise for me as a woman scientist. Since my advisor's wife was also a professor, I had a very positive role model of a woman scientist with a family and a dual-career couple, a particularly scarce commodity in the 1960s.

During my marriage at the beginning of my academic career, I did not want to have kids. At that time, less was known about the dangers of delaying too long before attempting to have children. Because I did not have my first child until I had become a full professor, I faced the balancing career and family issues at a somewhat different time under different circumstances than women who have their children at an earlier stage of their careers. I believe that some don't want to think about having kids until they are established. With the funding availability now, this has become a particularly salient issue. For some, the internal desire to do more service may motivate the delay.

Because I delayed childbearing until becoming a full professor, balancing career and family became a significant issue for me as a senior woman scientist. As a full professor woman scientist, I encountered expectations to undertake significant service. I faced an extreme workload and intense time pressures. Often I had to turn down opportunities for administration. My choice of a supportive mate facilitated my coping with the extreme pressures.

I have seen many senior women who understandably become angry when they see men getting through the system faster, being paid more, and receiving more respect and invitations. This often leads to an angry phase. Coupled with the feelings of being overwhelmed by the work, negative reviews of grants, and other setbacks, some women in this phase end up burning their bridges so that they cannot be a leader. I am interested in trying to help other women get through that phase without burning their bridges and as an administrator have opportunities to help women in this phase. I recommend that they write down the things upsetting them in a book, rather than acting on them. When a department or discipline does not have lots of women, if one or a few are slightly eccentric, she is seen by others as the example of all women scientists. I try to help departments realize that more numbers allow people to see that women scientists also fall along the same spectrum as men scientists from difficult to OK to great.

In her interview, another successful woman scientist who chose to become dean of the Graduate School emphasized the help she could give to others, particularly women scientists, by working with department chairs to influence their interactions in hiring women faculty. As documented in the book, *Women Don't Ask* (Babcock and Laschever 2003) and reinforced in the interview with Joanne excerpted above, women tend to ask for less than their male counterparts when negotiating. This often puts them at a disadvantage without the equipment, facilities, and help they need to get their laboratory up and running efficiently; ultimately, this undercuts the quantity and perhaps the quality of science they can produce in time to meet the demands of tenure. Janet's efforts to help chairs understand the importance of insuring that women faculty receive the resources they need during start-up negotiations provides a considerable service to both the women and the department. The ability to use her position to help the women scientists in this way clearly influenced Janet's decision to leave the laboratory to go into administration.

Dean Janet Anthony

I believe that going to an oceanographic institution immediately after graduate school stands out as the most significant factor that prepared me for success in the academy. My experiences at the Institution immersed me in research, providing me with focus, contacts, and knowledge of how to obtain grants. Because of the several years I spent there, by the time I took an academic position, I already had a well-established research career. Being on the right trajectory for research distinguished me from others new to academia; if anything, I had to work harder on learning to teach.

Contrary to the popular myth that a lengthy postdoctoral period is negative, I found it crucial to my research and thus ultimately, my academic success. While a postdoc, I met all of the influential people in the field; they provided valuable opportunities and served as contacts after I entered academia. I also credit my postdoctoral experience with making me extremely independent. Independence proved instrumental to my success, since in my academic department, my colleagues were independent and cubby-holed; those seeking collaborators find the departmental environment difficult. Not only did independence help me fit into the male-dominated department, but my interest in sports made it easier to interact with colleagues and fit in.

Although I personally did not have to worry about balancing career and family, I feel that constitutes the primary issue for most junior women faculty. I also believe in the significance of critical mass, since having only one or two women in a department of all men faculty creates weird dynamics.

Because senior women remain so few in numbers in departments and in the university as a whole, they easily become overburdened. Excessive service on committees and trying to save the junior women faculty leads to burnout for many senior women scientists.

I believe that institutions need to introduce policies to stop the tenure clock and to increase flexibility, especially for women tied to laboratory or field research. People must also feel that they will not be stigmatized if they use the policies.

This position has allowed me to see that negotiation stands as an issue for both junior and senior women. Although women may receive competitive salaries, often other things such as space, equipment, and graduate students are equally or more important. Neither senior nor junior women play the game of negotiation well; women simply do not ask for as much as men do.

In my role as an administrator, I try to educate the chairs to negotiate fairly with the women. I tell them to think about what a man coming into the position would ask for to be successful and suggest that the chairs offer that to the women. I also make it clear to chairs who try to hire senior women by hiring them from another institution that they do not deserve a "targeted opportunity" hire because they have done nothing to increase the numbers of women in science overall.

From the position of dean of the graduate school, an institution-wide administrative position that works with all colleges and departments with graduate programs, Janet can exert considerable influence to educate and persuade the department chairs to negotiate with new women faculty hires in ways that would put them on more equal footing with the men hires who tend to negotiate harder and ask for more. This possibly made a significant difference in the careers of those individual women scientists, as well as impacting the skills of the chair and overall department climate with ultimate benefits to science.

At most institutions, the Dean of the Graduate School does not directly control hiring, promotion and tenure, retention negotiations, and large budgets for personnel and programs. Chairs, deans, provosts, and presidents tend to have the authority and responsibility for these matters. Having more women in these significant leadership positions, as underlined by the goals of NSF's ADVANCE Initiative, could provide a powerful mechanism to transform institutions to attract and retain more women scientists and engineers. Women in significant leadership positions may also help to insure that new barriers are not erected that remove women scientists from cutting-edge national and global science as it moves toward applied research and innovation. As the next chapter outlines, some indicators such as the gender gap in patenting suggest that vigilance will be necessary to make certain that women are not excluded from technology transfer and the newer interdisciplinary fields of nanotechnology, biotechnology, and information technology.

Recommendations for Institutions to Advance Women Scientists to Leadership Positions

1. Appoint women to the top leadership positions of president, provost, vice president for research and dean.
2. Apply for a NSF ADVANCE Institutional Transformation grant.
3. Permit leaves of absence for limited periods for faculty to accept significant leadership positions in government or industry that will enhance their academic scientific productivity and credibility.
4. Make certain that standing committees exist for nominations for institutional and national awards and that women and under-represented minorities serve on those committees.
5. Foster a culture that does not track women and under-represented minorities into lower-level administrative positions until they have become full professors.
6. Provide leadership training that includes information on possible differential criteria used to judge women and men administrators.
7. Encourage women administrators to attend HERs, ACE Women in Leadership, or other appropriate programs where they can receive support for unique difficulties faced by women administrators.

Recommendations for Women Seeking to Become Leaders in Administration

1. Develop and maintain state and federal contacts to provide leadership in your area of expertise in setting priorities and agendas.
2. Establish appropriate collaborations with industry, government, and other academic institutions.
3. Accept leadership positions on boards and in professional societies.
4. Accept appropriate positions in government or industry that will enhance contacts and administrative skills without undercutting academic scientific productivity and credibility.
5. Achieve promotion to full professor before taking on major administrative positions such as associate dean, associate provost, or department chair.
6. Seek help outside the institution immediately if you believe you are encountering difficulties in your position.
7. Consider the positive impacts on policies and practices that you can have because of your experiences as a woman.

Recommendations for Mentors Seeking to Advance Women Scientists to Administrative Leadership

1. Nominate women for awards.
2. Nominate women to serve on significant institutional and national committees.
3. Nominate women for leadership positions such as dean, vice president for research, provost, and president at your institution as well as other universities.
4. Do not appoint women to time-consuming administrative positions such as associate dean, associate provost, or chair of the department until they have become full professors.
5. Insure that the criteria by which you assess the performance of women candidates in administrative positions are not more harsh and stringent than those used to judge men administrators.
6. Watch for signs that a woman new to a leadership position is experiencing difficulties and intervene appropriately and immediately.
7. Spell out to women and under-represented minority mentees the positive impacts that they can have for others in their institution.

6

The Gender Gap in Patents

Software engineer Joan Jetma works at a very large global information technology company that prides itself on innovation and rewards its employees for patenting innovative discoveries. Joan had observed that very few women in the company where she worked obtained patents. When she did some research to determine whether her observations were correct, she learned that data are scarce on the number of women who patent both inside and outside her company. She discovered that about 10 percent of the women obtained patents at her company. When her own patent came up for review, she realized that all of the reviewers were men.

> Patents weigh heavily for some promotions and career advancement in the company, which considers itself a leader in innovation. Not only do individuals who patent receive financial rewards, but patenting can be a make or break difference for certain promotions. For example, it's impossible to become a Fellow or Distinguished Engineer without having patented at the company where I work.

My own career and research had long made me aware of the importance of mentoring, institutional barriers, and leadership in the careers of women scientists and engineers, but it was not until recently that a young male faculty member in a different department made me aware of a new issue, critical for women in science, of which I had previously been ignorant. When he first brought the issue of gender and patents to my attention, my reactions ranged from how boring to who cares? Fortunately the new faculty member was persistent, bringing up the issue again at a reception, when he bumped into me in the hall, and finally when he made an appointment to discuss it with me.

Parts of this chapter were taken from a published journal article written by the author: Sue V. Rosser, 2009, "The gender gap in patenting: Is technology transfer a feminist issue?" *NWSA Journal* 21(2): 65–84.

On some level, I wondered if my resistance came from the realization that a gender gap in patents would mean that women had been left out of the leading edge of science yet again. Was this yet another new face of this old issue? After more than 30 years of studying issues of women, science, and technology, and working actively on the national and local levels to implement programs (Rosser and Lane 2002b) to increase the numbers of women scientists and engineers, I couldn't bear to recognize the old pattern of women achieving parity in one area, just as the men lead the shift to a new, different arena.

As a dean, of course, I felt obligated to take the research interests of my faculty member seriously. The more I investigated the gender gap in patents, the more I began to see that it represents a very critical issue for women in science today. Although I didn't know very much about patents, as a dean at a doctoral research extensive technological institution, I was keenly aware of the increasing significance of technology transfer and commercialization of science. In the United States, Japan, and many European countries, most research universities are placing increasing emphasis upon innovation and applied research. This results in blurring of boundaries between academia and industry. Technology transfer and licensing offices and increased percentages of total research funding coming from industry, as well as conflict of interest policies that spell out ethical ways for faculty to commercialize the products that result from their federally funded research conducted at the university, mark the evidence of the commercialization of science and this blurring. Even the most distant faculty colleagues in humanities and fine arts become aware of the trend when they read about the unanimous 2006 decision of Texas A&M University to include inventions in tenure and promotion decisions (Zaragoza 2008); when they serve on a university tenure and promotion committee where a lengthy discussion emerges over how much weight patents should be given compared to peer-reviewed publications in a promotion decision; or when they serve on the committee to determine how to modify existing policies on sabbaticals and research leaves for faculty who wish to take one or more years away from the classroom for a "start-up" company.

Most faculty also recognize the drivers for this trend toward applied research and increasingly closer relationships between the corporate world and academia. The exciting work emerging from new interdisciplinary fields such as biotechnology, nanotechnology, and information technology have spawned many of these stimulating intellectual relationships. Those very names suggest the application (technology) to basic science discoveries in molecular biology, materials, and computer science. These new fields have experienced remarkable growth. For example, patents in information technologies have shown a fivefold increase from the early eighties (1980–1985) to the early twenty-first century (2000–2005) (Ashcraft and Breitzman 2007).

De-funding of higher education, particularly by state legislatures, has forced public institutions into closer relationships with corporations. Relatively flat funding from the federal government for research and education in physical sciences and engineering until the President's proposed 2009 budget, combined with flattening of the National Institutes of Health (NIH) budget after its doubling from 1998–2003 to support health and bioscience, provided further impetus for the university-industry relationship. The economic crash beginning in 2008 has led to budget cuts for universities that will ultimately impact research productivity; the results of the Stimulus Package remain to be seen.

Spurred by several reports produced by the National Science Board (NSB 2004), the National Academy of Sciences (2007), and the Council on Competitiveness (2005), the U.S. Congress has begun to recognize science, technology, and innovation as crucial keys for insuring the competitive edge of the United States in the global economy. The tightening on visa restrictions in the wake of September 11 underlined the dependence of the U.S. science and technological enterprise on students from other countries and professionals who are immigrants on H-1B visas. Globalization and the flattening of the world described by Thomas Friedman uncovered the possibilities for loss of U.S. innovative competitiveness. In August 2007, the U.S. Congress held hearings on future directions for science and technology in general and on ways to improve the 1980 Bayh-Dole Act in particular, to rebalance incentives for patents, transfer, and licensing between corporations and universities. The focus on patents reflects their significance as a measure of innovation. In September, 2011 a U.S. patent reform was signed, changing the law from first to invent to first to file or publish.

Much of the current funding available from federal agencies, along with corporate funding, is now allocated to fund applied research, commercialization, and technology transfer. The funding as well as the bonuses, stock options, and hefty salaries paid to scientists who serve on advisory boards to start-up companies means that a gender gap in patents signals the old dilemma of women again being left behind, since patents are a primary indicator of technology transfer.

Women in Science and Technology

Just as globalization, constraints brought on by September 11, and new interdisciplinary fields in science and technology have increased focus on commercialization of science and innovation in the United States, they have also brought renewed attention back to issues of women in science and technology. Reports released from the National Academy of Sciences (2007) such as *Rising Above the Gathering Storm*, as well as *Innovate America* (Council on Competitiveness 2005), and *Science and Engineering Indicators* (National Science Board 2004), spell out the anticipated workforce shortage. They also underline the extent to which the U.S. science and engineering workforce has depended upon students from other countries to provide well-qualified and motivated graduate students and immigrant scientists and engineers to keep both U.S. industrial and academic science staffed. September 11, 2001 not only caused entry problems via H-1B and student visas, but it also changed the desire of many scientists, engineers, and students to come to the United States. The projected dearth of scientists and engineers resulting from the decrease in immigrant scientists has caused the focus to shift to underutilized sources within the U.S. population to fill the gap. Women represent the largest underutilized source. (See chapter 1 for the statistics on women in STEM.)

Juxtaposing the increasing emphasis of global science and technology on innovation with the data on gender participation in the science and technology workforce reveals an additional issue of potential consequence both for women scientists and engineers as well as for the competitiveness of the United States. The percentage of women granted patents ranks significantly lower than that of their male peers. Not only is the percentage of women obtaining patents lower than men, but it also ranks very low relative to the percentage of women in the STEM disciplines.

Curiosity drove me to explore the gender gap data in different disciplines, sectors, and countries. The evidence proved overwhelming. In all countries, in every discipline, including those such as biology, in which women had begun to approach parity, the gender gap remained substantial, whether in government, academic, or private sector.

Measures of Productivity:
Patents and Publications Obtained by U.S. Women

A patent is a set of exclusive rights granted by a national government to an inventor for a time-limited period in exchange for public disclosure of the invention. Usually a patent application includes one or more claims defining the invention, which must be new, inventive, useful, or industrially applicable. Since national laws and international agreements govern patents, the procedures for granting them, as well as the requirements and extent of exclusive rights, vary quite a bit depending upon where the patent was granted.

Quantifying gender and patents becomes a difficult exercise. Many patents bear the names of several individuals, often including lawyers and other individuals who work for the company but who have little to do with the invention itself. Some counts include all patents with at least one woman inventor. For example, a 2007 study from the National Center for Women and Information Technology reported that from 1980 to 2005, approximately 9% of U.S.-invented IT patents had at least one female inventor. Others use fractional counts. When the fraction of the patent that can be counted as female is calculated, the overall percentage of female U.S.-invented IT patents drops to 4.7%, although the fractional percentage has increased from 1.7% in 1980 to 6.1% in 2005 (Ashcraft and Breitzman 2007). This positive increase in percentage of patents by women occurred during a period when the percentage of women employed in IT decreased slightly, from 32% in 1983 to 27% in 2005 (Ashcraft and Breitzman 2007). Nonetheless, these data underline that 93.9% of U.S. origin patents come from men, who constitute approximately 70% of the U.S. IT workforce. The percentage of U.S. origin patents obtained by women in IT ranks well below their percentage in the IT workforce.

Although women are closer to parity in numbers and percentages in the life sciences, a similar gender gap pattern found in other fields with regard to patenting appears to occur in the life sciences (Ding, Murray, and Stuart 2006). A study of more than 1,000 recipients of NIH training grants in cellular and molecular biology revealed that 30% of men compared to 14% of women recipients had patented (Bunker Whittington and Smith-Doerr 2005). In contrast, this same study revealed that women's patents are more frequently cited than those of the men, suggesting a similar pattern to that found in earlier studies of publication rates in which men published more than women but that women's publications were cited more frequently (Long 1993). Citation, in both patents and publications, reflects the significance or importance of the work and how much other scientists or engineers use it as a basis for reference for their work.

A study restricted to a sample of 4,227 life science faculty found that 5.65% of the women and 13.0% of the men held at least one patent, despite no significant differences in publication patterns (Thursby and Thursby 2005). The lower percentage of women obtaining patents appears to hold across sectors of government, academia, and industry (Stephan and El-Ganainy 2007; U.S. Patent and Trademark Office 2003) with the exception of science-based network firms in the biotechnology industry (Whittington and Smith-Doerr 2008), where women are equally as likely as men to become involved in patenting, but still do not patent as frequently as men.

Women also tend to have lower publication rates than men, but the gender disparities in publication rates are not as significant as those for patents. For the United States, Yu Xie and Kimberlee Shauman (2003) document that women publish at about 70– 80% of the rate of men, based on 1988 and 1993 databases. In her study of tenured or tenure-track faculty in doctoral granting departments in computer science, chemistry, electrical engineering, microbiology, and physics in 1993–1994, Mary Frank Fox (2005) found that men are twice as likely as women to publish 20 or more papers, while women are almost twice as likely as men to publish zero or one paper. Fiona Murray and Leslie Graham (2007) found that men at "Big School" had higher total publication counts (82 vs. 55) and higher publication counts per year (3.7 vs. 2.6) than women, although these were not statistically significant; however, the citation counts per paper were very similar (42 for men vs. 41 for women). The significant difference between men and women was that men published 16% of their publications jointly with industry, while women published only 6% jointly with industry (Murray and Graham 2007, table 1).

An additional issue, not exactly paralleled in citation counts for papers, arises surrounding quality or impact of patents. Patents are obtained both to protect new inventions or ideas, as well as in business to prevent others from using or developing linked components critical to the basic operation of the invention. It is the latter type of patent, particularly common in computing, that many claim are "junk patents" that are "putting too many patents of dubious merit in the hands of people who can use them to drag companies and other inventors to court" (Tessler 2008, 1). One possible way to read the higher citation count for women's patents is to assume that women hold fewer patents of "dubious merit" compared to men.

International Comparisons of Patents Obtained by Women

Unfortunately, the gender gap also appears to hold internationally. Since patent offices do not record the gender of inventors for each patent (Ashcraft and Breitzman 2007), relying on names makes determination of gender difficult in some instances, particularly for gender-ambiguous names (Chris) or for names commonly applied to women in some countries and men in others (Jean in the United States compared to France). Using complicated and labor-intensive techniques, researchers have evolved methodologies to match gender with patents for large databases internationally. This reliance on names constitutes a further complication to studying the gender gap in patents. Catherine Ashcraft and Anthony Breitzman (2007) compared female IT patenting rates in the United States and Japan. Fulvio Naldi and Ilaria Prenti (2002) used large databases to study gender differences in patenting and publications in the United Kingdom, France, Germany, Italy, Spain, and Sweden in biology, biomedical research, chemistry, clinical medicine, earth and space, engineering, mathematics, and physics. Frietsch et al. (2007) studied gender differences in patenting and publications in those same fields and in those same six countries plus eight others: Australia, Austria, Belgium, Denmark, Ireland, New Zealand, Switzerland, and the United States.

Using the Scopus database that covers more than 15,000 peer-reviewed journals in the life sciences, health sciences, physical sciences, and social sciences, Rainer Frietsch and colleagues (2007) found that the share of female authors varied by country between 21.5% (Switzerland) through 28.3% (United States) to 38.6% (Italy). He also found considerable variation by field, with biology (33.9%), biomedicine (32.2%), and medicine (28.3%) having the largest share of female authors, while engineering (20.4%), physics (18.1%), and mathematics (16.3%) had the least. Chemistry (25.3%) and geosciences (21.8%) were intermediate. His data of share of female authors by discipline and country suggest that women publish somewhat less than men in each field but that women's publication rates are significantly higher than their patenting rates in all countries and all fields.

All these studies document that in all of these countries in all of the different areas, the percentage of women obtaining patents is significantly lower than that of their male counterparts. Considerable variation exists among the technological fields, with pharmaceutical (24.1%) and basic chemicals (12.5%) tending to have higher percentages of patents obtained by women, and machine-tools (2.3%) and energy machinery (1.9%) having lower percentages in 2001 (Frietsch et al. 2007). Within the IT industry, some variation occurred among subcategories, with women obtaining about 8% (fractional count) of the computer software patents in the United States and about 6% (fractional count) of patents in other fields such as hardware, semiconductors, communications, and peripherals. Relatively the same subcategory distributions held for Japanese women, but at lower percentages overall, since Japanese women obtained about 3.0–3.6% (fractional count) of patents overall but 5.6% (fractional count) of the software patents.

As suggested by the comparison of U.S. and Japanese women in IT, considerable differences in the percentage of women obtaining patents occur among countries. The study of patenting in 14 countries (Frietsch et al. 2007) documented that in general the percentage of women's patenting has increased during the past decade in all countries. However, substantial variations exist among countries, even within Europe. Australia (13.7%), Spain (17.5%), and New Zealand (14.0%) rank highest; Switzerland (7.4%), Germany (5.9%), and Austria (4.5%) rank lowest. The United States (11.1%), Sweden (9.3%), and Denmark (11.4%) rank about midway in percentage of women obtaining patents (Frietsch et al. 2007). In all countries, the percentage of women obtaining patents is less than the percentage of women in the STEM workforce.

Issues surrounding quantification, quality, and association of some names with a particular gender might raise doubts if the gender gap in patents were small or not evident in all sectors, disciplines, or countries. But the gap is substantial. In short, in all countries across all sectors and in all fields, the percentage of women obtaining patents is not only less than their male counterparts but it is less than the percentage of women in STEM in the field in the country. This raises the following questions: what are the impacts and nature of the gender gap, and what can be applied from women's studies and gender studies to close this gender gap in patenting?

Both in the United States and internationally, the focus for scientific research has shifted from basic to applied research and innovation, for which one of the primary indicators is patents granted. If women scientists and engineers are not obtaining patents at rates comparable to their participation in the STEM workforce and at significantly lower rates than their male peers, then women are not participating in the new areas and directions for science and technology. This hurts women scientists and engineers who are left out of the leading-edge work in innovation. Women are then not seen as leaders in their field, which hurts women financially and in their professional advancement. Commercialization of science can be extremely lucrative, if the patent results in a product that is developed, brought to market, and is successful. Since patents "count" as a marker of success, similar to publications, and may even be required for some bonuses and "fellow" status in some industries, women's small percentages of patents also inhibit their professional advancement. Although men dominate patenting in all fields, some relative gender differences in fields of patents exist.

What Is the Impact of Gender Inequity in Patents?

Having a relatively small number of women obtaining patents hurts scientific innovation, technology, and competitiveness overall. As feminist critiques (Keller 1983; 1985) of science have revealed, science is gendered in ways that bind objectivity with masculinity so that a latent, diffuse assumption that scientists are working toward the common good permeates approaches and results of science, when in fact it may be working for the good of only some races, classes, and one gender. When women entered science in larger numbers, they revealed androcentric approaches that included biased questions, approaches, and theories and conclusions drawn from data. Similarly, the predominance of men in patenting may mean that innovations useful for a broader population may not be developed.

Having large numbers of male engineers and creators of technologies often results in technologies that are useful from a male perspective. In addition to the military origins for the development and funding of much technology (Barnaby 1981; Norman 1979), which makes its civilian application less useful for women's lives (Cockburn 1983), technology for the home that is designed by men frequently focuses on issues that are less important to women users. For example, Anne-Jorunn Berg's (1999) analysis of "smart houses" reveals that such houses do not include new technologies; instead they focus on "integration, centralized control and regulation of all functions in the home" (306). "Housework is no part of what this house will 'do' for you" (307). Knowledge of housework appears to be overlooked by the designers of smart houses. As Ruth Schwartz Cowan's (1983) work suggests, the improved household technologies developed in the first half of the twentieth century actually increased the amount of time housewives spent on housework and reduced their role from general manager of servants, maiden aunts, grandmothers, children, and others, to an individual who worked alone doing manual labor aided by household appliances.

Although men do dominate patenting in all fields, some relative gender differences in fields of patents exist. Since ideas for patents often arise out of personal experience, it is not surprising that studies (Macdonald 1992) of the patents obtained by women and of women inventors document that women invent more technologies related to reproduction or children. Women also have invented many technologies for the home (a patented house that cleans itself, using 68 separate devices), and for caretaking, particularly of children (disposable diapers and the pull-down-from-the-wall baby-changing stations found in public restrooms). If more women were involved in commercialization, imagine the new, useful products that might be developed to benefit society.

Reasons for the Gender Gap in Industry

Exclusion or self-exclusion of women from commercialization of science and patenting hurts both women and science, while also shortchanging society. Patenting has been integral to technical and scientific firms for more than two centuries and remains central and significant for the culture of most science and technology corporations. As noted previously, not only do those who patent reap significant financial rewards and recognition, but a track record in obtaining patents is required for individuals to attain certain positions in their fields. As suggested in the previous chapter, some scientists and engineers move back and forth among the private, academic, and government sectors. Since the gender gap in numbers of patents obtained by women remains in industry, where the rewards, incentives, and motivations for patenting are more positive and clear, I thought that attempting to understand some of the reasons behind the gap in industry might help begin to understand the gap in academia, where the impact of patents on the academic career path may be mixed or not well understood.

Interview Data and Methods

I conducted interviews with ten people, two men and eight women, who served as software engineers, vice presidents, chief executive officers, or presidents of technology companies in the metro New York City area and in California's Silicon Valley. Although two individuals had worked at the same company in different positions during their entire careers, most had worked at a variety of companies, both large and established and small and start-up. Interviewees were obtained using the snowball method; at the close of each interview, I asked who else in another company in the area I should ask these same questions to help me better understand the gender gap in patenting. All names and other identifiers of interviewees have been changed.

Each interviewee was asked the following five questions:

1. What is the percentage of women, compared to men, obtaining patents at the company(ies) with which you have been associated? How does that compare with the overall percentage of women in the company?
2. What role do patents play in advancing one's career in the company? Are patents becoming more or less important than they were 10 years ago?
3. Why don't women patent at the same rates as men? What are the barriers?
4. How can we increase opportunities for women to patent? What actions is your company taking to facilitate this?
5. What (else) should I have asked about women and patents?

The quotations that follow from three interviews are representative of the broader set of data collected.

I conducted an interview with technology sector CEO Sharlane Levitan.* Sharlane finds from her experience in both large and small technology companies that women have different motivations and interests that may make them less likely to patent.

CEO Sharlane Levitan

Sharlane Levitan has worked in very large technology companies in a variety of roles, mostly on the marketing and development sides, as well as serving as CEO of two small technology companies. She believes that one reason women patent at lower rates than their workforce numbers in the IT industry is that most women move to the marketing, development, and human resource sides of the company. Although they may start in engineering or software development, many women move into the operationally oriented roles, which are less likely to be areas from which patents emanate.

> In general, women are less interested in technology and more inter-ested in socially oriented areas. I believe that the way to motivate women and retain them in technology is to emphasize context, cre-ativity, and the arts side of technology for which women may be more hard-wired. Simultaneously, I believe that most women do take a risk-averse approach to their career that inhibits their ability to think boldly and persistently about one big idea that might be patent-able. To overcome these differences in motivation and risk aversion, companies should make mentoring others in the process of patent-ing part of performance plans and develop R&D training programs to teach women about the process of patenting. That would help to change the climate and motivation for women to patent.

Levitan's notions of women's risk aversion also seemed to stem from the fact that women are more interested in and occupied with children and family, which might lead them to develop more patentable ideas in these arenas than in IT. Indeed, her contention receives some support from evidence derived from the studies of inventions by women and sur-veys of patents obtained by women (Macdonald 1992) which suggest that many women develop technologies related to reproduction (e.g., Nystatin to prevent vaginal yeast infections), secondary sex characteristics (back-less bra), or babies/children (folding crib).

When I pressed her a bit, Sharlane admitted that it might not be the biological differences between men and women, but the societal views of gender based on biological differences as suggested by existentialist Sim-one de Beauvoir (1949) that resulted in this gender gap in patenting in IT.

When I interviewed women in industry about the gender gap in patent-ing, they immediately knew what I was talking about and told me what they believed to be the reasons the gap persists. In contrast, when I spoke with men in industry, most of the interview was spent challenging the data that the gap existed at all. After they became convinced that the gap might be real, they stated that it might hold for other companies, but they were pretty sure it was not true for theirs, although they had never thought about it or looked into it, as the my interview with Rick Foot* reveals.

President Rick Foot

Rick Foot currently serves as president and founder of a very successful IT innovation company. He has started up other companies and headed several research and development operations. Friendly and generous with his time for the interview, he began by explaining the patenting process.

He told me that he didn't think there was a gender gap in patenting in the industry but that it must result from the persistently low numbers of women in the industry. When I explained the NCWIT study and the data showing that women patented at much lower rates than their participation in the IT workforce, he challenged the data with other questions about sector, publication rates, incentives, and age. When he finally accepted that the data for the gender gap might be solid, he said, "I'm pretty sure that the women in R&D in my company patent at the same rate as their many male counterparts." He did admit, though, that he had never thought about gender or checked the data for his company, which he became intrigued to examine. Rick Foot was quite convinced that his view—that there could not be a gender gap in patenting or if a gap did exist, it was proportional to the low number of women in IT—was absolutely true.

I conducted the following interview with Sal Calfit*, a software engineer who works at one of the largest global information technology companies in the world. Concerned about the dearth of women obtaining patents in the company, she formed a community to support them and help them learn the process.

Software Engineer Sal Calfit

Sal had observed that very few women in the company where she worked obtained patents. That stimulated her to start the support community for women. She sent an email to about 20 women in the company; she immediately received responses from all around the globe. In two years, the community has grown to 600 women who represent all sectors and all countries where the company is located.

I believe that a variety of factors account for the low numbers of patents obtained by women. Women look critically at themselves and their ideas, wondering whether they are meritorious. They need someone both to encourage and to guide them through the process.

Women also tend to be the workhorses on the team; they are more focused on getting the job done than the external rewards.

I also believe that women have less access to networks, which is why the network I created provides a lifeline for these women. The women seem to love the community atmosphere; they appear to crave the brainstorming, support, and nurturing atmosphere. Communities of the company are now springing up in China and India with large memberships of women.

In setting up the online support community for women in her company, Sal Calfit tries to provide access and level the playing field for women in other countries. The interest of women in India and China working for the corporation in the online communities to support patenting reflects the varying complex aspects of the inter-relationships among developed and developing countries in general and between the particular cultures of the colonized and colonizing country.

The particular forms and ways that these shape and play out vary, depending upon the history, culture, geography, and duration of colonization for both the colonized and colonizing countries. For example, the IT industry uses subcontracted female labor in developing countries, particularly for software development. Practically, the ties developed between colony and colonizer, as well as the language of the colonizer learned by the colonized during the period of colonization, means that former relationships continue in the neocolonial modern world (Rosser 2005, 15–16).

Using feminist theoretical frameworks to contextualize responses of interviewees provides some further insights into the gender gap in patenting in industry. Some of the studies about the gender gap in patenting for academic women also point to issues of access and discrimination. For example, Murray and Graham (2007) conducted semi-structured interviews of 56 life science faculty about their experiences with commercial science at "Big School." Only 23% of women faculty had patented, while 74% of men faculty hold at least one patent. Women faculty reported fewer opportunities and referrals from collegial networks to participate in the commercial marketplace by being asked to consult, serve on science advisory boards, and interact with industry, resulting in women becoming less socialized to commercial science. This led to women having fewer chances, relative to their male colleagues, to resolve ambiguities that many life scientists hold about commercial science.

Murray and Graham (2007) then appear to move beyond issues of access to explore what might be described as almost a psychoanalytic approach, reminiscent of the work of Evelyn Fox Keller. They state, "Partly because of the dearth of women, the practices of commercial science, including those surrounding money and competition, became constructed as male" (Murray and Graham 2007, 682). Murray and Graham found that male constructions of "these intersections were reinforced across generations by homophily in mentoring and networks, work-family issues, and broader societal stereotypes towards women in commercial roles" (Murray and Graham 2007). Although the effects were more severe on senior women, in the "entire population of junior faculty, 44% of men have been granted patents compared to only 11% of women." Although not stated explicitly, the presence of the continuing gap even among junior women implies that the liberal feminist approach of eliminating barriers will not be sufficient, as long as organizational and societal stereotypes remain unchallenged.

Paula Stephan and Asmaa El-Ganainy (2007) suggest that one aspect of the organizational context argument—that more men than women are employed at higher ranks at doctoral research extensive institutions where most patenting occurs—only partially accounts for the gender gap. Although they appear to recognize some of the structural and power issues surrounding why doctoral research extensive institutions with high prestige and better salaries are dominated by men, they do not really critique these organizational structures. The predominance of men employed at research I institutions, where wages are higher and hours are longer, results partly from a culture that is less family-friendly than that found at many less elite higher education institutions.

Stephan and El-Ganainy (2007) provide evidence from various studies to suggest the following explanations for the gap, in addition to employment at doctoral research extensive institutions:

- Women are more risk averse than men regarding financial decisions and may have less interest in money and a lower comfort level with financial transactions.
- Women dislike competition more than men, and commercial science is perceived as competitive.
- Women are less comfortable selling themselves and their science in the entrepreneurial manner needed for commercialization.

- Women are less likely to seek out opportunities to participate in commercial science.
- Women may choose areas for research that are less compatible with commercialization.
- Women have fewer characteristics such as high productivity and a "title" that venture capitalists like.
- Compared to men, women have more family constraints which they perceive as a tradeoff with their entrepreneurial activities.
- Women faculty may be less likely to be located in one of the three commercialization geographic "hot spots" in California, Massachusetts, or North Carolina.
- Women tend to have fewer peers involved in commercialization, partly because their collegial networks are likely to include more women than those of men. Women scientists may have fewer graduate students and postdocs than men and less diverse networks than men.

Some women, particularly those coming from a socialist feminist perspective, purposely avoid commercialization of their research which they view as "selling their science" to pander to capitalism. Current intellectual property rights agreements and laws provide opportunities for choices in technology development that further exacerbate class differences by transferring technologies developed using public moneys to the private realm through patents. The decisions regarding which products are developed falls under the influence of capitalist interests in profit margins. Such intellectual property rights function as a form of privatization (Mohanty 1997). They allow decisions about which products will be developed to occur in the private, rather than the public, realm. This results in capitalist interests in the bottom line, rather than public needs and interests, dictating which "products" are developed. New technologies in computer science and engineering are often developed using federal grants (paid for by taxes). In the patenting of intellectual property, rights (and profits) get transferred from the public who paid for the research with their tax dollars, to the private company, institution, or individual who controls the patent. Socialist feminists might view this as a transfer from the pockets of the working class, who pay the taxes to underwrite federal research, to the patent holders in the private sector who will reap massive profits, serving the interests of bourgeois capitalists.

Understanding that middle- and upper-class men create and design most new technology, along with serving as the sources of money for design and creation, explains much about whose needs are met by current technology and its design. The male norm is often used in technology design, resulting in the exclusion of women even as users of the technology. For example, military regulations often apply Military Standard 1472 of anthropometric data so that systems dimensions use the 95th and 5th percentile of male dimensions in designing weapons systems. This led to the cockpits of airplanes being designed to fit the dimensions of 90 percent of the male military recruits (Weber 1997). This worked relatively well as long as the military was entirely male. In the case of the Joint Primary Aircraft Training System (JPATS), used by both the navy and air force to train the pilots, the application of the standard accommodated the 5th through 95th percentile (90 percent) of males, but only approximately the 65th through 95th percentile (30 percent) of females. The policy decision by Secretary of Defense Les Aspin (1993, 10) to increase the percentage of women pilots, uncovered the gender bias in the cockpit design. Designed to exclude only 10 percent of male recruits by its dimensions, the cockpit excluded 70 percent of women recruits, making it extremely difficult to meet the military's policy goal of increasing the number of women pilots. The officers initially reacted by assuming that the technology reflected the best or only design possible and that the goal for the percentage of women pilots would have to be lowered and/or the number of tall women recruits would have to be increased. This initial reaction, which represented the world viewpoint of men, changed over time. When political coalitions, the Tailhook scandal, and feminist groups reinforced the policy goal, a new cockpit design emerged which reduced the minimum sitting height from 34 to 32.8 inches, thereby increasing the percentage of eligible women (Weber 1997, 239).

Imagining women as designers, as well as users, of technology suggests that more technologies might meet the needs of women and be adapted for the spaces where women spend time. Socialist feminism would suggest that the allocation of resources for technology development should be determined by greatest benefit for the common good. For example, now that a larger percentage of the population is older, perhaps more technology to ease daily life for the elderly will be invented.

Venture capitalists may have a higher comfort level with men than women since most venture capitalists are men (Murray and Graham 2007).

Gender discounting (viewing the accomplishments of women differently from those of men, when all else is equal) of women's work by industry may lead to fewer women being asked to participate in commercialization.

In brief, although more research on the reasons for the gender gap needs to be undertaken, it appears that a variety of factors concerning attitudes and socialization of women, balancing work and family, sexist attitudes of venture capitalists and industrial partners, as well as women's differing collegial networks and research focus, may serve as major contributors. Gender discounting of women's scientific work by industry, greater comfort level of venture capitalists with men than women, fewer opportunities for commercialization open to women, broader and more varied collegial networks available to men, and a boy's club atmosphere imply exclusion and being locked out, if not actual discrimination against women in commercialization of science. These suggest that the gender gap in patents is a feminist issue to which theories from gender and women's studies might usefully be applied.

What Can We Apply from Gender and Women's Studies to Close the Patenting Gender Gap?

These "explanations" given by Stephan and El-Ganainy parallel many of the "reasons" elaborated during the last quarter century for why women do not participate in science. Many scholars who study women in science and engineering have suggested solutions or policy initiatives that mentors, departments, and institutions can undertake to attract and retain women in science.

In 1990, I suggested ideas to make science more female-friendly (Rosser 1990). Considering this list makes me wonder if adapting some of these ideas to issues raised about gender and patenting could be useful in attracting more women to commercialization of science. Murray and Graham (2007) suggest policy interventions for faculty PhD advisors, for institutions and their institutional technology transfer offices, and for the industrial and investment communities to facilitate women's participation in commercial science to "ensure that those scientific ideas with important commercial relevance are not squandered" (Murray and Graham 2007, 583). These interventions include suggestions to make certain that commercially active PhD advisors provide women and men students with the same, appropriate mentoring experiences including encouraging all students to look into commercial science, facilitating ties to industrial and other sponsors who want to "buy" their ideas, and demonstrating, especially to women, how to sell their science without violating their scientific integrity. They suggest that institutions appoint more qualified women to high-level administrative positions to encourage industry to look more carefully at their science and leadership capabilities, and appoint them to scientific advisory boards. Technology transfer offices should provide legitimacy and support for women faculty to navigate the commercial science marketplace. After being made aware of the data documenting their leadership role in fostering old boy networks, the industrial and investment community should actively seek out and assess ideas from women, as well as men, scientists.

Using the policy interventions suggested by Murray and Graham, the "explanations" for the gender gap provided by Stephan and El Ganainy, who offer no explicit policy interventions, coupled with evidence of different areas in which women have patented (MacDonald 1992; Frietsch et al. 2007) as a basis, I modified my earlier ideas of ways to make patenting more female-friendly. They are divided into suggestions for faculty, institutions and their technology transfer offices, corporations and venture capitalists, and women scientists.

Suggestions for Women Scientists

1. Consider expanding your scientific research agenda to include commercialization. This may mean overcoming notions about the purity of what counts as good science.
2. Formulate hypotheses that focus on gender as a crucial part of the commercialization/patenting decision. For example, in initial experimental design, ask whether a particular drug works differently in males and females. Might a drug cure an illness in both men and women or just men? Might an invention be adapted for a new product, especially useful to women?
3. Consider basic research problems that might lead to patents and commercialization of products to help with complex problems more commonly dealt with by women in the home, such as child caregiving, housecleaning, and care for the elderly.
4. Make a conscious effort to broaden networks to include both older and younger men and women scientists.

Suggestions for Corporations and Venture Capitalists

1. Collect data, disaggregated by gender, on who patents.
2. Expand the scientific research agendas open to commercialization by seeking out the work of women scientists to explore its potential.
3. Explore science and ideas that have not traditionally been considered for commercialization because of gender discounting.
4. Focus on gender as a crucial part of the commercialization/patenting decision. Does a particular drug work differently in males and females or cure an illness in both men and women or just men? Could this invention be adapted for a new product, especially useful to women, children, or the elderly?
5. Include women on scientific advisory boards of corporations.
6. Make a conscious effort to overcome the boys' club atmosphere of commercialization and to broaden networks to include both men and women scientists.
7. Expand recruitment for commercialization ideas beyond males who self-promote very aggressively to include women who may initially appear less entrepreneurial.
8. Move beyond the signal shock stage of only inviting women with very high-level titles such as dean, provost, vice president, or president of the university to serve on scientific advisory boards to seek out women scientists who have not chosen the administrative career path but who have excellent ideas for commercialization.
9. Use national and international conferences to seek out scientific research ideas ripe for commercialization, recognizing that this may be an excellent way to reach women scientists in particular, who are more likely than their male colleagues to live outside one of the geographic hotspots for commercialization.
10. Consider other ways to find ideas for commercialization that rely less on self-promotion and competition with others and more on understanding the potential based upon solid explanation of the science.
11. Make technology transfer and commercialization companies more family-friendly through on-site day care, holding meetings during business hours, and use of conferencing technology to limit necessity for travel.
12. Articulate the goals for commercialization of science to link them directly with making society better and helping people to provide powerful incentives for women to patent.

Suggestions for Male Faculty, Institutions, and Technology Transfer Offices

1. Make transparent all stages of the commercialization process, and provide both male and female students with equal access, mentoring, and connections to each stage of the process.
2. Incorporate discussion of how to build a business plan and how to understand financial risks in commercialization into scientific training for all students, both male and female, just as learning to write grants, build budgets, and manage a laboratory are now considered necessary constituents of graduate training in science and engineering.
3. Encourage all students to undertake research agendas that include some "high-risk" ideas and experiments and some "lower-risk" ideas and experiments. This insures that women have experience with higher-risk ideas and learn that it's OK to fail. In contrast, some risk-seeking male students may need to learn to balance their high-risk research agenda with the benefits of some lower-risk ideas.
4. Alternate discussion, experiments, and problems assigned between basic and applied science in the classroom and laboratory to facilitate students' perceiving a less sharp dichotomy between science and technology transfer and overcome their aversion to commercialization.
5. Include information from economics, business, and policy, along with science courses in training to socialize students to commercialization and how big science works.
6. Insure that mentoring of students is gender-neutral by inviting all students, both male and female, to explore commercialization potential of their ideas, and by making all parts of the process transparent. Mentoring should also be gender appropriate, in recognizing that women may be more risk averse, less inclined to sell science, and have different constraints. Provide women and men with a variety of approaches to address their particular constraints.
7. Include women in significant administrative positions in the university. This not only provides leadership opportunities and role models for women in the institution, but it also sends the shock signal corporations use to identify women with outstanding credentials.

8. Provide courses and online training and apprenticeship models/ mentors to teach scientists how to sell their ideas to venture capitalists, angel funders, and corporations.
9. Emphasize the social usefulness, especially to help human beings and the environment, of technology transfer and commercialization.

Timing and a Model to Close the Gender Gap

Why was the gap discovered so recently? Now that we've noticed the gap, when, if ever, will it be closed? How long will it take for women scientists, corporations, venture capitalists, male faculty, technology transfer offices, and institutions to implement the policies others and I have suggested as a way to close this gap? Since the commercialization of science only began to explode in academia in the 1970s and was particularly fueled by the passage of the Bayh-Dole Act in 1980, encouraging academics to claim intellectual property and work with universities to license these rights to firms, in some ways it is not surprising that the "gender gap" has relatively recently been identified (Ding, Murray, and Stuart 2006; Bunker Whittington and Smith-Doerr 2005) and that researchers are only beginning to explore the dimensions of the gap across different fields, sectors, and countries (Ashcraft and Breitzman 2007; Frietsch et al. 2007; Naldi and Prenti 2002, 2004).

To someone like me, who has focused on women in science, women's studies, and curriculum transformation for more than 30 years, it smacks of a familiar pattern: women are excluded until someone "discovers" their absence. Then women become integrated over time in what can be described as a series of stages or phases.

In *Female Friendly Science* (1990), I proposed a five-stage model for curriculum transformation to aid in including more information on women and men of color. Built on models developed by feminist scholars working in other disciplines (McIntosh 1984; Schuster and Van Dyne 1985; Tetreault 1985), the following model is specific for science and mathematics.

Stage 1. Absence of women not noted. This is the traditional approach to science and the curriculum from the perspective of the white, Eurocentric, middle- to upper-class male in which the absence of women is not noted. The assumption is that gender affects neither those who become scientists nor the science produced.

Stage 2. Women as an add-on. This stage recognizes that most scientists are male and that science may reflect a masculine perspective on the physical, natural world. A few exceptional women such as Nobel laureates who have achieved the highest success as defined by the traditional standards of the discipline may be accepted in the scientific community and included in the curriculum.

Stage 3. Women as a problem. Barriers that prevent women from entering science are identified. Women are recognized as a problem, anomaly, or absence from science and the curriculum. Women may be seen as victims, as protesters, or as deprived or defective variants, who deviate from the white, middle- to upper-class norm of the male scientist.

Stage 4. Women as the focus. Women scientists and their unique contributions are sought. The extent to which the role of women has been overlooked, misunderstood, or attributed to male colleagues throughout the history of science is explored to determine women's scientific achievements. Questions are asked about new perspectives that might result when women become the focus in topics chosen for study. New methods may be used and language in which data and theories are described may shift, improving the quality of science.

Stage 5. Inclusive science. Scientists, scientific research, and science curriculum are redefined and reconstructed to include diversity in terms of gender, as well as race, class, age, and other factors.

Thinking of the stage model and its possibilities for explaining phenomena of curriculum drew my attention to the possibility of its application to the gender gap in patents. My junior colleague's interest in the reasons for, and parameters surrounding, the gender gap in patents, coupled with several recent high-profile studies (Ashcraft and Breitzman 2007; Ding et al. 2006; Murray and Graham 2007; Stephan and El Ganainy 2007) which focused on women's low rates of patenting suggest that we are currently moving toward stage 3, centering on barriers or problems that prevent women from patenting. A 2008 article on the dearth of women in high positions in Silicon Valley (Ross 2008) exemplifies the problem stage. The article states that "almost one-third of women at the 'middle-level' of their high-tech careers are planning to quit primarily because of perceived barriers to advancement" (2008).

The time when commercialization and technology transfer began to take off in the late 1970s to the early 1980s until the "discovery" of the gender gap in about 2004–2005 constitutes stage 1, when the absence of women is not noted. Occasional articles highlighting star women who patent at high rates exemplify stage 2, exceptional women who patent at the same rates under the same conditions as men in male-dominated fields. Stephanie Louise Kwolek exemplifies such a stage 2 woman. She invented Kevlar, a synthetic material used in bullet-proof vests that is five times stronger than the same weight of steel, while she worked as a chemist at DuPont and obtained 28 patents during her 40 year career (About. com.Inventors 2006). A recent spate of attention to the gender gap as demonstrated by publications, NSF-funded projects, and conference presentations begins to encroach on stage 4: focus on the gender gap, although it seems unlikely that more than a few individuals have reached stage 4.

In short, most scientists, engineers, and academia have not noticed the gender gap and remain in stage 1. Even individuals involved in technology transfer appear unaware of the absence of women until it is brought to their attention. Once they think about it, they typically agree that very few women patent in the fields with which they are familiar. After some thought, they'll often mention one or two women in their field who do obtain patents, exemplifying stage 2. Most will then begin to move to stage 3 when they wonder what prevents women from patenting at the same rate as men. The 2008 study from Stanford's Clayman Institute and the Anita Borg Institute, titled *Climbing the Technical Ladder: Obstacles and Solutions for Mid-level Women in Technology* (Simard, et al. 2008) highlights the problem aspect of this stage 3.

A gender gap also seems to apply in the recognition of the gender gap in patents. Men and women outside of fields where technology transfer and commercialization occur are equally ignorant of the gender gap in patents. In fields where technology transfer and commercialization are prevalent, men appear much less aware of the gender gap than women. Most women in these same fields are completely aware of the gap and immediately articulate the number of women who patent in their particular area and their personal theories about why women do not patent at the same rate as men. In contrast, men in those same fields typically state that they were unaware of the gap, deny its existence, or declare that it may exist elsewhere but not in their laboratory or department (Rosser 2009).

Implications for Closing the Gender Gap:
What Are the Implications of Stage Theory for Technology Transfer?
What Will It Mean for Closing the Gender Gap in Patenting?

A stage or phase theory implies that the final stage of inclusion won't be reached without taking the time to go through each of the earlier stages. Evidence of narrowing the gender gap among younger cohorts of women suggests progression through the stages. First, the numbers and percentages of women obtaining patents have increased over time. Overall, the U.S. Patent and Trademark Office reports that the percentage of U.S. origin patents in all categories which include at least one woman inventor has increased from 3.7% (1977–1988) to 10.9% in 2002, and that the number of U.S. origin patents that include at least one woman inventor has also been increasing (U.S. Patent and Trademark Office 2003). From 1977 to 2002, women inventors showed the greatest participation in U.S. origin patents in design (11.5%) and plant (11.7%) patenting. By 2002, 12.9% of the design patents and 21.2% of the plant patents had at least one woman inventor. In 2002, 19.6% of chemical utility patents had at least one woman inventor, but electrical (7.0%) and mechanical (7.8%) utility patents with one woman inventor ranked much lower.

Second, younger women are patenting more than senior women colleagues. In a study at "Big School," only 23% of women faculty had patented, while 74% of men faculty held at least one patent. Among the younger cohort the gap is less; in the "entire population of junior faculty, 44% of men have been granted patents compared to only 11% of women" (Murray and Graham 2007).

Third, limited evidence suggests that women are becoming involved with patenting at the same rates as their male peers in some venues. In a study of science-based network firms in the biotechnology industry, Kristin Whittington and Laurel Smith-Doerr (2008) documented that women were as likely as men to become involved in patenting, although the women were still patenting less frequently than the men.

Overall, both nationally and internationally, the gender gap in patents has shown some signs of closing over time. These studies provide some evidence for progression through the stages. Reaching stage 5 of inclusion seems distant, although some fields and sectors, such as the biotech start-ups, appear to be closer to inclusion.

In order to reach inclusion (stage 5), not only will all disciplines, but all sectors and individuals involved, have to pass through these stages. As I worked in projects on curricular transformation occurring in the sciences, I recognized that the phases applied to more than curriculum. These stages describe steps of personal development through which individuals progress as they become aware of biases due to gender and race in curriculum and pedagogy. In an early book (Rosser 1986), I suggested that an individual must progress personally through, or at least to, a stage of development before he or she can develop curriculum and pedagogical techniques at that stage. For example, a faculty member cannot teach a stage 5, inclusive course in which the primary focus shifts from the white male experience to include women, men of color, and disabled persons, if she or he is only at the add-on phase (stage 2) in her or his own thinking.

Just as phase theory may be applied to personal development and transformation toward inclusion as well as curriculum, it also may be applied to programs, departments, institutions, and/or agencies. As is the case with individuals, even with a well-conceived (stage 5) plan for diversity and inclusion and the best of intentions on the part of all faculty, staff, and/or employees, a university cannot jump from stage 1 to 5 without going through the intermediate stages. Moving an entire department and curriculum toward gender inclusion is difficult. Transforming an entire college or university has proved a long-term challenge.

Technology transfer and commercialization involve interactions with many individuals outside the university from a variety of sectors with quite different cultures from that of academia. Corporations and their boards, venture capitalists, marketing specialists, and angel funders, in addition to students, men and women faculty, and technology transfer personnel in universities will all need to progress through these stages to close the gender gap. Not only is the group involved in technology transfer very large and diverse in terms of backgrounds and expertise, but different components and individuals hold competing interests and cultures.

More significant than understanding the stage theory and process is the desire of each individual and each group, as well as that of corporate power and elite educational institutions, to want to close the gender gap. Since technology transfer and patenting involve substantial amounts of money, such a desire cannot be taken for granted. Indeed, one study of the gender gap noted that part of the appeal of technology transfer for some academics may have been to create an elite male-only club: As Stephan and El-Ganainy suggest, "entrepreneurial science opened the possibility of having a 'boys' club' when it emerged on campuses in the late 1970s" just at the time when larger numbers of women and under-represented minorities were entering academic science (Stephan and El-Ganainy 2007, 486.)

Aside from the obvious issues of fairness and discrimination, what other problems and losses result from the boys' club that excludes women and leads to a gender gap in patenting? First, women who are scientists lose. Studies (Stephan and El-Ganainy 2007) document that women scientists, compared to their male peers, have fewer graduate students and postdocs and smaller, less diverse collegial networks. Compared to their male peers, women are asked less frequently to consult or serve on scientific advisory boards, and have their work discounted more frequently by industry (Murray and Graham 2007). This means that women scientists lose out not only on higher salaries, stock options, awards, and promotions, but also on opportunities to work in some of the most cutting-edge fields on the frontiers of science such as information technology, biotechnology, and nanotechnology.

Second, science loses in attracting more individuals with creative ideas. Fewer women are attracted to science because of the perceived chilly atmosphere of exclusion (Rosser 2004). As indicated in the recent Clayman Institute and Anita Borg Study (Simard et al. 2008), perceived barriers and obstacles cause women either to not enter the field, to drop out, or to switch fields mid-career.

Third, society loses because fewer products are developed. Having very few women obtaining patents hurts scientific innovation, technology, and competitiveness overall. Although men dominate patenting in all fields, some relative gender differences in fields of patents exist. Since ideas for patents often arise in areas with which the innovators have experiences, small numbers of women patenting suggests fewer products to solve problems and facilitate daily life for women and children in particular. If more women were involved in commercialization, imagine the new, useful products to benefit society that might be developed. Simultaneously, increasing the percentage of women scientists and engineers who patent is also likely to increase their economic equality as technology transfer and commercialization of science increase in the United States and globally.

In contrast, if the percentage of patents awarded to women remains far lower than the percentage of women scientists and engineers in the science, engineering, technology, and mathematics (STEM) workforce, this may represent another example of old wine in new bottles. Does exclusion of women from these leading-edge fields in innovation simply represent the twenty-first century version of the mid-twentieth-century phenomenon of women not holding major leadership positions in big science? Such exclusion represents a major loss, since women scientists have focused on different problems, used new approaches, and produced new theoretical perspectives that have benefitted science, technology, and society, as documented in the next chapter.

%%   7   %%

The Impact That Women Have
Made on Science and Technology

*As founding director of San Francisco State's Health
Equity Institute, (Cynthia) Gomez brings academic
prowess as well as community-based solutions to the
daunting problem of health disparities...Her expertise
and ability to bring different ideologies to the same
table led to her serving as an appointed member to the
Presidential Advisory council on HIV/AIDS under both
Presidents Bill Clinton and George W. Bush. In 2008,
California governor Arnold Schwarzenegger appointed
her to the first California Public Health Advisory Committee. . . . A self-described "Latina mutt," Cynthia
Gomez is a third-generation Mexican American whose
older siblings do not speak Spanish.*

*A teacher and researcher whose work has zeroed in
on barriers to HIV-prevention strategies for women and
particularly Latina women, Gomez also has a passion for
building bridges when it comes to applying that research
to real-world problems...While visiting the Native American migrant blueberry pickers in northern Maine, Gomez
learned one woman created an HIV-education-themed
bingo night because bingo was a popular activity. Gomez
was on hand to help peer educators articulate their inten-
tion when it comes to HIV education and prevention,
both to help find funding support and so other tribes
can replicate the program. And she also wanted to help
group members understand the science behind behavior
change so barriers and solutions could come to the fore-
front. "Some of our public health can't just be instinctual,"
Gomez said. "You have to bring in the science."*

—Currie 2010, 2030–32

What difference does it make to have women scientists and engineers? The last two chapters suggested significant effects from having more women in key administrative positions in academic institutions, and possible losses in innovation from having fewer women involved in inventions, technology transfer, and patenting. What impact have women had on basic science and technology becomes an especially significant question. Although scientists may note contributions of individual women scientists to their discipline or subdiscipline, scholars from the field of women's studies have explored the question in greater depth.

As this wave of feminism and women's studies marks its fourth decade, the cross-fertilization of the interaction among science, technology, medicine, and feminism has continued to blossom and bear fruit. Science, technology, and medicine have come to accept feminist perspectives and gender analyses, and particularly their extension to experimental methods, more slowly than did the humanities and social sciences. Those of us who had one foot in science and the other in women's studies worked hard to build the two-way streets between science and feminism articulated by Anne Fausto-Sterling in her article by that title (1992a).

Most researchers in the behavioral, biomedical, and physical sciences are trained in the scientific method and believe in its power. Few, however, are aware of its historical and philosophical roots in logical positivism and objectivity that lead to the belief in the possibilities of obtaining knowledge that is both objective and value free, the cornerstones of the scientific method.

Longino (1990) has explored the extent to which methods employed by scientists can be objective and lead to repeatable, verifiable results while contributing to hypotheses or theories that are congruent with nonobjective institutions and ideologies of the society. The institutions and beliefs of our society reflect the fact that the society is patriarchal. Even female scientists have only recently become aware of the influence of patriarchal bias in the paradigms of science (Rose and Rose 1980; Rosser 1992).

A first step for women scientists, especially feminists, was recognizing the possibility that androcentric bias would result from having men hold virtually all theoretical and decision-making positions in science (Keller 1983). Not until a substantial number of women had entered the profession (Rosser 1986) could this androcentrism be exposed. As long as only a few women were scientists, they had to demonstrate or conform to the male view of the world to be successful and have their research meet the criteria for "objectivity."

By excluding females as experimental subjects, focusing on problems of primary interest to males, using faulty experimental designs, and interpreting data based on language or ideas constricted by patriarchal parameters, scientists have introduced bias or flaws into their experimental results in several areas, including biology. These flaws and biases were permitted to become part of the mainstream of scientific thought and were perpetuated in the scientific literature for decades. Because most scientists were men, values they held as males were not distinguished as biasing; rather, they were congruent with the values of all scientists and thus became synonymous with the "objective" view of the world (Chodorow 1978; Keller 1982, 1985) and the aspects of it studied.

The demonstration that contextual values, including gender, bias not only the scientific research of individuals but also what is accepted as valid science by the entire scientific community represents one of the major contributions that feminism has made to science. In *Feminism in Twentieth-Century Science, Technology, and Medicine* (Creager, Lunbeck, and Schiebinger 2001), the contributing authors, responded to the question of what difference feminism has made to the fields of science, technology, and medicine. It built on co-editor Londa Schiebinger's (1999) book, *Has Feminism Changed Science?* In that volume, Schiebinger examined how the presence of women in traditionally male disciplines has altered scientific thinking and awareness, concluding that feminist perspectives have had little effect on mathematics and the physical sciences but more impact on biology, including medicine, archaeology, reproductive and evolutionary biology, and primatology.

Although the degree and the specifics of the impact of feminism on science, medicine, and technology vary from one subdiscipline to another, as the co-editors of the 2001 volume state, "Feminism connects gender to other systems that structure our lives and individual identities" (Creager et al. 2001, viii).

Feminism and feminist perspectives have increased in variety and complexity over time. Major advances in science, technology, and medicine such as new uses of IT and improvements in gene sequencing have further impacted and complicated the interactions between these fields and feminist theories and methods. Some of the impacts appear positive for women, while others seem neutral or negative.

The Internet and new technologies that exploit its use through increased online journal publishing, Twitter, Facebook, and other social networking mechanisms tend to have positive effects of expanding access to science, technology, and medicine to more individuals and beginning to level the playing field among richer and poorer institutions. Simultaneously, a negative impact may be that revelation of information about location and habits that may occur with some sites and technologies may make women especially vulnerable.

Cheaper, faster gene sequencing techniques increase the emphasis upon biological determinism, while opening new venues for exploring genealogical narrations and ancestry. The increasing emphasis upon technology transfer and translational research from basic science opens the door to invention of new products, many of which will benefit women. In contrast, as discussed in the last chapter, the percentages of women involved in creating new inventions through technology transfer remain extremely low, thus suggesting that women are excluded yet again from the leading edge of science and technology.

All feminist theories place women and gender in central focus, but each one brings a specific perspective to that focus. Many feminist theories evolved in response to correct a deficiency or add a dimension that had been missing from previous theories. The particular theories I have chosen to discuss here represent those I find most influential in understanding the impact of feminism on the natural, physical, and social sciences. Although feminist analyses have had greatest exploration and impact in biology and health-related fields where gender applies directly to experimental subjects and results, I will also attempt to include examples from the physical sciences, engineering, and newer technologies such as gene sequencing and IT under each feminist theory.

Liberal Feminism

A general definition of liberal feminism is the belief that women are suppressed in contemporary society because they suffer unjust discrimination (Jaggar 1983). Liberal feminists seek no special privileges for women and simply demand that everyone receive equal consideration without discrimination on the basis of sex.

Most scientists would assume that the implications of liberal feminism for biology and other disciplines within the sciences are that scientists should work to remove the documented overt and covert barriers (National Academies 2006; National Science Foundation [NSF] 2002; Rosser 2004; Rossiter 1982) that have prevented women from entering and succeeding in science. Although they might hold individual opinions as to whether or not women deserve equal pay for equal work, access to research resources, and equal opportunities for advancement, most scientists do not recognize that the implications of liberal feminism extend beyond employment, access, and discrimination to the acceptance of positivism as the theory of knowledge and belief in the ability to obtain knowledge that is both objective and value free (Jaggar 1983).

Given the high costs of sophisticated equipment, maintenance of laboratory animals and facilities, and salaries for qualified technicians and researchers, little experimental research is undertaken today without governmental or foundation support. While the Internet has increased access to research results for individuals distant from major research libraries and has even allowed more scientists from less research-intensive institutions to contribute to major projects, the choice of problems for study in research is substantially determined by a national agenda that defines what is worthy of study (i.e., worth funding). Members of Congress and the individuals in the theoretical and decision-making positions within the medical and scientific establishments, overwhelmingly white, middle- or upper-class, and male, set priorities and allocate funds for research. The lack of diversity among congressional and scientific leaders may allow unintentional, undetected flaws to bias the research in terms of what we study and how we study it. Examples from research studies demonstrate that unintentional bias may be reflected in at least three stages of application of the scientific method: (1) choice and definition of problems to be studied; (2) methods and approaches used in data gathering, including whom we choose as subjects; and (3) theories and conclusions drawn from the data.

Feminist critiques revealed the impact of distinct gender bias in choice and definition of health research problems. For example, many diseases that occur in both sexes have been studied in males only or with a male-as-norm approach. Cardiovascular diseases serve as a case in point. Research protocols for large-scale studies (Grobbee et al. 1990; Multiple Risk Factor Intervention Trial Research Group [MRFIT] 1990; Steering Committee of the Physicians' Health Study Group 1989) of cardiovascular diseases failed to assess gender differences. Women were excluded from clinical trials of drugs because of fear of litigation from possible teratogenic effects on fetuses. Exclusion of women from clinical drug trials was so pervasive that a meta-analysis surveying the literature from 1960 to 1991 on clinical trials of medications used to treat acute myocardial infarction found that women were included in less than 20% and the elderly in less than 40% of those studies (Gurwitz, Nananda and Avorn 1992). A 2009 study by Zucker and Beery found that many articles across all science and medical fields failed to report subject sex at all, while two-thirds of the studies that included both males and females failed to analyze the data by sex (Wald and Wu 2010).

Using the white, middle-aged, heterosexual male as the "basic experimental subject" ignores the fact that females may respond differently to the variable tested; it also may lead to less accurate models even for many men. For example, the standard dosage of certain medications is not only inappropriate for many women and the elderly, but also for most Asian men, because of their smaller body size and weight. Certain surgical procedures such as angioplasty and cardiac bypass initially resulted in higher death rates for women (Kelsey et al. 1993) and Asian men and required modification for the same reason (Chinese Hospital Medical Staff and University of California School of Medicine 1982; Lin-Fu 1984). Studies of the use of statins to prevent cardiovascular disease reveal that in men, stroke is the major cardiovascular event most often prevented by statin use, while in women it is unstable angina (Mora et al. 2010).

Male dominance in engineering and the creative decision-making sectors of the IT workforce may result in similar bias, particularly design and user bias. Shirley Malcom (personal communication, October 1997) suggested that the air bag fiasco the U.S. auto industry experienced serves as an excellent example of gender bias reflected in design; this fiasco would have been much less likely had a woman engineer been on the design team. Because, on the average, women tend to be smaller than men, women on the design team might have recognized that a bag that implicitly used the larger male body as a norm would be flawed when applied to smaller individuals, killing, rather than protecting, children and small women.

Many studies have explored the overt and covert links between the military, whose origins and current directions conjoin with masculinity in our culture, and the theories for applications drawn from the research funded for the military. For example, Janet Abbate (1999) studied the origins of the Internet in ARPANET (Advanced Research Projects Agency Network), funded by the Department of Defense. The unique improvement of the Internet was that it was a network, overcoming the vulnerability to nuclear attack of the previous star configuration computer network.

Although liberal feminism suggests that true equity of women in the science and technology workforce would lead to inclusion of women in clinical trials and correct bias in design to better serve women's interests, by definition, liberal feminism does not address the potential of gender to affect "fundamentals" (i.e., Do women scientists define, approach, or discover different fundamentals such as string theory?). Liberal feminism accepts positivism as the theory of knowledge and assumes that human beings are highly individualistic and obtain knowledge in a rational manner that may be separated from their social conditions, including conditions of race, class, and gender. Because liberal feminism reaffirms, rather than challenges, positivism, it suggests that "fundamentals" would always remain the same. Now that they have become aware of potential bias, both male and female scientists and engineers can correct for such biases previously resulting from failure to include women and their needs and interests.

Socialist Feminism

In contrast to liberal feminism, socialist feminism rejects individualism and positivism. Although socialist feminists argue that women's oppression predated the development of class societies, Marxist critiques form the historical precursors and foundations for socialist feminist critiques and define all knowledge, including science, as socially constructed and emerging from practical human involvement in production. Because knowledge is a productive activity of human beings, it cannot be objective and value free because the basic categories of knowledge are shaped by human purposes and values. In the early twenty-first-century United States, capitalism, the prevailing mode of production, determines science and technology and favors the interests of the dominant class.

Different societies construct their material worlds, including the artifacts created and used, in different ways. The culture of a certain society may use the artifacts or attach particular meanings to them differently at different times or historical periods. Thus, particular technology and science are situated in place, time, and culture (Lerman, Oldenziel, and Mohun 2003).

Feminist scholars rightly point out that science and technology and the social shaping of technology (Wajcman 1991; Webster 1995) and science (Rose 1994) have often been conceptualized in terms of men, excluding women at all levels. Socialist feminist critiques include women and place gender on equal footing with class in shaping science and technology.

The social and technological shape each other. This so-called mutual shaping at times of technological change leads to contests over social categories, such as gender being reflected in new interactions with the material world (Lerman et al. 2003). Some scholars (Fox, Johnson, and Rosser 2006) have also referred to this "mutual shaping" of the social and technological aspects as the "co-evolution of gender and technology."

Considerable research focus and dollars target diseases, such as cardiovascular disease, that are especially problematic for middle- and upper-class men in their prime earning years. Although women die from cardiovascular disease with the same frequency as men, on average women die at later ages. Hence, until recently most cardiovascular disease research targeted white, middle-class men. Many of these studies, including the Physicians' Health Study, were flawed not only by the factors of gender and age but also by factors of race and class. Susceptibility to cardiovascular disease is known to be affected by lifestyle factors such as diet, exercise level, and stress, which are correlated with race and class. Because physicians in the United States are not representative of the overall male population with regard to lifestyle, the results may not be applicable even to most men. Factors linked with class interact with the other variables such as age and gender to determine likely candidates for cardiovascular disease. For example, the statin Crestor is now approved for men age 50 and over and women age 60 and over with normal LDL cholesterol but elevated C-reactive protein (an inflammation marker) and one additional cardiac risk factor, such as high blood pressure, low HDL cholesterol, or smoking (correlated with class) (Mora et al. 2010).

Significant amounts of time and money are expended on clinical research on women's bodies in connection with aspects of reproduction. Substantial clinical research has resulted in increasing medicalization and control of pregnancy, labor, and childbirth. Feminists have critiqued (Ehrenreich and English 1978; Holmes 1981) the conversion of a normal, natural process controlled by women into a clinical, and often surgical, procedure controlled by men.

Class appears to affect prices paid to egg donors. Women at U.S. universities are routinely offered more for their eggs than the $10,000 limit suggested by the American Society for Reproductive Medicine. The exact sums offered, obtained from a survey of 300 advertisements in college newspapers, varied, with a $2,000 increase in the fees advertised for potential egg donors for each 100-point difference in a university's average SAT score (Levine 2010).

Designation of certain diseases as particular to one gender, race, or sexual orientation leads to overuse of that group for research protocols and the neglect of other groups. This not only cultivates ignorance in the general public about transmission or frequency of the disease, but also results in research that does not adequately explore the parameters of the disease. Most of the funding for heart disease has been appropriated for research on predisposing factors for the disease (such as cholesterol level, lack of exercise, stress, smoking, and weight) using white, middle-aged, middle-class males. Much less research has been directed toward elderly women, African American women who have had several children, and other high-risk groups of women. Virtually no research has explored predisposing factors for these groups, who fall outside the disease definition established from the dominant perspective.

Biases in populations sampled and choice and definition of problems raise ethical issues. Health care practitioners treat the majority of the population, which consists of females, minorities, and the elderly, based on information gathered from clinical research in which women and minorities are undersampled or not included. Bias in research thus leads to further injustice in health care diagnosis and treatment.

Understandings of class relations emerging under capitalism and gender relations under patriarchy help to explain the intertwining of military and masculinity (Enloe 1983, 1989; MacKenzie and Wajcman 1999), which drives much technological innovation in this country and elsewhere. These understandings also explain the choices made to develop technologies in a certain way, including engineering decisions that favor fewer rich people over relatively less expensive technologies such as devices for the home to aid many people, especially women.

Caro's (1974) work revealed that Robert Moses, the master builder of New York's roads, parks, bridges, and other public works from the 1920s to the 1970s, had overpasses built to specifications to discourage buses on parkways. White upper- and middle-class car owners could use the parkways, such as Wantagh Parkway, for commuting and for accessing recreation sites, including Jones Beach. Because the 12-foot height of public transit buses prohibited their fitting under the overpass, blacks and poor people dependent on public transit did not have access to Jones Beach (Winner 1980).

Socialist feminist approaches also suggest why men dominate the creation of new technologies. Stephan and El-Ganainy (2007) suggest that the fact that more men than women are employed at higher ranks at research I institutions, where most patenting occurs, partially accounts for the gender gap in patenting. Class becomes an issue because research I institutions with high prestige and better salaries are dominated by men. These institutions provide more access to venture capital, geographic mobility, and ability to work long hours which may be as critical as technological expertise is for the success of start-ups.

African American/Womanist Feminism

African American or black/womanist (Collins 1990; hooks 1992) feminism also rejects individualism and positivism for social construction as an approach to knowledge. It is based on African American critiques of Eurocentric approaches to knowledge (Harding 1998). Whereas socialism posits class as the organizing principle around which the struggle for power exists, African American critiques maintain that race is the primary oppression. African Americans critical of the scientific enterprise may view it as a function of white Eurocentric interests with the methodology a reflection of those interests.

African American feminist critiques uncover the place or role of race in combination with gender. Racism intertwines and reinforces differing aspects of capitalism and patriarchy. African American feminists have examined the respective intersection of race and gender to provide a more complex, comprehensive view of reality. Many African American and other women of color are also uncomfortable with the word feminism, because of its historical association with white women and disregard of racial/ethnic diversity. Womanism (Steady 1982), critical race theory (Williams 1991, 1998), and black feminism (Collins 1990), while all placing race in central focus, provide slightly differing critiques. Just as their African American sisters have done, Latina, Asian American, and American Indian women and women from other racial or ethnic perspectives have developed critiques that place race/ethnicity and gender in central focus.

Just as many studies fail to report or analyze gender differences, studies also neglect to report and analyze racial/ethnic differences. These failures hold significant implications for both practitioners and patients, particularly for women of color, as documented with the history of AIDS in the United States. In 1981, the first official case of AIDS in a woman was reported to the Centers for Disease Control and Prevention (CDC). By

1991, $80 million had been spent since the inception of the Multicenter AIDS Cohort Study (MACS), designed to follow the natural history of HIV among gay and bisexual males (Faden, Kass, and McGraw 1996). Although by 1988 the case reports for women were higher than the number for men in 1983, the year the MACS began (Chu, Buehler, and Berelman 1990), it was not until the final quarter of 1994 that the first study on the natural history of HIV infection in women began. In 1998, the CDC reported AIDS as the leading cause of death among black females aged 25 to 44, and the second leading cause of death overall among those aged 25 to 44 (CDC 1998). In the twenty-first century, the majority of women diagnosed with AIDS remain black or Hispanic.

A 2009 study of 97,253 women—89,259 white women and 7,994 black women—aged 50–79 participating in the Women's Health Initiative focused on the possible health effects of optimism and cynical hostility in postmenopausal women. Overall, optimism decreased the risk of dying from cardiovascular causes or any other cause, while cynical hostility increased the risk of dying from cancer. Among black women, the associations were more pronounced. Among the most optimistic, black women had a 33% lower risk of death from all causes and a 44% lower risk of cancer death, compared to white women's 13% and no effect respectively on these same measures. Among the most cynical and hostile women, black women had a 62% higher risk of death from all causes, a 102% higher risk from heart disease, and a 142% higher risk of death from cancer; comparable figures for white women were 13%, 18%, and 18% respectively. (Tindle et al. 2009).

When women of color are used as experimental subjects, clinicians often hold stereotypical and racist views that limit accurate diagnosis. For example, numerous research studies have focused on sexually transmitted diseases in prostitutes in general (CDC 1987; Cohen, Alexander, and Woofsey 1988; Rosser 1994), and African American women prostitutes in particular. Several studies have also revealed that practitioners recognize and report at higher rates both crack-cocaine abuse in African American women and alcohol abuse in American Indian women, compared with white women, seeking prenatal care. In many cases, the women lost their children after they were born or had to serve jail time for detoxification. An American Civil Liberties Union study revealed that in 47 out of 53 cases brought against women for drug use during pregnancy in which the race of the woman was identifiable, 80% were brought against women of color (Pattrow 1990).

The popularity of the now relatively low cost gene-sequencing techniques permits individuals to trace their genealogy and ancestry. In the PBS documentary miniseries *Faces of America*, co-producer, host, and writer Henry Louis Gates, Jr., the director of the W.E.B. Du Bois Institute for African and African American Research and professor at Harvard, collaborates with genetic scientists to discover the genealogy of famous individuals. The show sometimes uncovers revelations of shocking information, as for example that Malcolm Gladwell's Jamaican maternal ancestor, a free woman of color, owned slaves of African descent. Perhaps because of the possibilities of these sorts of revelations being taken out of context and because of questions about use of ownership of such DNA, some refuse to submit to gene sequencing. For example, the Native American writer Louise Erdrich refuses to assent to genetic ancestry testing because she understands her DNA to belong to her community (Nelson 2010).

Frequently it is difficult to determine whether women are treated disrespectfully and unethically due to their gender or whether race and class are more significant variables. From the Tuskegee syphilis experiment (1932–1972), in which the effects of untreated syphilis were studied in 399 men over a period of 40 years (Jones 1981), it is clear that men who are black and poor may not receive appropriate treatment or information about the experiment in which they are participating. Scholars (Clarke and Olesen 1999) now explore the extent to which gender, race, and class become complex, interlocking variables that may affect access to and quality of health care.

Just as humanities Professor Gates has collaborated with genetic scientists of differing ethnicities and races, a growing recognition has evolved of the strength and necessity for diversity on teams (Knights 2004). Diversity in gender and race are beginning to be understood to be critical, along with the long-established recognition of the importance of having an engineering team representing varied intellectual and technical backgrounds, for designing complex technologies. Because knowledge and consideration of the user, client, or customer are central to the technology design, a design team with racial and gender diversity coupled with surveys of demographically diverse customers will increase diversity in technology design.

African Americans and Hispanics are underrepresented in engineering and in the upper end of the technology workforce, relative to their percentage in the overall U.S. population (27.3%) (NSF 2010). In 2007, African Americans constituted 4.6% of engineers and 9.8% of computer and mathematical scientists (table H-4); 5% of engineers and 7.1% of mathematical and computer scientists identified as Hispanic (table H-4). Although engineering has been traditionally defined as a career path for mobility from the working class to the middle class, engineering is pursued by disproportionately fewer blacks and Latinos than whites. Even fewer African American women and Latinas than their male counterparts become engineers or scientists, despite the higher percentage of African American women (compared with African American men) in college.

In stark contrast, women of color are disproportionately represented in the lowest paying and highest health risk portions of the technology labor force. Studies demonstrate that women of color occupy the ghettos in the cities where the electronic assembly occurs (Hesse-Biber and Carter 2005). Outside the technology production workforce, women of color also represent the group most likely to be replaced by technology when automation takes over the work formerly done by their hands. Although technology has not resulted in the extreme reductions in female clerical workers once feared, increasing automation has forced some women of color from higher paying assembly line factory work into lower paying service sector jobs (Hesse-Biber and Carter 2005; Mitter 1986).

Essentialist Feminism

African American and socialist feminist critiques emphasize race and class as sources of oppression that combine with gender in shaping and being shaped by science and technology. In contrast, essentialist feminist theory posits that all women are united by their biology. Women are also different from men because of their biology, specifically their secondary sex characteristics and their reproductive systems. Frequently, essentialist feminism may extend to include gender differences in visuospatial and verbal ability, aggression and other behaviors, and other physical and mental traits based on prenatal or pubertal hormone exposure.

The biomedical model, although too restricted for an approach to most diseases, remains especially inadequate for women's health, particularly for exploring causes, treatments, and prevention of events such as menopause that occur as part of the life cycle course and that are influenced by biology as well as a variety of social, environmental, and other factors. Until the Women's Health Initiative, very little research on women's menopausal experience existed. As the baby boom generation aged, the pharmaceutical companies developed an extreme interest in capturing the market of consuming women approaching menopause. These companies redefined menopause as a disease that required hormones to cure it and made large amounts of money by selling hormone replacement therapy (HRT) to women before, during, and after menopause. This tradition places responsibility at the level of the individual rather than the society as a whole.

Using only the methods traditional to a particular discipline may result in limited approaches that fail to reveal sufficient information about the problem being explored. On July 9, 2002, NIH announced that the hormone replacement therapy (HRT), estrogen/progestin portion of the Women's Health Initiative (WHI) would be stopped. The study had shown that women taking HRT had a 26% increase in breast cancer, a 41% increase in strokes, and a 200% increase in the rates of blood clots in the legs and lungs (National Women's Health Network 2002). Subsequent studies also revealed that HRT did not improve "quality of life" issues or memory, although women taking HRT did have 37% less colon cancer and 34% fewer hip fractures.

Focusing basic research at the level of the cell and below has consequences for the types of treatments developed. Many women expressed outrage against the pharmaceutical companies after the announcement that the HRT portion of the Women's Health Initiative was halted (Worcester 2009). Until the Women's Health Initiative, very little research compared the health of menopausal women who took HRT with those who did not take HRT. Women wanted to know why they had been given HRT before such research had been done.

The approach to HRT reveals the American health care system's focus on individual responsibility rather than on overall societal responsibility for the increasingly significant proportion of the population that consists of elderly women, who will need a disproportionately large amount of health care. Will research on diseases, maintenance of health and well-being, and successful, cost-efficient health care practices appropriate for elderly women be accorded high priority on the national health care agenda?

Ecofeminism, sometimes defined as a type of essentialist feminism, suggests that men, because of their biology and inability to conceive, also develop technologies to dominate, control, and exploit the natural world, women, and other peoples (Easlea 1983). In contrast, because of our biology, women not only have less testosterone, but also have the ability to give birth. Giving birth gives us less direct control over our bodies and connects us more closely with nature, other animals, and life (King 1989; Merchant 1979). In its most simplistic extreme form, essentialism implies that men use technologies to bring death and control to other people, women, and the environment, while (or because) women give birth and nurture life in all its forms. In his study of the discovery and development of nuclear weapons and the atomic bomb, Easlea (1983) examines the language and behavior of the scientists. Analyzing the aggressive sexual and birth metaphors the scientists use to describe their work, he argues that men "give birth" to science and weapons to compensate for their inability to give birth to babies.

Both ecofeminism and essentialism suggest that because of our biology, women would design different technologies and use them differently. The studies of inventions by women and surveys of patents obtained by women (Macdonald 1992) suggest an essentialist feminist theoretical approach to these invention and patent data studies showing that many women develop technologies related to reproduction, secondary sex characteristics, or babies or children such as the medicine Nystatin, the backless bra, or the folding crib, because of differences in women's, compared with men's, biology. They suggest that differences such as hormone levels, menstruation, giving birth, and ability to lactate to nourish offspring lead to women designing different technologies and using technologies differently from men. The dearth of women currently involved in technology transfer and patenting suggests why fewer technologies and products useful to women continue to be developed.

The 2000 AAUW Report documented that girls said they use computers to communicate and perform specific tasks, while boys have underdeveloped social skills and use computers to play games and "fool around" (American Association of University Women 2000). This use of technology for communication suggests why women and girls use Twitter, Facebook, and other forms of social networking as much or more than men, while men continue to be the major users of most videogames.

Essentialism can be used to support either superiority or inferiority of women compared with men, as long as the source of difference remains rooted in biology. Essentialism was seen as a tool for conservatives who wished to keep women in the home and out of the workplace. Eventually, feminists reexamined essentialism from perspectives ranging from conservative to radical (Corea 1985; Dworkin 1983; MacKinnon 1982, 1987; O'Brien 1981; Rich 1976) with a recognition that biologically based differences between the sexes might imply superiority and power for women in some arenas.

Existentialist Feminism

Existentialist feminism, first described by Simone de Beauvoir (1949/1989), suggests that women's "otherness" and the social construction of gender rest on society's interpretation of biological differences. Existentialists see "women's and men's lives as concretely situated" and emphasize concepts like "freedom, interpersonal relations, and experience of lived body" (Larrabee 2000, 187). In contrast to essentialist feminism, existentialist feminism purports that it is not the biological differences themselves, but the value that society assigns to biological differences between males and females, that has led woman to play the role of the Other (Tong 1989).

Research on conditions specific to females receives low priority, funding, and prestige, although women make up half of the population and receive more than half of the health care. The Women's Health Initiative launched by NIH in 1991 to study cardiovascular diseases, cancers, and osteoporosis attempted to raise the priority of women's health and provide baseline data on previously understudied causes of death in women (Pinn and LaRosa 1992). Cardiovascular diseases (Healy 1991b) and AIDS (Norwood 1988; Rosser 1994) stand as classic examples of diseases studied using a male-as-norm approach.

Examples of reproductive technologies suggest that considerable resources and attention are devoted to women's health issues when those issues are directly related to men's interest in controlling production of children. Contraceptive research may permit men to have sexual pleasure without the production of children; research on infertility, pregnancy, and childbirth has allowed men to assert more control over the production of more "perfect" children and over an aspect of women's lives over which they previously held less power.

Demographic projections reveal that the majority of the U.S. population soon will come from the current racial "minorities"; as the baby boom generation ages, the elderly populations, predominantly female, will increase dramatically. Perceiving the flaws in the male-as-norm approach in its applications to the "other" of women opens the door to understanding the diversities among women. Lesbians, women of color, women from non-U.S. cultures, disabled, and elderly women remain the "other" compared to white, middle-aged, heterosexual, able-bodied U.S.-born women upon whom much of the research has been done. To rectify this dearth of research and avoid problems from failing to include the health of the majority of U.S. women, research and needs of diverse women must become a central focus.

An existentialist feminist framework might be used to explain the higher frequency of inventions by women of technologies useful for menstruation, childbirth, lactation, and hormones. In contrast to essentialism, rather than placing the emphasis for the origin of the technology on the biology itself, existentialism would suggest that it is value assigned by society to women as other that leads to the technology. Women serve as the predominant caretakers of babies and children, perhaps because they give birth to them and nurse them. Existentialist feminism would suggest that this assignment of the role as other, based on the biological reasons, would lead to women having more experience caring for babies and children. In turn, this experience would lead them to invent more technologies useful for child care, such as the baby changing stations found in public bathrooms, disposable diapers, and folding cribs (Macdonald 1992).

The Clayman Institute for Gender Research at Stanford University, through its gendered innovations project (http://www.stanford.edu/group/gender/GenderedInnovations/index 2010), seeks to bring attention to the need for changes in both technology and policy to fit the needs and requirements for women, such as a different seat belt design for pregnant women and a requirement that the new design be tested on appropriate subjects (pregnant women) before wearing the belt is required by law.

Frequently, designing products or technology for the needs of a particular group viewed as the "other" yields a design or product that is better for the "norm" as well as the other. For example, the curb cuts designed for wheelchairs also facilitate street crossing for people with strollers, suitcases on wheels, and other wheeled devices. Since the number of people in the United States over age 65 is estimated to double in 20 years, with those over 80 quadrupling in 40 years worldwide, we stand poised for a major demographic shift (Monaghan 2010). Universal design to accommodate the needs of this increase in the elderly and disabled population now defined as "other" should cater to a wider range of human capability.

Psychoanalytic Feminism

Evelyn Keller (1982, 1985) applied the work of Chodorow (1978) and Dinnerstein (1977) to suggest how science, populated mostly by men, has become a masculine province in its choice of experimental topics, use of male subjects for experimentation, and interpretation and theorizing from data, as well as the practice and applications of science undertaken by the scientists. Keller suggests that because the scientific method stresses objectivity, rationality, distance, and autonomy of the observer from the object of study (i.e., the positivist neutral observer), individuals who feel comfortable with independence, autonomy, and distance will be most likely to become scientists. Feminists have suggested that the objectivity and rationality of science are synonymous with a male approach to the physical, natural world.

The particularly reductionistic version of the biomedical model currently in vogue, in which extreme attention is drawn to genetic causes for diseases, has been critiqued by feminists as positivist and enforcing distance and autonomy between the observer and object of study. Interdisciplinary approaches might most effectively target women's health issues, including dysmenorrhea, incontinence in older women, nutrition in postmenopausal women, and effects of exercise level and duration on alleviation of menstrual discomfort. Although these issues would not require high-tech or expensive drug testing as solutions, effective research would include methods, such as interviews and case studies, from the social and natural sciences that shorten the distance between the observer and the object of study.

The distant, autonomous approaches of science become reflected in medical tests that do little to connect with the realities for women susceptible to cancers such as ovarian cancer. Because symptoms typically develop after the disease has become incurable, ovarian cancer has been called a "silent killer." In a National Cancer Institute study, more than 75,000 healthy women were randomly assigned to undergo either usual care or annual CA-125 testing plus transvaginal ultrasound. If a woman's CA-125 testing or ultrasound was positive, she was referred to a gynecologist. After annual screening for more than four years, on average, 19.5 women had undergone surgery for each identified case of ovarian cancer; 72% of the cancers detected were already at late stage (Robb-Nicholson 2010).

Carriers of the BRCA-1 or BRCA-2 gene mutations, or women with a mother, sister, daughter, grandmother, aunt or niece who had, or are at high risk genetically, for ovarian cancer can benefit from CA-125 and transvaginal ultrasound. However, most experts recommend combination screening of high-risk women with CA-125 and trans vaginal ultrasound every six months. If they obtain a positive result, they must undergo invasive surgery. It is also recommended that high-risk women past child-bearing consider having their ovaries removed. These alternatives seem unappealing and appear as high-risk solutions to many of these high-risk women. For non-high-risk women, the danger of general screening with CA-125 alone far outweighs the benefit since current screening misses half of all women with early stage cancer, due to lack of test-specificity. Not surprisingly, many women find the existence of this test of minimal help in making everyday health decisions (Robb-Nicholson 2010).

A psychoanalytic feminist framework might provide the theoretical backdrop for Cockburn's (1981, 1983, 1985) work documenting the intertwining of masculinity and technology. Encouraged to be independent, autonomous, and distant, male engineers and computer scientists design technologies and IT systems reflecting those characteristics. As Bodker and Greenbaum (1993) suggest, the "hard-systems" approach to computer systems developments follows the positivist, linear, and technicist approach compatible with Western scientific thought. The technical capabilities, constraints of the machines, and rational data flow become the focus and driver of the technology design.

This "hard-systems" design approach used by developers (mostly male) of computer systems assumes separation, distance, and independence on several levels: (1) between the abstract systems development and the concrete real world of work—separation ignores the often circular and interconnected forces of organization, assuming that they remain linear and unaffected by other hierarchical power relations; and (2) between the developers and users—because users do not contribute to the design of the system, their needs and suggestions that might make the system function more smoothly in the real world of work are ignored. The problems caused by this abstraction, objectivity, autonomy, and separation have spawned methods such as "soft-systems" human factors approaches to solving the problems and mediating the gap. Twitter, Facebook, and other social networking sites provide a mechanism that allows users to contribute to the design of a system.

The gender constellation predicted by psychoanalytic feminism also becomes transparent in technology: The men who design hardware systems design them in ways reflective of their perspective on the world with which they feel comfortable. Such system designs tend to place priority on data and ignore relationships between people. Women, socialized to value connections and relationships, tend to feel uncomfortable with the hard-systems approach. As users, they find that the technology fails to aid much of the real-world work. The design inhibits or fails to foster good teamwork and other relationships among co-workers. Because the design does not reflect their view of priorities in the organization and work, and actively ignores the reality of power and gender relations, women tend to be excluded, and exclude themselves, from hard-systems design.

Critiques of information technologies from a psychoanalytic feminist perspective raise the very interesting question of how systems design might change if more feminine values and connection became priorities. Sorenson (1992) explored whether male and female computer scientists worked differently. He found that men tended to focus on mathematical models and computer programming, while women spent more time running experiments, reading scientific literature, and plotting data. After studying the technological and political values of men and women engineering students, graduate students, and junior R&D scientists at the Norwegian Institute of Technology, Sorenson found that women brought "caring values" to research in computer science. "Caring values" included empathy and rationale of responsibility. "In computer science, this means that women have a caring, other-oriented relationship to nature and to people, an integrated, more holistic and less hierarchical world-view, a less competitive way of relating to colleagues and a greater affinity to users" (10).

The popularity of "apps," often created by users, represents another way of shortening the distance between the designers and users. Although some might view this as an example of Harding's "strong objectivity," this shortening of distance between the user and the system design mimics Keller's (1983) description of McClintock's work in "A Feeling for the Organism." In the shortening of the distance between the observer and the object of study, Keller describes less autonomy, independence, and separation as classic hallmarks of psychoanalytic feminism when applied to the work of women scientists.

Radical Feminism

Radical feminism, in contrast to psychoanalytic feminism and liberal feminism, rejects the possibility of a gender-free science or a science developed from a neutral, objective perspective. Because men dominate and control most institutions, politics, and knowledge in our society, they reflect a male perspective and are effective in oppressing women. Radical feminism rejects most scientific theories, data, and experiments precisely because they not only exclude women but also are not women centered.

The theory that radical feminism proposes (Tong 1989) is not as well developed as some of the other feminist theories. The reasons that its theory is less developed spring fairly directly from the nature of radical feminism itself. First, it is radical. That means that it rejects most currently accepted ideas about scientific epistemology— what kinds of things can be known, who can be a knower, and how beliefs are legitimated as knowledge. Radical feminism also rejects the current methodology—the general structure of how theory finds its application in particular scientific disciplines. Second, unlike the feminisms previously discussed, radical feminism does not have its basis in a theory such as Marxism, positivism, psychoanalysis, or existentialism, already developed for decades by men. Because radical feminism is based in women's experience, it rejects feminisms rooted in theories developed by men based on their experience and worldview. Third, the theory of radical feminism must be developed by women and based in women's experience (MacKinnon 1987).

Because radical feminism maintains that the oppression of women is the deepest, most widespread, and historically first oppression (Jaggar and Rothenberg 1994), women have had few opportunities to come together, understand their experiences collectively, and develop theories based on those experiences. Perhaps because of this dearth of opportunities, radical-libertarian feminists (Firestone 1970; Rubin 1984) view sexuality as a powerful force that society seeks to control, and they encourage women to violate sexual taboos and use artificial means to control reproduction. In contrast, radical-cultural feminists (Dworkin 1983; Ferguson 1984) view heterosexual relations as forms of male domination as evidenced in pornography, prostitution, rape, and sexual harassment; they encourage elimination of patriarchal institutions and care in using artificial intervention in reproduction, which they see as a source of power for women.

The implications of radical feminism for science and experimental methods are much more far-reaching than those of other feminist theories. Radical feminism implies rejection of much of the standard epistemology of science. Radical feminism posits that it is women, not men, who can be the knowers. Because women have been oppressed, they know more than men. They must see the world from the male perspective to survive, but their double vision from their experience as an oppressed group allows them to see more than men. However, radical feminism deviates considerably from other feminisms in its view of how beliefs are legitimated as knowledge.

Because radical feminists believe in a connection with and a conception of the world as an organized whole, they reject dualistic and hierarchical approaches. Linear conceptions of time and what is considered to be "logical" thinking in the Western traditions are frequently rejected by radical feminists. Cyclicity as a conception of time and thinking as an upward spiral seem more appropriate approaches to studying a world in which everything is connected in a process of constant change (Daly 1978, 1984). Radical feminists view all human beings, and most particularly themselves, as connected to the living and nonliving worlds. Consequently, radical feminists view themselves as "participators" (Jagger 1983) connected in the same plane with, rather than distanced from, their object of study. Many radical feminists also believe that because of this connection, women can know things by relying on intuition or spiritual powers.

The male bias in research—male-as-norm approach and exclusion of women from clinical trials—persists in animal studies. Both because of the cost and because of the tradition of studying males, almost no one uses female animals in basic research (Wald and Wu 2010). "It's cuckoo that for diseases such as asthma, stroke, pain, immune diseases, where there are huge sex differences, people are just studying male animals," says behavioral neuroscientist Irving Zucker, a professor emeritus at UC Berkeley (Wald and Wu 2010, 1571).

A 2001 Institute of Medicine report published by the National Academy Press pointed to evidence that just as women and minorities had been excluded from clinical trials, the same was true for research using animal models: the sex of the animal can lead to qualitatively different results. This bias may compromise the safety and effectiveness of drugs in women. For example, between 1997 and 2000, ten drugs were withdrawn from the market due to adverse health effects. Eight of the ten posed higher risks for women than men, at least half of which were due to physiological differences. "Silver suspects that lack of adequate pre-clinical testing in female animal models could partly explain the result ...Increasing the use of female animals in research could increase the trend toward personalized medicine for women and insure we're not left behind" (Wald and Wu 2010, 1571).

In addition to the focus on women and seeking to empower women, MacKinnon (1987) adds a further criterion to radical feminism. She suggests that the consciousness-raising group provides a methodology for radical feminism. Because patriarchy pervades and dominates all institutions, ideologies, and technologies, women have difficulty placing their experiences, lives, and needs in central focus in everyday life and environments. Using their personal experiences as a basis, women meet together in communal, nonhierarchical groups to examine their experiences to determine what counts as knowledge (MacKinnon 1987). Internet feedback sites, chat-rooms, Twitter, blogs, Facebook, and other social networking sites provide a twenty-first-century mechanism for women to compare their personal experiences virtually without meeting in the consciousness-raising groups popular in the 1970s.

Another aspect of hierarchy appears in the organization of the specialties within medicine, which may contribute to the dearth of research and lack of focus on certain diseases such as breast cancer. The breast does not "fit" into the territory of any particular specialty. The breast fails to fit the traditional location of obstetrics or gynecology, usually considered to be a woman's reproductive system below the waist—the ovaries, oviduct, uterus, vagina, urethra, and their associated glands; even its involvement in sexual activity has not resulted in its being claimed as the province of obstetrics or gynecology. After birth, during lactation, the breast may briefly fit under pediatrics. For palpation to detect changes or lumps, it may fall into the territory of the obstetrician or gynecologist, general practitioner, or internist during the course of a physical examination. Radiologists claim the breast for mammography screening.

Only after the breast becomes cancerous does it intersect with the territory of other specialists—the surgeon for lumpectomy or mastectomy, the pathologist for determination of malignancy, the oncologist to oversee chemotherapy, and the radiologist who delivers radiation to kill cancerous cells. Eventually, a plastic surgeon may undertake reconstruction using implants. In brief, the breast is the territory of virtually all specialists and of none. Although the notion of a team of specialists now enjoys recognition as the favored approach for patient treatment, the typical breast cancer research project does not routinely use such a large, interdisciplinary team of researchers. Because the organization of NIH correlates with the medical specialties, it is not remarkable that breast cancer research has fallen through the cracks until recently. New online publications such as the *International Journal of Women's Health* (http://www.dovepress.com/international-journal-of-womens-health 2010) may help to overcome this issue of silos through its interdisciplinary focus and providing access to more women.

Because it originates from women's discourse on computer science problems and methods, some might define the work of Bratteteig (2002) and her co-workers as radical feminism. They insist on prioritizing applicability of systems and putting users and developers in the same plane as collaborators in systems development. This starting from the understanding of a woman worker and her abilities and then focusing on how her professional competence can be augmented by the use of a system does begin with women's experience and is consistent with feminist principles. The use of instant messages and other forms of cybercommunication to create rapid public protests that appear to occur spontaneously, such as the coordination of protests of the G20 summit in London that used social networking sites such as Facebook and Twitter, might be seen as representing such cyclicity (Beaumont 2009).

Radical feminists examining information technologies might interpret the binary 0,1 foundation of computers and computing as based on the primary dichotomy/dualism of male-female. The "switchers," "controls," and "operations" language of computing fit the patriarchal mode of control. The dichotomy receives reinforcement by the domination of men and relative absence of women from the design process. "So, the domination of men and the absence of women from the design process is one factor which creates technologies which are closely geared to the needs of men and which are inappropriate to women's requirements" (Webster 1995, 179).

Lesbian Separatism

To understand the complete, comprehensive influence of patriarchy and begin to imagine alternative technologies, lesbian separatism would suggest that women must separate entirely from men (Frye 1983; Hoagland 1988). Lesbian separatism, often seen as an offshoot of radical feminism, would suggest that separation from men is necessary in a patriarchal society for females to understand their experiences and explore the potential of science and the impact of technologies. Although some lesbian separatists also now identify with queer theory, because queer theory also embraces gay men (Butler 1990; de Lauretis 1991), some lesbians prefer to retain a more separate stance.

As women and as non-heterosexuals, lesbians are doubly distanced from the heterosexual male norm focus of health research and care. Although often lesbians are ignored in studies, when they are recognized, they may be subsumed as a subset of women or homosexuals, thereby lumping lesbian health issues with those of heterosexual females or male homosexuals. In fact, lesbians may be at higher risk for certain diseases such as breast and uterine cancer since many lesbians do not have children, have higher body fat, and limit their access to regular health care checkups relative to heterosexual women because of fear of discrimination (Campbell 1992). Very few studies have focused on lesbians as a separate population for health studies.

Cockburn (1983) advocates women-only organizations in information technology:

> In my view, by far the most effective principle evolved to date is a separate, woman-only organisation. It enables us to learn (teach each other) without being put down. Provide schoolgirls with separate facilities and the boys won't be able to grab the computer and bully the girls off the console. Provide young women with all-women courses so that they can gain the experience to make an informed choice about an engineering career. (132)

The establishment of engineering at Smith College, a women's college, may provide a site where ideas, curriculum, and pedagogy in technology can be explored in an environment somewhat separate from men.

Radical feminism would suggest that the reason no truly feminist alternative to technology exists is that men, masculinity, and patriarchy have become completely intertwined with technology and computer systems in our society. Imagining technology from a woman-centered perspective in the absence of patriarchy becomes extremely difficult, if not impossible. Because engineering and technology development in the West/ North foreground control—control over nature, over people, and over machines— imagining a technology premised on cooperation, collaboration, and working with nature, people, and machines runs contrary to our image of the technology that evolved in a patriarchal, heterosexist society. Brun (1994) suggests that the creation and protection of human life should be the point of departure for technological development for women: "Women's ethics . . . is not sentimental. It is practical. It implies a concrete and holistic consideration of people's need for a sustainable environment and that basic security which is the precondition of common responsible action" (79).

Queer and Transgender Theories

Queer and transgender theories, seen by some as successors to theories of radical feminism and lesbian separatism, question links among sex, gender, and sexual orientation (Butler 1990; de Lauretis 1991; Stryker 1998). They raise additional challenges about the links among economic, racial, and dominance factors with gender in our society. As Judith Butler (1990, 1992, 1994) argues, the very act of defining a gender identity excludes or devalues some bodies and practices, while simultaneously obscuring the constructed character of gender identity; describing gender identity creates a norm.

When lesbians are lumped together with heterosexual women in studies of incidence or cause of sexually transmitted diseases or other gynecological problems from which they are exempt or for which they are at low risk because they do not engage in heterosexual intercourse, both lesbians and nonlesbians suffer. Defining such studies generally as research on "women's health issues" rather than on "health issues for women engaging in heterosexual sex" leads the general population and some health care workers to think that lesbians are at risk for diseases that they are unlikely to contract, while obscuring the true risk behavior for heterosexual women.

The creators of *The Turing Game,* a computer game modification of Alan Turing's suggestion of ways to differentiate machines from people and men from women, explain their goals and methodologies in the following terms:

> Do men and women behave differently online? Can you tell who is a man and who is a woman based on how they communicate and interact with others on the Internet? Can you tell how old someone is, or determine their race or national origin? In the online world as in the real world, these issues of personal identity affect how we relate to others. Societies are created and destroyed by these understandings and misunderstandings in the real world. Yet, as the online world becomes increasingly a part of our lives, identity in this new medium is still poorly understood. (Berman and Bruckman 2000)

The Georgia Institute of Technology developed the Turing Game, an online game of identity deception, expression, and discovery. Available on the Internet, it has been played by thousands of people. Players on all seven continents have used the game to learn about issues of identity and diversity online through direct experience. At the same time, they have created communities of their own, and explore the boundaries of electronic communication (Berman and Bruckman 2000). This Turing Game explores the creations of these norms and how the Internet opens possibilities for identity changes or deception. The use of avatars with a different race, gender, or sexual orientation allows individuals to assume and explore different identities online.

Postmodern or Poststructural Feminism

Liberal feminism suggests that women have a unified voice and can be universally addressed (Gunew 1990). Poststructuralists (Derrida 2000; Foucault 1978; Lacan 1977, 1998) have challenged some of the fundamental assumptions about knowledge, subjectivity, and power through transforming the theory of meaning and the assumptions about subjectivity found in structural linguistics. Feminist poststructuralists (Irigaray 1985; Kristeva 1986) critiqued the absence of women and the feminine in these assumptions.

Like poststructuralists, postmodernists (Jameson 1981; Lyotard 1986) question fundamental assumptions of the Enlightenment, with postmodern feminists critiquing the absence of women. Postmodernism dissolves the universal subject and postmodern feminism dissolves the possibility that women speak in a unified voice or that they can be universally addressed. Postmodern perspectives stress that due to her situatedness—the result of her specific national, class, and cultural identities—the category of woman can no longer be regarded as smooth, uniform, and homogeneous. Although postmodern feminists (Grosz 1994; Irigaray 1985) see the material body as significant and a site of resistance to patriarchy, postmodern feminist theories imply that no universal health research agenda or application of technologies will be appropriate and that various women will have different reactions to science and technologies, depending on their own class, race, sexuality, country, and other factors.

A limitation of the biomedical model with its cellular, hormonal, and genetic approaches becomes its tendency to center on the individual and her body, while bringing less attention to surrounding social, economic, and political factors that may contribute to disease and its progress. The incidence of breast cancer has increased about 30% in the past 25 years in western countries, according to the American Cancer Society. This is due in part to increased screening, leading to detection in earlier stages. The reduction in the use of hormone replacement therapy led breast cancer rates to decrease by 10% between 2000 and 2004. The lifetime probability of developing breast cancer in developed countries is about 4.8%; in contrast, the lifetime probability is about 1.8% in developing countries, mostly because of lifestyle and dietary differences (American Cancer Center 2007).

Inclusion of social, psychological, and public health perspectives is needed for a more comprehensive research base to explore why poor women and women of color have higher death rates from breast cancer than middle-class white U.S. women. Epidemiological approaches include these perspectives; they reveal factors important for disease prevention. Because "the poor, in general, have a 10 to 15 percent lower cancer survival rate regardless of race" (Altman 1996, 37), research that relies on biology alone and ignores socioeconomic factors will be unlikely to uncover the best way to remove this survival differential. White, Hawaiian, and African American women have almost four times the incidence of invasive breast cancer in the United States compared to Korean, American Indian, and Vietnamese women. African American women have the highest death rate from breast cancer and are more likely to be diagnosed with a later stage of breast cancer than white women (American Cancer Center 2007). Interdisciplinary approaches may tease apart the relative effects that more exposure to workplace and environmental carcinogens and less access to high-quality medical care, nutritious food, and decent living conditions have on the higher incidence and lower survival rates experienced by African Americans with regard to breast cancer.

Studies focused on women in the technology workforce have tended to imply a universalist stance that all women have similar needs for uses of technology and that the employment categories and effects within technology industries affect women uniformly. Interviews with women at a major multinational company in the computer industry revealed an even greater desire of women in India and China working for the company to join women-only groups to increase their knowledge and access to patenting (Rosser 2009). Similarly, the "flexibility" and "casualization" of the workforce, which telecommuting permits, may hurt wages, benefits, and long-term stability overall. Although it creates or increases the double burden for women who can mind children while working at home, some women prefer this option to no work at all.

Women may react differently to technologies, depending on their race, class, age, ability status, parental status, urban-rural location, or other factors. Coupled with the rapid and changing pace of technology, postmodern feminism suggests why universal theories fail to fit the reality of women's lives. The lack of universalism may inhibit gender-based coalitions and organizing, making it also easier to understand the political inactivism of which individuals who articulate postmodern perspectives may be accused (Butler 1992).

Just as women's needs for IT or technology designs differ and vary, depending on class, nationality, culture, age, and other factors, employment of women in technology industries also does not fit a universal or uniform pattern. Some groups of women have improved or lost ground in their employment in technology industries. For example, some women have benefited from programs designed to increase female representation in IT and other technology industries. These equity and access programs (based in liberal feminist theories) have benefited some professional middle-class women whose educational backgrounds position them to capitalize on better employment opportunities (Phipps 2008).

Although relocation and temporization of work have tended to hurt employees in general and women in particular, the effects may depend on urban location. For example, closing offices in city centers and metropolitan areas has tended to hurt urban women, more likely to be of lower socioeconomic status and of color, while creating employment for women in the suburbs (Greenbaum 1995). In contrast, development of offshore information processing has improved employment for women in poorer countries. Information and data processing functions, once performed by women in the First World, have now been exported to low-cost economies because telecommunications and satellite technologies make this possible (Webster 1995, 182).

Postcolonial Feminism

Beginning in 1947, following various campaigns of anticolonial resistance, often with an explicitly nationalist basis, many colonial empires formally dissolved and previously colonized countries gained independence (Williams and Crissman 1994). The continuing Western influence, particularly in the economic arena, but also in the political, ideological, and military sectors, became known as neocolonialism by Marxists (Williams and

Crissman 1994). Feminists have suggested that patriarchy dominates post-colonial and neocolonial, much as it dominated colonial, everyday life.

Not surprisingly, science and technology reflect the varying complex aspects of the interrelationships among developed and developing countries in general and between the particular cultures of the colonized and colonizing countries. General themes include the underdevelopment of the southern continents by Europe and other northern continents (Harding 2006, 2008); ignoring, obscuring, or misappropriating earlier scientific achievements and history of countries in southern continents; the fascination with so-called indigenous science (Harding 1998); the idea that the culture, science, and technology of the colonizer or former colonizing country remains superior to that of the colony or postcolonial country; and the insistence that developing countries must restructure their local economies, to become scientifically and technologically literate to join and compete in a global economy (Mohanty 1997). Both post-colonialist and feminist discourses center on otherness or "alterity." Post-colonial feminism has focused generally around issues of cultural identity, language, nationalism, and the position of women in formerly colonized countries as they become nation-states (Mehta 2000).

The implementation and use of reproductive technologies demonstrate quite vividly the significance of diversity among women surrounding health issues. The use of low-technology techniques such as cesarean section and high-technology processes such as in vitro fertilization and rented uteri varies within countries and among countries. Pressures to make women conform to the norms of the patriarchal culture and class within which they are located provide similarities for women in the use of these technologies. Different cultures, classes, races, and nationalities provide the parameters for differences of use between women within a culture and among cultures.

Although differences and complexities among cultures represent one type of diversity, class differences represent another. Women in developed countries experience more use of such technologies than women in developing countries, possibly because of socioeconomic differences between less- and more-developed countries. Sometimes class serves as the most reliable predictor of the use of technologies on women across cultures. Wealthy individuals and couples often seek poorer women either in the United States or in developing countries to serve as egg donors or surrogates. The diffractions of reproductive health in modern global society define infertility as the health problem for women of certain races and classes in developed countries, while overpopulation is defined as the problem for women of other races and lower socioeconomic status in developing countries.

Using observation, trial and error, and sharing of information across generations, women in developing countries used methods of cleaning and cooking and fed their families food to maximize health and minimize disease; women learned which plants held medicinal properties. Part of their indigenous scientific knowledge included recognition of herbal remedies to enhance fertility, prevent conception, and cause abortion. The major efforts made by pharmaceutical companies to identify the plants used in traditional healing in indigenous cultures today constitute some recognition of the women's knowledge. However, just as when doctors obtained herbal remedies from midwives and witches in the nineteenth-century United States (Ehrenreich and English 1978), the modern pharmaceutical companies award the patent to the scientist who does the "work" of synthesizing the compound based on the extract from the medicinal plant, thereby defining the indigenous women's knowledge as nonscience and nonwork.

In many developing countries, cultural mores encourage adoption of only part of the health care practices from developed countries; mores prevent adoption of other practices. In overpopulated parts of Latin America, such as the favelas in the Nordest of Brazil, the culture of breast-feeding has been lost, because the father's provision of milk symbolizes paternity. To breast-feed her baby signifies that the woman has been abandoned by the baby's father. The adoption of some "modern" health practices such as bottle-feeding simultaneously with nonadoption of others such as contraception demonstrates the role of culture in mediating these diffracted reproductive health practices.

Many women in the so-called Third World or developing countries receive employment in technology industries or because of technological developments such as satellites that permit rapid data transmission over large geographic distances. The United States, Western Europe, and Japan house the corporate headquarters, owners, and decision makers of these global, multinational corporations; technological developments permit these companies to roam the globe and use women in offshore, formerly colonized, or developing nations as cheap sources of labor. Because new technologies transcend boundaries of time and space, they facilitate corporations in dispersing work around the globe to exploit sexual and racial labor divisions.

Information technology, satellites, and computerization become the glue that holds the global networks within a company together and permits them to function smoothly and efficiently. These technologies permit a 24/7 workforce. Work completed by the IT workforce in India dur- ing the day, while managers and developers sleep in the United States, is ready for review when they awaken.

The IT industry uses subcontracted female labor in developing coun- tries, particularly for software development. Western managements con- trol the conduct of software development projects, relying on women from India, China, Mexico, Hungary, and Israel as programmers. Tele- communications technologies ease the transmission of specifications and completed work between the workers in developing countries and client companies in the West. Women from these developing countries are pre- ferred as workers over those in developed countries because of their tech- nical skills and English proficiency, relatively high roles of productivity, and relatively low costs of labor.

These examples clearly demonstrate aspects of postcolonialism in that control of the economy of developing countries remains in the hands of developed countries. They demonstrate patriarchal control because women, not men, in the developing countries become the sources of cheap labor. Language becomes an interesting feature that continues to tie for- mer colony with colonizer. Theoretically, satellites and telecommunications transcend geographical barriers and permit any developed country to use labor in any developing country, but because of prior colonial relationships and a common language, former relationships continue in the neocolonial modern world. Innovations such as Twitter permit instant brief communi- cations to ascertain how a particular request is understood or received by workers around the world. Twitter and other social media proved critical to the movements towards democracy that occurred in 2011 in Egypt, Syria, and other countries. Technologies such as the cell phone are used differ- ently in developing, compared to developed, countries. For example, in Africa, most individuals use the cell phone for banking transactions, while in the United States the cell phone is used for this quite infrequently.

Cyberfeminism

Cyberfeminism stands not only as the most recent feminist theory but also as the theory that overtly fuses modern science and technology with gender. As the name suggests, cyberfeminism explores the ways that information technologies and the Internet provide avenues to liberate (or oppress) women. In the early 1990s, the term *cyberfeminism* first began to be used in various parts of the world (Hawthorne and Klein 1999), with VNS Matrix, an Australian-based group of media-based artists being one of the first groups to use the term.

The individuals who defined cyberfeminism (Hawthorne and Klein 1999; Millar 1998) saw the potential of the Internet and computer science as technologies to level the playing field and open new avenues for job opportunities and creativity for women. They describe cyberfeminism as "a woman-centered perspective that advocates women's use of new information and communications technologies of empowerment. Some cyberfeminists see these technologies as inherently liberatory and argue that their development will lead to an end to male superiority because women are uniquely suited to life in the digital age" (Millar 1998, 200).

In 1980, women represented 37% of computer science majors. The early history of computing reveals that Ada Lovelace contributed to the development of the protocomputer, and Grace Hopper created the first computer language composed of words and invented virtual storage (Stanley 1995). Women performed calculations and wired hardware for the first digital electronic computer, ENIAC (Electronic Numerical Integrator and Computer). In the late 1980s, a drastic change began to occur. The numbers of women majoring in computer science plummeted; in 2007, the percentage of U.S. women receiving computer science degrees was 18.6% (NSF 2010). This plunge coincided with the restructuring of the capitalist system on a global scale and with the rise of financial speculation.

Biomedicine fuses technology with the biological human body in the forms of artificial hips, heart valves, pacemakers, and implants to deliver drugs, creating the cyborgs discussed by Donna Haraway (1997). Simultaneously, new media technologies explore the reciprocity between science and media, where in this age of genetics as the life code, culture may become biology. Analyses of metaphors in genome research suggest that because researchers transpose literature on to biology, it is not possible to critique science without critiquing culture.

Haraway moves beyond the use of computers to sequence the human genome to explore how the image of the cyborg embodies the extent to which technoscience interventions have become part of us and of women's health. She uses the image of the "virtual speculum" in *Modest_ Witness@Second_Millennium. FemaleMan©_ Meets_OncoMouse: Feminism and Technoscience* to "open up observation into the orifices of the technoscientific body politic to address these kinds of questions about knowledge projects" (1997, 67). As the pioneer of feminist science studies, Haraway focuses on interdependencies and interrelationships among bodies, technologies, and cultures.

As Millar and other cyberfeminist critics point out, the existing elites have struggled to seize control and stabilize the commercial potential of digital technologies, as well as their research and development. Discontinuity, speed, symbolic and linguistic spectacle, and constant change characterize information technology and digital discourse. Although these characteristics of instability and indeterminacy because of the changing technology open the possibility for other changes in the social realm and power relations, it is very unclear that information technologies and cyberculture will result in such social changes.

Some critics suggest that the current information technology revolution has resulted in a rigidifying and reifying of current power relations along previously existing gender, race, and class lines. The Internet becomes a tool, making women more vulnerable to men who use it to order brides from developing countries, prostitution, cybersex, assumption of false identities, and pornography. A woman who "Twitters" that she's having coffee at Starbucks at Dupont Circle and P makes herself vulnerable to individuals to find her there or to rob her home from which she is absent.

Despite their postmodern veneer of fragmentation, shifting identities, and speed, information technologies rest on the power of science and technology to emancipate humans and a faith in abstract reason. Millar (1998) defines this situation as "hypermodern." Hypermodern describes the packaging of modernity power relations that are universally patriarchal, racist, and bourgeois in a postmodern discourse of discontinuity, spectacle, and speed.

This raises the question of whether cyberfeminism is really a feminist theory. In *Cyberfeminism: Next Protocols*, the Old Boys Network (2004) claims that "Cyberfeminism is not simply an evolution of historical feminism created as a more adequate answer to meet the changed conditions of the Information Age" (14). After describing cyberfeminism as a feminist intervention into the information age to explore how the conditions of the information age challenge political and social conditions of feminism, the authors raise questions about the parameters of cyberfeminism.

Could cyberfeminism merely represent an attempt to see information technology as the latest venue for women's liberation, much as Shulamith Firestone (1970) envisioned such liberation resulting from reproductive technologies? Although reproductive technologies have resulted in significant feminist critiques, theorizing, and discussion, no one considers them to be a feminist theory or method.

Conclusion

This chapter has used several feminist theoretical perspectives to examine the relationships among, and impact of women scientists upon, gender, science, and technology. Taken together, the spectrum of feminist theories provides different, new insights to explore these relationships. All of these perspectives have affected experimental methods by placing women in central focus. Each of the theories discussed here (and some not included) has contributed at least one new perspective or emphasis overlooked in other theories. Because many feminist theories emerged in response to critiques of a preceding theory or theories, successor theories tend to be more comprehensive and compensatory for factors or groups overlooked by previous theories.

Knowledge of the range of theories and the particular factors each emphasizes allow one to better understand the context in which each may be most useful. For example, in providing testimony before Congress or other legislative bodies, a liberal feminist approach remains the theoretical venue most likely to resonate successfully with the audience, because despite the failure to pass the Equal Rights Amendment (ERA), the universal equity and access underlined in liberal feminism are acceptable and familiar to those enmeshed in our judicial and legislative systems. Although raising issues of class (socialist feminism) or race (African American feminism), particularly if the testimony centers on health care or other issues known to he affected by income or ethnicity, may be successful, using radical feminist approaches would be unlikely to work in the congressional setting.

Just as the composition of the audience and the context of the setting make different feminist theoretical approaches more useful in some settings than others, the impact of feminism on experimental methods also varies with different disciplines. Feminism appears to affect experimental methods more significantly in fields such as the social sciences and biology, where sex or gender is prominent and evident. Feminism seems to have less effect in areas of basic research in the physical sciences and mathematics on fundamentals such as string theory.

In addition to the fact that sex and gender in the forms of males or females and associated masculinity and femininity are not overt in the physical sciences and technology, the disciplines in these fields also have significantly smaller percentages of women than the biological and social sciences (NSF 2010), where women now receive half of undergraduate degrees. In the humanities and many areas of the social sciences, increases in the numbers and percentages of women correlated with increases in emphases on women and gender in research and scholarship (Boxer 2000; Rosser 2002). A critical mass of women physicians was needed to push for medicine to provide increased attention to women's health (Dan and Rosser 2003) and basic research on gendered medicine (Wald and Wu 2010). When the percentage of women in physics, computer science, and engineering exceeds 30%, perhaps women may begin to explore the gendered nature of the questions asked, approaches, and theories and conclusions drawn from the data in those disciplines.

In the technological and applied areas of physics, math, and the natural sciences such as engineering, computer science, and medicine, the very powerful fusion of biology and computer science has created a new technoscience. Technoscience has facilitated sequencing the human genome and amazing advances in biomedical engineering, as well as cyberfeminism. Feminist theories must be used to place gender in central focus to critically evaluate the social and political implications of these new technosciences. Women scientists have played and will continue to play critical roles in both developing and critiquing the technosciences.

8

Conclusion

Women in Science Are

Critical for Society

When I began my undergraduate education in science more than 40 years ago, I experienced mentoring from faculty that encouraged me to continue in science as well as some that had a decidedly chilling effect to make me question my choice of major. For example, one faculty member, who noticed how well I had done in the genetics course for non-majors, asked me to work in his lab and then encouraged me every semester to major in science. In contrast, that same faculty member sexually harassed me in the lab, which of course made me question the whole endeavor.

As a graduate student and postdoc, I encountered a different set of mixed messages from mentors and society that left me with ambiguous feelings about beginning my career as a professor of biology. On the one hand, I regularly heard how well I was progressing toward my dissertation; indeed, I received my PhD four years after my undergraduate degree, while the average time in the Zoology Department at that time was seven years. Yet, I also had a U.S. museum-based research question selected for me by my major professor because he assumed that I would not wish to go to Africa since I was pregnant with my first child. Throughout my career in academia, I continued to face a variety of obstacles that made me determined to try to change both individual behaviors of unsupportive mentors and institutional structures to ease the way for junior women scientists and engineers.

The data from the responses and interviews of current women scientists, some junior and some about ten to twenty years younger than I, document that although the pipeline of women in most STEM fields has increased substantially, many of the same issues for women in science and engineering persist today. Although perhaps the obstacles appear to be slightly different or the experiences are expressed using different language, many basic issues remain unchanged. Because of legal changes, colleagues may not express their opinions as directly. Overt sexual harassment from a supervisor has become less frequent, yet the structures of institutions and science make junior women question whether they can balance career and family. Time management, isolation, lack of camaraderie, poor mentoring, gaining credibility and respectability from colleagues and superiors, as well as issues for dual-career couples in science, remain problematic. Sexual harassment and gender discrimination still occur all too frequently.

When women scientists and their mentors are aware of daily micro-inequities and their potential impact upon a career, they can attempt to contain or mitigate them. Spelling out some of the helpful and unhelpful actions of mentors toward women scientists serves as one impetus for this volume. I recorded what successful women scientists said about their experiences to help guide mentors in their individual behaviors, as simultaneously we seek to transform institutional structures to facilitate careers for academic women scientists. I also emphasize some of the choices that women themselves underline as making a significant difference in their professional lives. The importance of the mentor's willingness to permit flexibility in the research timetable and understand that sometimes, allowing a bit more time to complete a degree or postdoc because of childbearing or other family issues might permit a woman scientist with great potential to stay in the field became an issue that was raised very frequently. Perhaps the most surprising theme I heard was women's admission of the significant impact that the choice of a supportive partner or spouse had on their success as a scientist or engineer.

As I listened to the voices of successful women scientists, they not only articulated new ways of expressing some of the same old issues, but they also revealed many positive changes that have occurred. During the last 40 years, we have made documented progress on many fronts. The numbers and percentages of women have increased dramatically in all STEM fields and reached parity in degree attainment in the life sciences as well as many of the social sciences. Women represent more than 30% of STEM faculty at four-year institutions. Although the percentage drops precipitously at elite research institutions, particularly at the rank of full professor, the report from the National Academy of Sciences (2009) found improving opportunities nationally for women in tenure-track positions at those institutions. In addition to increases in the pipeline, partially because of federal and anti-discrimination legislation such as Title VII and Title IX, virtually all institutions have articulated policies banning discrimination in hiring and prohibiting sexual harassment as well as gender discrimination. Many institutions now have policies or practices such as parental leave and stop the tenure clock to facilitate balancing career and family during especially critical family transitions. Although old issues remain with new facets and faces, progress has definitely occurred both in terms of the pipeline of numbers of women scientists and changes in institutional structures. Vigilance will be required to insure that the deep recession that began in 2008 and its increasingly severe impacts on higher education do not erode these gains in numbers, practices, and policies. Many lessons can be learned from these successes, such as continuing to support family-friendly policies, dual-career hires, and monitoring the data to ensure that women receive tenure, promotion, and awards at the same rates as their male colleagues. This will go a long way toward building on the progress that has already been made.

Careful listening also revealed some suggestions that should probably be heard as new issues with potential danger signals. Interviews of AWIS Fellows underlined a primary point made in the 1999 MIT Report (Hopkins 1999), which is that the issues of successful senior women scientists have been overlooked and understudied. While the policy and practice changes by institutions, as well as the institutional structural transformations pushed by federal funding agencies through programs such as NSF's ADVANCE, have addressed flexibility in the tenure clock, parental leave, and other issues most relevant for junior women, the unique challenges faced by successful senior women scientists remain unaddressed. Although some senior women must balance career with family because of delayed childbearing, they more commonly need family friendly policies to cope with elder care for a parent or an ill partner or spouse. Noting that they do not appear to be receiving the same awards and perks that their male peers do, many senior women become marginalized, embittered, or seek early retirement. Individual institutions, coupled with help from the funding agencies and professional societies, need to address the issues for senior women to stanch the loss of this valuable, experienced group of scientists.

Successful senior women scientists serve as a prime source of leadership for top academic administrative positions. Their experience in obtaining funding and managing large budgets, major projects, and teams of personnel in their scientific laboratories translates well into the expectations and skills needed by deans, vice presidents of research, provosts and presidents. Some of the data and examples of women academic administrators that have received particularly harsh and harassing treatment make some individuals reluctant to explore these top leadership positions. In contrast, the possibility of helping other women scientists and impacting institutional priorities become strong incentives for administration for many women.

Although somewhat more problematic for senior women, both junior and senior women are not obtaining patents at the same percentages as their male peers. In all countries, across all sectors and in all fields, the percentage of women obtaining patents is not only less than their male counterparts but it is less than the percentage of women in science, technology, engineering, and mathematics in the field in the country. Patents, along with publications, serve as primary indicators of innovation and competitiveness. Since the focus of scientific research, both globally and nationally, has shifted from basic to applied research and innovation, the dearth of women receiving patents suggests a possible new twenty-first-century face on the old story of women's exclusion from the leading edge of science. Exclusion of women from commercialization of science and patenting hurts women's career advancement and deprives society of women's creative ideas for new and useful products.

Having women in key decision-making positions in the scientific and technological workforce is critical for the future of our society. The importance of the leadership of women in science has been illustrated in other areas such as health care; not until a substantial number of women had entered the professions of biology and medicine could biases from androcentrism be exposed. Once the possibility of androcentric bias was discovered, the potential for distortion on a variety of levels of research and theory was recognized: the choice and definition of problems to be studied, the exclusion of females as experimental subjects, bias in the methodology used to collect and interpret data, and bias in theories and conclusions drawn from the data. Since the practice of modern medicine uses a biomedical approach based in positivist research in biology and chemistry and depends heavily on clinical research, any flaws and ethical problems in this research are likely to result in poorer health care and inequity in the medical treatment of disadvantaged groups (Rosser 1994).

This realization uncovered gender bias which had distorted some medical research. Women's health had become synonymous with reproductive health and obstetrics gynecology, which meant that many diseases that occurred in both sexes, such as cardiovascular disease and even breast cancer, had been studied in males only and/or used a male-as-norm approach. Excessive focus on male research subjects and definition of cardiovascular diseases as "male" led to underdiagnosis and under-treatment of the disease in women. Studies demonstrated that women were significantly less likely than men to undergo coronary angioplasty, angiography, or surgery when admitted to the hospital with a diagnosis of myocardial infarction, unstable or stable angina, chronic ischemic heart disease, or chest pain. This significant difference remained even when variables such as race, age, economic status, and other chronic disease such as diabetes and heart failure were controlled. Similarly, women had angina before myocardial infarction as frequently as, and with more debilitating effects than men, yet women were referred for cardiac catheterization only half as often. These and other similar studies led Bernadine Healy, a cardiologist and first woman director of NIH, to characterize the diagnosis of coronary heart disease in women as the Yentl syndrome: "Once a woman showed that she was just like a man, by having coronary artery disease or a myocardial infarction, then she was treated as a man should be" (Healy 1991b, 274). The male-as-norm approach in research and diagnosis, unsurprisingly, was translated into bias in treatments for women. Women exhibited higher death rates from angioplasty and coronary bypass surgery because the techniques had been pioneered using male subjects (Rosser 1994). This provides an important lesson that can be applied to other fields, as increased leadership by women could potentially lead to new breakthroughs and discoveries.

Women scientists, consumers, physicians, and politicians brought these revelations and other examples of bias and gaps in research and practice to the attention of the health community. After the 1985 U.S. Public Health Service survey recommended that the definition of women's health be expanded beyond reproductive health, the General Accounting Office (GAO) reported that the NIH expended only 13.5 percent of its budget on women's health issues. In 1990, the GAO criticized the NIH for inadequate representation of women and minorities in federally funded studies and the Congressional Caucus for Women's Issues introduced the Women's Health Equity Act. In 1991, Bernadine Healy, MD, established the Office of Research on Women's Health and announced plans for the Women's Health Initiative. The Women's Health Initiative, designed to collect baseline data and look at interventions to prevent cardiovascular disease, breast cancer, colorectal cancer, and osteoporosis seeks to fill the gaps in research and practice.

In addition to providing the basic research for health care, science and technology hold the keys to solving many of the problems extant in the world today, as well as to maintaining long-term competitiveness and economic prosperity of the United States. Congress, state and local elected officials, and the lay public often do not understand the importance of not losing momentum and competitive edge for science, especially during this time of economic crisis and competing demands for scarce federal and local resources.

Faced with the current fiscal crisis and the longer term projections for the United States of vastly constricted resources, compared not only to the golden days of the 1960s but also in comparison with the 1990s and early twenty-first century, most teachers, researchers, and administrators recognize the significance of policy. Engineers and basic scientists now realize that access to the funding to carry out their research depends upon state and federal policies that give priority to their area of study.

During the last two decades, the United States has shifted its emphasis from funding basic research to increased support for applied research in the form of technology transfer, innovation, and translational research. This has occurred both in industry, where many companies have cut back, outsourced, or eliminated research and development (R&D) entirely, and in the national agenda, where federal priorities for funding reflect increases in support for technology transfer and translational research (Rosser and Taylor 2008).

The increasing corporatization of the universities links explicitly with this increasing concentration on translational research. With the decreased funding of public higher education, universities rely more on federal, state, and corporate grants for research and infrastructure support. The funding priorities that favor translational research over basic research push university research in this direction also. These changes make it even more essential that women reach parity with their male counterparts when it comes to attracting funding and securing patents in industry.

Because of their attraction to science as a way to help society and people, women can play a particular and significant role in articulating policies on the national level that can also benefit the public at the state and local government levels, especially in the three areas of increasing the investment in basic research, continuing to support the education and production of scientists from under-represented groups, and increasing the funding for public education.

Building upon the recommendations outlined in National Academies Reports, *Rising Above the Gathering Storm: Energizing and Employing America for a Brighter Economic Future* (2007) and *Rising Above the Gathering Storm Revisited: Rapidly Approaching Category 5* (2010), the federal government in particular must increase substantially its investment in basic research in the physical sciences, mathematics, and engineering, as well as the biomedical sciences. Women will need to play a continuing role in maintaining funding for basic research in the life and social sciences, as well as the physical sciences and technology, on the congressional agenda, particularly as the impact of the Stimulus Package recedes. Although total U.S. research and development (R&D) spending is higher now than it has ever been, U.S. R&D spending per gross domestic production (GDP) peaked in 2001 and has declined ever since. U.S. research and development outlays now trail behind the per GDP expenditures of eight of our high-tech competitors, including Japan, South Korea, Switzerland, Israel, and Taiwan (Rosser and Taylor 2008).

The decreased funding of public higher education affects curriculum and teaching, resulting in a parallel process to that found in research. Students face increasing tuition costs and fees to compensate for the dramatic decreases in state support for higher education that have occurred in the last two decades. Public funding for public higher education as a share of state outlays is now about two-thirds of what it was in 1980. In the early 2000s, per-student expenditures in public universities fell by 15 percent. For example, in the State of California, higher education is the only major sector of the California state budget that has grown more slowly than the population and the only sector to have less per capita funding (-12%) in the early 2000s than it had in 1984. In contrast, during that same period, K-12 education experienced a 26% increase, while the prisons experienced a 126% increase (Newfield 2008). In many institutions such as the University of Colorado and the University of Virginia, the state funds less than 10% of the cost of student education, thus using a corporate model to privatize education as well as research.

Continuing to support the education and production of scientists, particularly those from under-represented groups, builds the workforce of the future. The United States has drastically slowed its production of competitive STEM workers, with fewer college students receiving engineering degrees in 2005 than in 1985, despite a rising undergraduate population; in contrast, other countries are increasing the numbers of graduates with degrees in science and technology. The number of Americans earning PhD's in science and engineering peaked in 1997 and then declined steadily over the next five years. Although U.S. PhD's increased between 2002 and 2005, the number of new PhD's is still nearly 6% lower than it was in 1997. The events of September 11, 2001 and the current economic crisis have made the United States less attractive to scientists and engineers from other countries upon which the United States has depended for its science and technology workforce. The paucity of jobs and constraints on grant funding have caused some scientists already at the doctoral and postdoctoral stages to leave the profession and many in earlier stages of their education to re-evaluate a career in science. The dire consequences of losing an entire generation of scientists and the particular consequences of not attracting under-represented groups such as women and ethnic minorities need to be articulated to the nation.

A recent study from the National Bureau of Economic Research (Adams 2010) documents that the decline in research publication rates in the United States in the 1990s can be traced to a decreasing growth of resources for public universities. In published research, China now ranks second in chemistry and third in physics and mathematics. State and local officials must be made aware of the significance of state appropriations for the production of research and scientists to maintain economic competiveness at the state and national levels. High-tech production has begun to take advantage of the growing educated labor supply in China, making it the world's biggest exporter of equipment, computers, electronic components, and even of solar panels. Several recent studies have shown that high-tech multinational corporations heavily base their location and outsourcing decisions on the availability of a country's STEM workforce and of the research universities that produce them. Data reveal that the drop in the relative U.S. technological competitiveness is highly correlated with the decline in the U.S. STEM workforce.

A drop in numbers of individuals in the U.S. STEM workforce not only signals fewer numbers but a potential loss of ideas. Particularly with the increased emphasis upon translation of basic research into applications in terms of technology transfer and innovation, the presence of diversity in the STEM workforce becomes more critical. More than in basic research, applications for technology and inventions depend upon the experiences and ideas of the designers. Excessive dominance of one group, such as the overwhelming percentage of males in engineering and the creative decision-making sectors of the technology workforce, may result in bias in the technologies produced, such as the air bag disaster of the U.S. auto industry

(Malcom, personal communication, October 1997). More women, as well as more diversity in general, in the composition of the STEM workforce not only helps to guard against such bias but may increase the numbers of new ideas that will help people in their daily lives and improve society.

In January 2010, the play "Truth Values: One Girl's Romp Through M.I.T.'s Male Math Maze," played in San Francisco, sponsored by the Mathematical Science Research Institute of Berkeley, California, concurrent with the American Mathematical Association meeting. The play also had an extended run during the fall 2009 at the Central Square Theater in Cambridge, Massachusetts and a performance at the Graduate Center of the City University of New York.

Lawrence H. Summers is credited with helping to inspire the play, according to Gioia De Cari, the author of this autobiographical, one-woman drama and its sole actress. "The play's prologue discusses Summers, whose controversial 2005 remarks questioning the aptitude of women to study math and science, contributed to his ouster from Harvard." De Cari then tells the story of her math journey through a parade of real-life characters, including math nerds who wanted to paw her and professors who asked her to bring cookies to a meeting or wondered why she wasn't at home raising children. "The question is why a woman who graduates with top honors from Berkeley in math, and gets accepted into an MIT doctoral program, ends up leaving," she says in an interview. "'That's the play'" (Mooney 2010, B13).

I offer this book partially as an answer to that question. More importantly, I hope that the insights from so many successful women scientists will help to guide mentors and women scientists, mathematicians, and engineers along paths to help them remain in science and experience happy productive careers in areas so critical for society.

Appendix A

Grants to Support Women
Scientists Cited in This Book

TABLE A.1.

Grant Title	Funding Agency	Current Website For Funding Or Years Program Existed
Professional Opportunities for Women in Research and Education (POWRE)	National Science Foundation (NSF)	1997—2000
ADVANCE	NSF	http://www.nsf.gov/div/index.jsp?div=HRD
*Research on Gender in Science and Engineering (GSE)	NSF	http://www.nsf.gov/div/index.jsp?div=HRD
Visiting Professorships for Women (VPW)	NSF	1982—1997
Career Advancement Awards (CAA)	NSF	1986—1998
Faculty Awards for Women (FAW)	NSF	1990
Research on Causal Factors and Interventions that Promote & Support the Careers of Women in Biomedical and BSE (RFA-GM_09-012)	National Institutes of Health (NIH)	http://womeninscience.hih.gov/funding/index/asp
Clare Boothe Luce Professorships	Luce Foundation	http://www.hluce.org/cb/progrm/aspx
AAUW Fellowships	American Association of University Women	http://www.aauw.org/education/fga//index.cfm

*Beginning in 1993, this NSF program was known by a variety of names, beginning with Program for Women and Girls (PWG), followed by Program for Gender Equity in Science, Mathematics, Engineering and Technology (PGE) and then Gender Diversity in STEM Education (GDSE) before it became Research on Gender in Science and Engineering (GSE).

References

Abbate, Janet. 1999. Cold war and white heat: The origins and meanings of packet switching. In *The social shaping of technology*, 2nd ed. Edited by Donald MacKenzie and Judy Wacjman, 351–71. Philadelphia: Open University Press.

About.com.Inventors. 2006. Patent point to ponder—Mothers of Invention. Part 3: Women fighting germs, stronger than steel, and nearly me. http://inventors.about.com/library/inventors/blkidprimer6_12w3.htm. Retrieved January 12, 2009.

Adams, James D. 2010. Is the U.S. losing its preeminence in higher education? In *American universities in a global market*, ed. Charles T. Clotfelter. National Bureau of Economic Research. Chicago: University of Chicago Press.

Altman, Roberta. 1996. *Waking up/fighting back: The politics of breast cancer*. Boston: Little, Brown.

Ambrose, S., K. Kunkle, B. Lazarus, I. Nair, and D. Harkus. 1997. *Journeys of women in science and engineering: No universal constants*. Philadelphia: Temple University Press.

American Association of University Women. 2000. *Tech-savvy: Educating girls in the new computer age*. Washington, DC: AAUW Educational Foundation. www.awis.org. Retrieved June 23, 2006.

American Cancer Center. 2007. Breast cancer cases/Deaths per year (U.S. and world). http://www.imaginis.com/breast-health/breast-cancer-statistics-on-incidence. Retrieved May 7, 2010.

American Council on Education (ACE). 2009. The American College President. 2007 edition. http://wwwlacenet.edu/Content/NavigationMenu/ProgramsServices/CPA/ExecutiveSummary.htm. Retrieved July 13, 2011.

Arenson, K. 2005. Little advance is seen in Ivies' hiring of minorities and women. *New York Times*, March 1, p. 16.

Armstrong, B. and R. Doll. 1975. Environmental factors and cancer incidence and mortality in different countries, with special reference to dietary practice. *International Journal of Cancer* 15, 617–31.

Ashcraft, Catherine and Anthony Breitzman. 2007. *Who invents IT? An analysis of women's participation in information technology patenting*. Boulder, CO: National Center for Women in Technology (NCWIT).

Aspin, Les. 1993. April. *Policy on the assignment of women in the armed forces*. Washington, DC: Department of Defense.

Astin, Helen and Linda Sax. 1996 Developing scientific talent in undergraduate women. In *The equity equation*, ed. C. S. Davis, A. B. Ginorio, C. S. Hollenshead, B. B. Lazarus, P. M. Rayman and Associates. San Francisco: Jossey-Bass.

Babcock, Linda and Sara Laschever. 2003. *Women don't ask: Negotiation and the gender divide*. Princeton, NJ: Princeton University Press.

Barnaby, F. 1981. Social and economic reverberations of military research. *Impact of Science on Society* 31, 73–83.

Bar-Tal, D. and Irene Frieze. 1977. Achievement motivation for males and females as a determinant of attributions for success and failure. *Sex Roles* 3: 301–14.

Bartlett, T. 2005. "More time." *Chronicle of Higher Education* 52 (2): A-16.

Beaumont, Claudine. 2009. G-20: Protesters use Twitter, Facebook and social media tools to organise demonstrations. *The Telegraph.* http://www.telegraph.co.uk/ finance/g20-summit/5090003/G20-summit-Protesters-use-Twitter-Facebook-and-social-media-tools-to-organise-demonstrations.html. Retrieved May 17, 2010.

Berg, Anne-Jorunn. 1999. A gendered socio-technical construction: The smart house. In *The social shaping of technology*, 2nd ed. Edited by Donald MacKenzie and Judy Wacjman, 301–13. Philadelphia: Open University Press.

Berman, Joshua and Amy Bruckman. 2000. The Turing game: A participatory exploration of identity in online environments. *Proceedings of Directions and Implications of Advanced Computing (DIAL) 2000*. Seattle, WA: Computer Professionals for Social Responsibility.

Bodker, S. and J. Greenbaum. 1993. Design of information systems: Things versus people. In *Gendered by design: Information technology and office systems*, ed. J. Owen Green and D. Pain, 53–63. London: Taylor and Francis.

Boxer, Marilyn. 2000. Unruly knowledge: Women's Studies and the problem of disciplinarity. *NWSA Journal* 12 (2): 119–29.

Brainard, J. 2006. Earmarks may skew analysis of spending. *Chronicle of Higher Education* 52 (35): A-31.

Bratteteig, Tone. 2002. Bringing gender issues to technology design. In *Feminist challenges in the information age*, ed. C. Floyd, G. Kelkar, S. Klein-Franke, and C. P. Limpangog, 91–105. Opladen, Germany: Leske and Budrich.

Briggs, Thyra. 2010. More women than men in the first-year class at Harvey Mudd College: How did this happen? *University Business.* http://www.university business.com/newsletter/vertical/verticalnewss. Retrieved December 16, 2010.

Brun, E. 1994. Technology appropriate for women? In *Feminist voices on gender, technology, and ethics*, ed. E. Gunnarsson and L. Trojer. Lulea, Sweden: University of Technology Centre for Women's Studies.

Bunker Whittington, Kjersten and Laurel Smith-Doerr. 2005. Gender and commercial science: Women's patenting in the life sciences. *Journal of Technology Transfer* 30: 355–70.

Burroughs Wellcome Fund and Howard Hughes Medical Institute. 2004. *Making the right moves: A practical guide to scientific management for postdocs and new faculty.* Research Triangle, NC and Chevy Chase, MD: Burroughs Wellcome Fund and Howard Hughes Medical Institute.

Butler, Judith. 1990. *Gender trouble: Feminism and the subversion of identity.* New York: Routledge.

————. 1992. Introduction. In *Feminists theorize the political*, ed. J. Butler and J. Scott, xii–xvii. New York: Routledge.

————. 1994. *Bodies that matter: On the discursive limits of "sex."* New York: Routledge.

Campbell, Kristina. 1992. 1 in 3 lesbians may get breast cancer, expert theorizes. *Washington Blade*, October 2, pp. 1, 23.

Campbell, K. 2001. Leaders of 9 universities and 25 women faculty meet at MIT, agree to equity reviews. *MIT News Office*. http://web.mit.edu/newsoffice/nr/2001/gender.html. Retrieved January 31, 2001.

Caro, Robert. 1974. *The power broker: Robert Moses and the fall of New York*. New York: Random House.

Catalyst, Inc. 1999. *Women scientists in industry: A winning formula for companies*. Retrieved from http://www.catalyst.org/xcart/product.php?productid-16142.

Centers for Disease Control. 1987. Antibody to human immunodeficiency virus in female prostitutes and social change in the twentieth century, 1976. *Morbidity and Mortality Weekly Report* 36, 157–61.

————. 1998. Guidelines for evaluating surveillance systems. *Morbidity and Mortality Weekly Report* 37, 1–18.

Cheryan, Sapna, V. C. Plaut, P. Devier and C. M. Steele. 2009. Ambient belonging: How stereotypical cues impact gender participation in computer science. *Journal of Personality and Social Psychology* 97: 1045–60.

Chinese Hospital Medical Staff and University of California School of Medicine. 1982, May. *Conference on health problems related to the Chinese in America*, San Francisco: Author.

Chodorow, Nancy. 1978. *The reproduction of mothering: Psychoanalysis and the sociology of gender*. Berkeley: University of California Press.

Chu, S. Y., J. W. Buehler and R. L. Berelman. 1990. Impact of the human immunodeficiency virus epidemic on mortality in women of reproductive age, United States. *Journal of the American Medical Association* 264: 225–29.

Clarke, Adele E. and Virginia L. Olesen, eds. 1999. *Revisioning women, health, and healing: Feminist, cultural, and technoscience perspectives*. New York: Routledge.

Clewell, Beatriz and Angela Ginorio. 1996. Examining women's progress in the sciences from the perspective of diversity. In *The equity equation*, ed. C. S. Davis, A. B. Ginorio, B. Lazarus, P. Rayman and Associates. San Francisco: Jossey-Bass.

Cockburn, Cynthia. 1981. The material of male power. *Feminist Review* 9: 41–58.

————. 1983. *Brothers: Male dominance and technological change*. London: Pluto Press.

————. 1985. *Machinery of dominance: Women, men and technical know-how*. London: Pluto Press.

Cohen, Judith, Priscilla Alexander and Constance Woofsey. 1988. Prostitutes and AIDS: Public policy issues. *AIDS and Public Policy Journal* 3: 16–22.

Collins, Patricia Hill. 1990. *Black feminist thought*. New York: Routledge.

Corea, Gena. 1985. *The mother machine: Reproductive technologies from artificial insemination to artificial wombs*. New York: Harper and Row.

Council on Competitiveness. 2005. *Innovate America: National Innovation Initiative Summit and Report*. Washington, DC: Council on Competitiveness.

Cowan, Ruth S. 1983. *More work for mother: The ironies of household technology from the open hearth to the microwave*. New York: Basic Books.

———. 1985. The industrial revolution in the home. In *The social shaping of technology*, ed. D. MacKenzie and J. Wajcman, 181–201. Milton Keynes, UK: Open University Press. (Reprinted from The industrial revolution: In the home: Household technology and social change in the twentieth century, 1976. *Technology and Culture* 17: 1–23).

Creager, Angela N. H., Elizabeth Lunbeck and Londa Schiebinger, eds. 2001. *Feminism in twentieth-century science, technology, and medicine*. Chicago: University of Chicago Press.

Currie, Donya. 2010. Cynthia Gomez: On the road for health equity. *American Journal of Public Health* 100 (11): 2030–32.

Daly, Mary. 1978. *Gyn/ecology: The metaethics of radical feminism*. Boston: Beacon Press.

———. 1984. *Pure lust: Elemental feminist philosophy*. Boston: Beacon Press.

Dan, Alice and Sue Rosser. 2003. Editorial. *Women's Studies Quarterly* 31 (1–2): 6–24.

Daniell, Ellen. 2006. *Every other Thursday: Stories and strategies from successful women scientists*. New Haven: Yale University Press.

Dean, Donna. 2009. *Getting the most out of your mentoring relationships*. New York: Springer.

Deaux, K. and T. Emswiller. 1974. Explanation of successful performance on sex-linked tasks: What is skill for the male is luck for the female. *Journal of Personality and Social Psychology* 29: 80–85.

de Beauvoir, Simone. 1989. *The second sex*, trans. and ed. H. M. Parshley. New York: Vintage Books. (Original work published 1949.)

de Lauretis, Teresa. 1991. Queer theory: Lesbian and gay sexualities. *Differences: A Journal of Feminist Cultural Studies* 3 (2): iii–xvii.

Derrida, Jacques. 2000. *Limited, inc.* Evanston: Northwestern University Press.

Ding, Waverly, Fiona Murray and Toby Stuart. 2006. Gender differences in patenting in the academic life sciences. *Science* 313 (5787): 665–67.

Dinnerstein, Dorothy. 1977. *The mermaid and the minotaur: Sexual arrangements and human malaise*. New York: Harper Colophon Books. http://www.dovepress.com/international-journal-of-womens-health. Retrieved May 10, 2010.

Dworkin, Andrea. 1983. *Right-wing women*. New York: Coward-McCann.

Easlea, Brian. 1983. *Fathering the unthinkable: Masculinity, scientists and the nuclear arms race*. London: Pluto Press.

Ehrenreich, Barbara and Deirdre English. 1978. *For her own good: 150 years of the experts' advice to women*. New York: Anchor Press, Doubleday.

Eisenstein, Zillah. 1977. *Capitalist patriarchy and the case for socialist feminism*. New York: Monthly Review Press.

Engineers Dedicated to a Better Tomorrow. 2006. "Women in engineering and related fields—Diversity analysis of students earning bachelor's degrees" *D-E Communications—Critical Issues Series*. www.DedicatedEngineers.org. Retrieved July 6, 2006.

Enloe, Cynthia. 1983. *Does khaki become you? The militarism of women's lives*. London: Pluto Press.

———. 1989. *Bananas, beaches, and bases*. Berkeley: University of California Press.

Etzkowitz, Henry, C. Kemelgor, M. Neuschatz and B. Uzzi. 1994. *Who will do science? Educating the next generation*. Baltimore: Johns Hopkins University Press.

Evans, E. and C. Grant, eds. 2008. *Mama PhD: Women write about motherhood and academia.* New Brunswick, NJ: Rutgers University Press.

Faden, R., N. Kass and D. McGraw. 1996. Women as vessels and vectors: Lessons from the HIV epidemic. In *Feminism and bioethics: Beyond Reproduction*, ed. Susan Wolf, 252–81. New York: Oxford University Press.

Fausto-Sterling, Anne. 1992a. Building two-way streets: The case of feminism and science. *NWSA Journal* 4 (3): 336–49.

———. 1992b. *Myths of gender.* New York: Basic Books.

Ferguson, Anne. 1984. Sex wars: The debate between radical and liberation feminists. *Signs: Journal of Women in Culture and Society* 10 (1): 15–31.

Finder, A., P. Healy and K. Zernike. 2006. President of Harvard resigns, ending stormy 5-year tenure. www.nytimes.com/2006/02/22/education/22harvard.html. Retrieved April 3, 2006.

Firestone, Shulamith. 1970. *The dialectic of sex.* New York: Bantam Books.

Fleig-Palmer, M., J. Muirrin, D. Palmer and C. Rathert. 2003. Meeting the Needs of Dual-Career Couples in Academia. *CUPA-HR Journal* 54: 1–6.

Fogg, Piper. 2003. So many committees, so little time. *The Chronicle of Higher Education*, December 19.

———. 2005. Princeton gives automatic tenure extension to new parents. *The Chronicle of Higher Education Today's News*, August 19. http://chronicle.com/temp/email.php?id=unlwfuntjabwyhvh5whlr7usj. Retrieved August 20, 2005.

———. 2006. Stanford offers paid maternity leave to all graduate students. *Chronicle of Higher Education*, January 30.

Foucault, Michel. 1978. *The history of sexuality: Vol. I. Introduction*, trans. R. Hurley. New York: Pantheon Books. (Original work published 1976.)

Fox, Mary Frank. 2005. Gender, family characteristics, and publication productivity among scientists. *Social Studies of Science* 35 (1): 131–50.

Fox, Mary, Deborah Johnson, and Sue Rosser, eds. 2006. *Women, gender and technology.* Champaign: University of Illinois Press.

Frietsch, Rainer, Inna Haller, Melanie Vrohlings and Hariolf Grupp. 2007. Battle of the sexes? Main areas of gender-specific technological and scientific activities in industrialized countries. Unpublished paper presented at Georgia Tech, October 16.

Frye, Marilyn. 1983. *The politics of reality.* Trumansburg, NY: Crossing Press.

Gornick, Vivian. 2009. *Women in science: Then and now.* New York: Feminist Press.

Greenbaum, J. 1995. *Windows on the workplace: Computers, jobs and the organization of office work in the late twentieth century.* New York: Monthly Review Press.

Greene, J. P. Lewis and Geraldine Richmond. 2008. Promoting gender equity in academic departments: A study of department heads in top-rated chemistry departments. *Journal of Women and Minorities in Science and Engineering* 14 (1–27).

Grobbee, D. B., E. B. Rimm, B. Giovannucci, G. Colditz, M. Stampfer and W. Willett. 1990. Coffee, caffeine, and cardiovascular disease in men. *New England Journal of Medicine* 321: 1026–32.

Grosz, Elizabeth. 1994. *Volatile bodies: Towards a corporeal feminism.* Bloomington: Indiana University Press.

Gunew, Sneja. 1990. *Feminist knowledge: Critique and construct.* New York: Routledge.

Gurwitz, J. H., F. C. Nananda and J. Avorn. 1992. The exclusion of the elderly and women from clinical trials in acute myocardial infarction. *Journal of the American Medical Association* 268 (2): 1417–22.

Hall, Roberta M. and Bernice Sandler. 1982. *The classroom climate: A chilly one for women.* Washington, DC: Association of American Colleges.

Hanisch, Carol. 1970. The personal is political. In *Notes from the Second Year: Women's Liberation,* ed. Shulamith Firestone and Anne Koedt. New York: Radical Feminism.

Haraway, Donna. 1997. *Modest_Witness@Second_Millennium. FemaleMan©_Meets_OncoMouse™: Feminism and technoscience.* New York: Routledge.

———. 2008. *When species meet.* Minneapolis: University of Minnesota Press.

Harding, Sandra. 1993. Introduction. In *The racial economy of science,* ed. Sandra Harding, 1–22. Bloomington: Indiana University Press.

———. 1998. *Is science multicultural? Postcolonialisms, feminisms, and epistemologies.* Bloomington: Indiana University Press.

———. 2006. Science and social inequality: Feminist and post-colonial issues. Champaign: University of Illinois Press.

———. 2008. Sciences from below: Feminisms, postcolonialities, and modernities. Durham, NC: Duke University Press.

Harris, J. R., M. E. Lippman, U. Veronesi and W. Willett. 1992. Breast cancer. *New England Journal of Medicine* 327: 319–28.

Hartmann, Heidi. 1981. The unhappy marriage of Marxism and feminism. In *Women and revolution,* ed. Lydia Sargent, 1–41. Boston: South End Press.

Hawthorne, Susan and Renate Klein. 1999. *Cyberfeminism.* Melbourne, Victoria, Australia: Spinifex.

Healy, Bernadine. 1991a. Women's health, public welfare. *Journal of the American Medical Association* 266: 566–68.

———. 1991b. The Yentl syndrome. *New England Journal of Medicine* 325 (4): 274–76.

Hedges, E. 1997. Looking back, moving forward. Editorial in *Women's Studies Quarterly* 25 (1–2): 6–13.

Hesse-Biber, Sharlene Nagy and Gregg Lee Carter. 2005. *Working women in America: Split dreams.* Oxford: Oxford University Press.

Hoagland, S. L. 1988. *Lesbian ethics.* Chicago: Institute of Lesbian Studies.

Holmes, Helen B. 1981. Reproductive technologies: The birth of women-centered analysis. In *The custom-made child,* ed. Helen B. Holmes, B. B. Hoskins and M. Gross, 1–18. Clifton, NJ: Humana Press.

hooks, bell. 1992. *Race and representation.* London: Turnaround Press.

Hopkins, Nancy. 1999. MIT and gender bias: Following up on victory. *Chronicle of Higher Education* 46 (15): B–4.

Irigaray, L. 1985. *This sex which is not one,* trans. C. Porter and C. Burke. Ithaca, NY: Cornell University Press. (Original work published 1977.)

Ivie, Rachel and K. Nies Ray. 2005. *Women in physics and astronomy.* Retrieved from AIP Statistical Research Center Website: http://www.aip.org/statistics/trends/reports/women05.pdf.

Jaggar, Alison. 1983. *Feminist politics and human nature.* Totowa, NJ: Rowman and Allanheld.

Jaggar, Alison and Paula Rothenberg, eds. 1994. *Feminist frameworks*. New York: McGraw-Hill.

Jameson, Fredric. 1981. *The political unconscious: The narrative as a socially symbolic act*. Ithaca, NY: Cornell University Press.

Jaschik, Scott. June 3, 2009. "Faring well" or disappearing? *Inside Higher Ed*. http://www.insidehighered.com/layout/set/print/news/2009/06/03/gender. Retrieved June 3, 2009.

Jones, James H. 1981. *Bad blood: The Tuskegee syphilis experiment: A tragedy of race and medicine*. New York: Free Press.

Keller, Evelyn Fox. 1982. Feminism and science. *Signs: Journal of Women in Culture and Society* 7(3): 589–602.

———. 1983. *A feeling for the organism*. San Francisco: Freeman.

———. 1985. *Reflections on gender and science*. New Haven: Yale University Press.

Kelsey, Sheryl F., M. James, A. L. Holubkov, R. Holubkov, M. J. Cowley, K. M. Detre and Investigators from the National Heart, Lung, and Blood Institute Percutaneous Transluminal Coronary Angioplasty Registry. 1993. Results of percutaneous transluminal coronary angioplasty in women: 1985–1986. *Circulation* 87 (3): 720–27.

King, Ynestra. 1989. The ecology of feminism and the feminism of ecology. In *Healing the wounds: The promise of ecofeminism*, ed. J. Plant, 18–28. Philadelphia: New Society.

Knights, James J. 2004. Why the FBI seeks more women as special agents. *Women in Higher Education* 13 (3): 30–31.

Koertge, N. 1994. Feminist epistemology: Stalking an undead horse. *Annals of the New York Academy of Sciences* 775 (1): 413–19.

Kristeva, Julia. 1986. *The Kristeva reader*, ed. Toril Moi. Oxford: Blackwell.

Lacan, Jacques. 1977. The agency of the letter in the unconscious or reason since Freud. In *Ecrits: A selection*, trans. Alan Sheridan. New York: W. W. Norton. (Original work published 1957.)

———. 1998. *The four fundamental concepts of psychoanalysis*. New York: W. W. Norton.

Larrabee, Mary Jeanne. 2000. Existential feminism. In *Encyclopedia of feminist theories*, ed. Lorraine Code, 186–87. New York: Routledge.

Lerman, Nina, Ruth Oldenziel and Arwen Mohun. 2003. *Gender & technology*. Baltimore: Johns Hopkins University Press.

Levine, Aaron. 2010. Self-regulation, compensation, and the ethical recruitment of oocyte donors. *Hastings Center Report* 40 (2): 25–36.

Lin-Fu, J. S. 1984, July/August. The need for sensitivity to Asian and Pacific Americans' health problems and concerns. *Organization of Chinese American Women Speaks*, pp. 1–2.

Long, Scott. 1993. Women in science. Part 1. The productivity puzzle. *Essays of an Information Scientist* 15, p. 248.

———. 2001. *From scarcity to visibility: Gender differences in the careers of doctoral scientists*. Washington, DC: National Academy Press.

Longino, Helen. 1990. *Science as a social knowledge: Values and objectivity in scientific inquiry*. Princeton, NJ: Princeton University Press.

Lyotard, Jean-Francois. 1986. *The postmodern condition*. Manchester: Manchester University Press.

Macdonald, Anne L. 1992. *Feminine ingenuity: Women and invention in America.* New York: Ballantine Books.

MacKenzie, D. and J. Wajcman. 1999. *The social shaping of technology*, 2nd ed. Milton Keynes, UK: Open University Press.

MacKinnon, Catharine. 1982. Feminism, Marxism, and the state: An agenda for theory. *Signs: Journal of Women in Culture and Society* 7 (3): 515–44.

———. 1987. *Feminism unmodified: Discourses on life and law.* Cambridge: Harvard University Press.

Marasco, C. A. 2006. Women faculty gain little ground. *Chemical and Engineering News* 84: 58–59.

Mason, Mary A. and Eve M. Ekman. 2007. *Mothers on the fast track.* Oxford: Oxford University Press.

Mason, Mary A. and Mark Goulden. 2004. Do babies matter (Part II). Closing the baby gap. *Academe*, November–December.

Mason, Mary A., Mark A. Goulden and K. Frasch. 2009. Why graduate students reject the fast track. *Academe Online.* http://www.aaup.org/AAUP/pubsres/academe/2009/JF/Feat/maso.htm. Retrieved June 15, 2009.

McIntosh, Peggy. 1984. The study of women: Processes of personal and curricular revision. *Forum for Liberal Education* 6(5): 2–4.

Mehta, Brinda J. 2000. Postcolonial feminism. In *Encyclopedia of feminist theories*, ed. Lorrain Code, 395–97. New York: Routledge.

Merchant, Carolyn. 1979. *The death of nature.* New York: Harper and Row.

Millar, Melanie. 1998. *Cracking the gender code: Who rules the wired world?* Toronto, Ontario, Canada: Second Story Press.

Miller, Patricia H., Sue V. Rosser, Joann P. Benigno and Mireille Zieseniss. 2000. A desire to help others: Goals of high achieving female science undergraduates. *Women's Studies Quarterly* 28 (1–2): 128–42.

Mitter, S. 1986. *Common fate, common bond.* London: Pluto.

Mohanty, Chandra T. 1997. Women workers and capitalist scripts: Ideologies of domination, common interests, and the politics of solidarity. In *Feminist genealogies, colonial legacies, democratic futures*, ed. M. Jacqui Alexander and Chandra T. Mohanty, 3–29. New York: Routledge.

Monaghan, Peter. 2010. Design for disability will become the norm. *Chronicle of Higher Education* (February 12): B6–B7.

Monosson, E., ed. 2008. *Motherhood, the elephant in the laboratory.* Ithaca, NY: Cornell University Press.

Mooney, Carolyn. 2010. Math + women + MIT = dramatic tension. *Chronicle of Higher Education*, January 17 (19): B–13.

Mora, Samia, Robert Glynn, Judith Hsia, Jean MacFadyen, Jacques Genest, and Paul Ridker. 2010. Statins for the primary prevention of cardiovascular events in women with elevated high-sensitivity C-Reactive protein or dyslipidemia. *Circulation* 121: 1069–77.

Multiple Risk Factor Intervention Trial Research Group (MRFIT). 1990. Mortality rates after 10.5 years for participants in the multiple risk factor intervention trial: Findings related to a prior hypothesis of the trial. *Journal of the American Medical Association* 263: 1795.

Murray, Fiona and L. Graham. 2007. Buying and selling science: Gender stratification in commercial science. *Industrial and Corporate Change Special Issue on Technology Transfer* 16 (4): 657–89.

Naldi, Fulvio and Ilaria Vannini Prenti. 2002. *Scientific and technological performance by gender. A feasibility study on patents and biometric indicators.* Luxembourg: European Union Commission.

———. 2004. "Performance by Gender." http://ec.europa.eu/research/infocentre/export/success/article_721_en.html. Retrieved April 13, 2009.

National Academies. 2006. *Beyond bias and barriers: Fulfilling the potential of women in academic science and engineering*, ed. Donna E. Shalala et al. Washington, DC: National Academies Press.

———. 2010. *Rising above the gathering storm, revisited: Rapidly approaching category 5.* Washington, DC: National Academies Press.

National Academy of Sciences. 2007. *Rising above the gathering storm.* Washington, DC: National Academies Press.

———. 2009. *Gender differences at critical transitions in the careers of science, engineering, and mathematics faculty.* Washington, DC: National Academies Press.

National Science Board. 2004. *Science and engineering indicators-2004* (NSBB 04-01). Arlington, VA: Author.

National Science Foundation (NSF). 2001. *ADVANCE. Program solicitation.* Arlington, VA: Author.

———. 2002. *Women, minorities, and persons with disabilities in science and engineering: 2002* (NSF 03-312). Arlington, VA: Author.

———. 2005. *ADVANCE. Program solicitation.* Arlington, VA: Author. www.nsf.gov. Retrieved July 31, 2006.

———. 2007. *Women, minorities, and persons with disabilities.* Washington, DC: National Science Foundation.

———. 2010. *Science and Engineering Indicators.* www.nsf.gov/sbe/srs/seind10/. Retrieved July 13, 2011.

———. 2011. ADVANCE. http://www.nsf.gov/funding/pgm.summ.jsp?pims_id=5383. Retrieved July 11, 2011.

———. 2010. *Women, Minorities, and Persons with Disabilities.* Washington, DC: NSF. http://www.nsf.gov/statistics/women. Retrieved December 16, 2010.

National Women's Health Network. 2002. The truth about hormone replacement therapy: How to break free from the medical myths of menopause. Roseville, CA: Prima Publishing.

Nelson, Alondra. 2010. Henry Louis Gates's extended family. *Chronicle of Higher Education* (March 5): B12–B13.

Nelson, Donald. 2005. *A national analysis of diversity in science and engineering faculties at research universities.* Retrieved from http://cheminfo.chemou.edu/~djn/diversity/briefings/Diversity%20REport@20Final.pdf.

Newfield, Christopher. 2008. *Unmaking the public university.* Cambridge, MA: Harvard University Press.

Nobelprize.org. 2009. Retrieved January 15, 2010.

Norman, C. 1979, July 26. Global research: Who spends what? *New Scientist*, pp. 279–81.

Norwood, Chris. 1988, July. Alarming rise in deaths. *MS*, pp. 65–67.

NSF ADVANCE website: www.nsf.gov/advance. 2009. Retrieved January 10, 2010.

NSF. 2009. *Survey of earned doctorates.* www.nsf.gov/statistics/infbrief/nsf11305. Retrieved December 7, 2010.

O'Brien, Mary. 1981. *The politics of reproduction.* Boston: Routledge and Kegan Paul.

Old Boys Network. 2004. Call for contributions. In *Cyberfeminism: Next protocols,* ed. Claudia Reiche and Verena Kuni. Brooklyn, NY: Autonomedia.

Pattrow, Lynn M. 1990. When becoming pregnant is a crime. *Criminal Justice Ethics* (Winter/Spring).

Phipps, Alison. 2008. *Women in science, engineering and technology: Three decades of UK initiatives.* Stoke on Trent: Trentham Books.

Pinn, Vivian and Judith LaRosa. 1992. *Overview: Office of research on women's health.* Bethesda: National Institutes of Health.

Pope, J. 2005. Harvard to commit $50M to women's programs. *Boston Globe,* May 17. www.boston.com/news/education/higher/articles/2005/05/17/html.

Reiche, Claudia. 2004. On/off-scenity: Medical and erotic couplings in the context of the visible human project. In *Cyberfeminism: Next protocols,* ed. Claudia Reiche and Verena Kuni, 159–84. Brooklyn, NY: Autonomedia.

Reskin, Barbara and P. A. Roos. 1990. *Job queues, gender queues: Explaining women's inroads into male occupations.* Philadelphia: Temple University Press.

Rich, Adrienne. 1976. *Of woman born: Motherhood as experience.* New York: W. W. Norton.

Robb-Nicholson, Celeste. 2010. Progress on ovarian cancer screening. *Harvard Women's Health Watch* 17(8): 1–3.

Rose, Hilary. 1994. *Love, power, and knowledge: Towards a feminist transformation of the sciences.* Bloomington: Indiana University Press.

Rose, Hilary and Steven Rose. 1980. The myth of the neutrality of science. In *Science and liberation,* ed. Rita Arditti, Pat Brennan and Steve Cavrak, 17–32. Boston: South End Press.

Ross, A. S. 2008. Few women at the top in Silicon Valley. *San Francisco Chronicle,* November 24, p. D-1.

Rosser, Sue V. 1986. *Teaching science and health from a feminist perspective: A practical guide.* Elmsford, NY: Pergamon Press.

———. ed. 1988. *Feminism in the science and health care professions: Overcoming resistance.* Elmsford, NY: Pergamon Press.

———. 1990. *Female friendly science.* Elmsford, NY: Pergamon Press.

———. 1992. *Feminism and biology.* New York: Twayne/Macmillan.

———. 1994. *Women's health: Missing from U.S. medicine.* Bloomington: Indiana University Press.

———. 1999. Different laboratory/work climates: Impacts upon women in the workplace. In *Women in science and engineering: Choices for success, Annals of the New York Academy of Sciences,* ed. C. Selby, 869: 95–101.

———. 2000. Editorial on women and science. *Women's Studies Quarterly* 28 (1–2): 61.

———. 2001. Balancing: Survey of fiscal year 1997, 1998, and 1999 POWRE awardees. *Journal of Women and Minorities in Science and Engineering* 7 (1): 1–11.

———. 2002. Twenty-five years of NWSA: Have we built the two way streets between women's studies and women in science and technology? *NWSA Journal Special 25th Anniversary Issue* 14 (1): 103–23.

———. 2004. *The science glass ceiling: Academic women scientists and the struggle to succeed.* New York: Routledge.

———. 2005. Through the lenses of feminist theories: Focus on women and information technology. *Frontiers* 26 (1): 1–23.

———. 2006. Senior women scientists: Overlooked and understudied? *Journal of Women and Minorities in Science and Engineering* 12 (4): 275–93.

———. 2007. Leveling the playing field for women in tenure and promotion. *NWSA Journal* 19(3): 190–98.

———. 2009. The gender gap in patenting: Is technology transfer a feminist issue? *NWSA Journal* 21(2): 65–84.

Rosser, Sue V. and Jean-Lou Chameau. 2006. Institutionalization, sustainability, and repeatability of ADVANCE for institutional transformation. *Journal of Technology Transfer* 31: 335–44.

Rosser, Sue V. and Jane Daniels. 2004. Widening paths to success, improving the environment, and moving toward lessons learned from experiences of POWRE and CBL awardees. *Journal of Women and Minorities in Science and Engineering* 10 (2): 131–48.

Rosser, Sue V., Jane Z. Daniels and Lan Wu. 2006. Institutional factors contributing to dearth of women STEM faculty: Classification and status matter; location doesn't. *Journal of Women and Minorities in Science and Engineering* 12 (1): 79–93.

Rosser, Sue V. and Eliesh Lane. 2002a. Key barriers for academic institutions seeking to retain women scientists and engineers: Family unfriendly policies, low numbers, stereotypes, and harassment. *Journal of Women and Minorities in Science and Engineering* 8 (2): 163–91.

———. 2002b. Funding for women's programs at NSF: Using individual POWRE approaches for institutions to ADVANCE. *Journal of Women and Minorities in Science and Engineering* 8 (3–4): 327–45.

Rosser, Sue V. and Mark Zachary Taylor. 2008. Economic security: Expanding women's participation in US science. *Harvard International Review* 30 (3): 20–24.

———. 2009. Why women leave science: Fixing the leaky pipeline has become a matter of national competitiveness. *Technology Review* (January–February). Cambridge, MA: MIT News. M-17-19.

Rosser, Sue V. and Mireille Zieseniss. 1998. *Final report on professional opportunities for women in research and education (POWRE) workshop.* Gainesville, FL: Center for Women's Studies and Gender Research.

———. 2000. Career issues and laboratory climates: Different challenges and opportunities for women engineers and scientists. Survey of FY 1997 POWRE Awardees. *Journal of Women and Minorities in Science and Engineering* 6 (2): 1–20.

Rossiter, Margaret. 1982. *Women scientists in America: Struggles and strategies to 1940.* Baltimore: Johns Hopkins University Press.

Rowe, Mary. 1974. Saturn's rings: A study of the minutiae of sexism which maintain discrimination and inhibit affirmative action results in corporations and nonprofit institutions. *Graduate and Professional Education of Women.* Washington, DC: American Association of University Women, pp. 1–9.

———. 1975. Saturn's Rings II, with racist and sexist incidents from 1974 and 1975. *Harvard Medical Alumni Bulletin* 50 (1): 14–18.

Rubin, Gayle. 1984. Thinking sex: Notes for a radical theory of the politics of sexuality. In *Pleasure and danger*, ed. C. Vance, 267–319. Boston: Routledge and Kegan Paul.

Sandler, Bernice. 1986. *The campus climate revisited: Chilly for women faculty, administrators, and graduate students.* Washington, DC: Association of American Colleges.

San Jose Mercury News. 2006. Obituary: Denice Dee Denton. http://www.legacy.com/obituaries/mercurynews/obituary.aspx?n=denice-dee-dentonpid=18221720. Retrieved July 20, 2006.

Schiebinger, Londa. 1999. *Has feminism changed science?* Cambridge: Harvard University Press. http://www.stanford.edu/group/gender/GenderedInnovations/index. Retrieved May 12, 2010.

Schiebinger, Londa, Andrea D. Henderson and S. Gilmartin. 2008. *Dual career academic couples: What universities need to know.* Stanford: Stanford University Michelle R. Clayman Institute for Gender Research.

Schneider, Anne. 2000. Female scientists turn their backs on jobs at research universities. *Chronicle of Higher Education* (August 18): A-12-14.

Schrecker, E. 2009. The bad old days: How higher education fared during the Great Depression. *Chronicle of Higher Education* 55 (40): B9–11.

Schuster, Marilyn and Susan Van Dyne. 1985. *Women's place in the academy: Transforming the liberal arts curriculum.* Totowa, NJ: Rowman and Allanheld.

Seymour, Elaine and Nancy Hewitt. 1994. *Talking about leaving: Factors contributing to high attrition rates among science, mathematics, and engineering undergraduate majors.* Final report to the Alfred P. Sloan Foundation. Boulder: University of Colorado.

Simard, C., A. D. Henderson, S. Gilmartin, L. Schiebinger and T. Whitney. 2008. *Climbing the technical ladder: Obstacles and solutions for mid-level women in technology.* Palo Alto, CA: Michelle Clayman Institute for Gender Research and the Anita Borg Institute.

Sonnert, Gerhardt and Gerald Holton. 1995. *Gender differences in science careers.* New Brunswick, NJ: Rutgers University Press.

Sorenson, K. 1992. Towards a feminized technology? Gendered values in the construction of technology. *Social Studies of Science* 22 (1): 5–31.

Stanley, Autumn. 1995. *Mothers and daughters of invention: Notes for a revised history of technology.* New Brunswick, NJ: Rutgers University Press.

Steady, Filomena. 1982. *The black woman culturally.* Cambridge, MA: Schenkman Publishing.

Steering Committee of the Physicians' Health Study Group. 1989. Final report on the aspirin component of the ongoing physician's health study. *New England Journal of Medicine* 321: 129–35.

Stephan, Paula and Asmaa El-Ganainy. 2007. The entrepreneurial puzzle: Explaining the gender gap. *Journal of Technology Transfer* 32: 475–87.

Stewart, Abigail, Janet Malley and Danielle LaVaque-Manty. 2007. *Transforming science and engineering: Advancing academic women.* Ann Arbor: University of Michigan Press.

Stryker, S. 1998. The transgender issue: An introduction. *glq: A Journal of Lesbian and Gay Studies* 4 (2): 145–58.

Suiter, Marilyn. 2006. Wisdom on mentoring: Sharing the methods of exemplary science and engineering mentors. *AWIS Magazine* (Winter) 35 (1): 17–25.

Summers, Laurence. 2005a. Retrieved from www.president.harvard.edu/speeches/2005/nber.html, Retrieved June 13, 2005.

———. 2005b. Remarks at NBER Conference on Diversifying the Science and Engineering Workforce. January 14, 2005. http://www.president.harvard.edu/speeches/2005/nber.html. Retrieved June 6, 2008.

Swim, J. K. and L. J. Sanna. 1996. He's skilled, she's lucky: a meta-analysis of Observers' attributions for women's and men's successes and failures. *Personality and Social Psychology Bulletin* 22: 507–19.

Tessler, Joelle. 2008. Program turns to online masses to improve patents.http://www.sfgate.com/cgi-bin/article.cgi?f=/n/a/2008/09/14financia...

Tetreault, Mary K. 1985. Stages of thinking about women: An experience-derived evaluation model. *Journal of Higher Education* 5 (4): 368–84.

Thursby, Jerry and Marie Thursby. 2005. Gender patterns of research and licensing activity of science and engineering faculty. *Journal of Technology Transfer* 30: 343–53.

Tierney, John. 2008. A new frontier for Title IX: Science. *New York Times*, July 15, http://www.nytimes.com/2008/07/15/science/15tier.html. Retrieved July 15, 2008.

———. 2010a. Daring to discuss women in science. *New York Times*, July 7. http://www.nytimes.com/2010/06/08/science/08tier.html. Retrieved July 8, 2010.

———. 2010b. Legislation won't close gender gap in sciences. *New York Times,* July 15. http://www.nytimes.com/2010/06/15/science/15tier.html. Retrieved July 16, 2010.

Tindle, Hilary, Yue-Fang Chan, Lewis Kuller, JoAnn Manson, Jennifer Robinson, Milagros Rosal, Greg Siegle and Karen Matthews. 2009. Optimism, cynical hostility, and incident coronary heart disease and mortality in the Women's Health Initiative. *Circulation* 120 (8): 649–55.

Tong, Rosemarie. 1989. *Feminist thought: A comprehensive introduction.* Boulder, CO: Westview Press.

U.C. Santa Cruz chancellor jumps to her death in S.F. *San Francisco Chronicle.* http://sfgate.com/2006/062).

U.S. Patent and Trademark Office. 2003. *U.S. Patenting by women.* Washington, DC: U.S. Patent and Trademark Office.

Valian, Virginia. 1998. *Why so slow? The advancement of women.* Cambridge: MIT Press.

Wajcman, Judy. 1991. *Feminism confronts technology.* University Park: Pennsylvania State University Press.

———. 2004. *Technofeminism.* Cambridge: Polity.

Wadwha, Vivek, Ben Rissing and Gary Gereffi. 2006. *Industry trends in engineering offshoring.* http://ssrn.com/abstract=1015839. Retrieved May 10, 2009.

Wald, Chelsea and Corinna Wu. 2010. Of mice and women: The bias in animal models. *Science* 327 (26 March): 1571–72.

Weber, Rachel. 1997. Manufacturing gender in commercial and military cockpit design. *Science, Technology and Human Values* 22: 235–53.

Webster, Juliet. 1995. *Shaping women's work: Gender, employment and information technology.* New York: Longman.

Weiss, Tara. 2008. "Science and the Glass Ceiling." *Forbes.* http://www.forbes. come/2008/05/10/science-women-careers-lead-cx_tw_0512athenastudy.html. Retrieved May 13, 2008.

Whittington, Kristin B. and Laurel Smith-Doerr. 2008. Women inventors in context: Disparities in patenting across academia and industry. *Gender and Society* 22: 194.

Wickham, J. and P. Murray. 1987. *Women in the Irish electronic industry.* Dublin: Employment Equality Agency.

Williams, Patricia. 1991. *The alchemy of race and rights.* Cambridge: Harvard University Press.

———. 1998. *Seeing a color-blind future.* New York: Noonday Press.

Williams, Patrick and Laura Crissman. 1994. Colonial discourse and post-colonial theory: An introduction. In *Colonial discourse and post-colonial theory*, ed. Patrick Williams and Laura Crissman, 1–20. New York: Columbia University Press.

Wilson, R. 2006. Just half of professors earn tenure in 7 years, Penn State study finds. *Chronicle of Higher Education* 52 (46): A-10.

Wilson, Robin. 2004. Louts in the lab: Duke U. looks for ways to stop the discrimination and harassment that women continue to face in physics; some male professors call it a smear campaign. *Chronicle of Higher Education*, January 23: A7–A9.

Winner, Langdon. 1980. Do artifacts have polities? *Daedalus* 109: 121–36.

Worcester, Nancy. 2009. Hormone replacement therapy (HRT): Getting to the heart of the politics of women's health? In *Diversity and women's health*, ed. Sue V. Rosser. Baltimore: Johns Hopkins University Press.

Xie, Yu and Kimberlee Shauman. 2003. *Women in science.* Boston: Harvard University Press.

Zaragoza, S. 2008. State wants added path to tenure at Texas universities. *Austin Business Journal*, February 8. http://austin.bizjournals.com/austin/stories/2008/02/11/stroy5.html.

Zuckerman, Harriet, Jonathan Cole and J. Bruer. 1991. *The outer circle: Women in the scientific community.* New York: W.W. Norton.

Index

About the Author

SUE V. ROSSER is Provost and Professor of Women's and Gender Studies and Sociology at San Francisco State University. She is the author or editor of many books, including *Diversity in Women's Health*; *Women, Gender, and Technology*; and *The Science Glass Ceiling: Academic Women Scientists and the Struggle to Succeed*.